BONAPARTE

BONAPARTE

❖

Correlli Barnett

WORDSWORTH EDITIONS

This edition published 1997
by Wordsworth Editions Limited
Cumberland House, Crib Street, Ware,
Hertfordshire SG12 9ET

ISBN 1 85326 678 7

Reprinted 1998

Wordsworth® is a registered trade mark of
Wordsworth Editions Limited

Printed and bound in Great Britain by
Mackays of Chatham PLC, Chatham, Kent

CONTENTS

AUTHOR'S FOREWORD

There is no lack of books on Napoleon Bonaparte. In venturing to add yet another to the stack the author has sought to examine anew both Bonaparte's personal character and his performance as soldier and politician; he has sought to place Bonaparte in a fresh historical perspective. He has not, however, attempted to describe in detail either Bonaparte's campaigns, the institutions Bonaparte created, or the foreign, domestic and economic policies he pursued, but instead to bring out their essential anatomy and show how they all reflected Bonaparte's own nature and ideas. For the emphasis throughout the book lies on Bonaparte himself – and Bonaparte seen in the even light of reality rather than the theatrical brilliance of legend.

C.B.

AUTHOR'S ACKNOWLEDGMENTS

In the first place, I wish to express my particular gratitude to John Terraine, Antony Brett-James and Felix Markham who kindly read the typescript and saved me thereby from many errors and omissions.

I would like to express my appreciation of the helpfulness and courtesy of the staffs of the London Library, the Library of the Royal United Services Institute for Defence Studies, the Central Library of the Ministry of Defence, the University of East Anglia Library, the British Library, the Bibliothèque Nationale in Paris, and of Monsieur Jean Humbert of the Musée de l'Armée, Paris.

I am indebted to Miss Georgina Dowse for her resourcefulness in finding illustrations, together with Miss Fiona Roxburgh; to General B. P. Hughes and Brigadier R. G. S. Bidwell for their advice on military organization and tactics, with especial reference to artillery; to Mr John Hadfield, Mr John Bright-Holmes and Mr Paul Brown for their shrewd advice and criticism; and to Mr Tom Stalker Miller, who turned my rough sketches into exemplary maps.

And once again I must thank my wife Ruth for typing the first draft, for her helpful criticisms of the style and content of the narrative, and for being in all ways the perfect chief-of-staff.

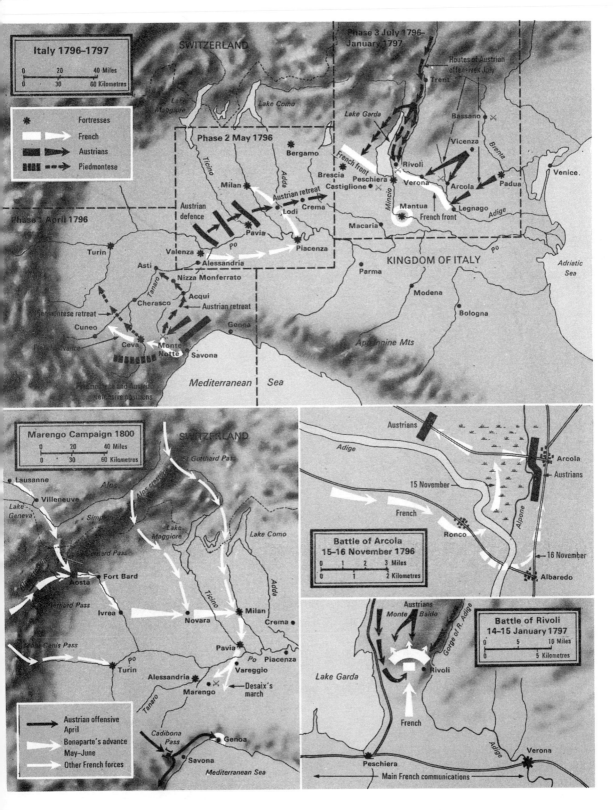

Italy 1796–1797

0	20	40 Miles
0	30	60 Kilometres

Fortresses

French

Austrians

Piedmontese

SWITZERLAND

Phase 3 July 1796–January 1797

Routes of Austrian offensive July

Trent

Lake Garda

Bassano

Vicenza

Phase 2 May 1796

Bergamo

Brescia

Castiglione

Peschiera

French front

Rivoli

Verona

Arcola

Padua

Milan

Adda

Ticino

French front

Mincio

Mantua

Legnago

Venice

Austrian retreat

Lodi

Crema

Macaria

Adige

Austrian defence

Pavia

Po

Phase 1 April 1796

Turin

Valenza

Alessandria

Piacenza

Asti

Nizza Monferrato

Acqui

Po

KINGDOM OF ITALY

Parma

Adriatic Sea

Cherasco

Austrian retreat

Modena

Piedmontese retreat

Cuneo

Genoa

Bologna

Piedmontese advance

Ceva

Monte Notte

Savona

Apennine Mts

Piedmontese and Austrian defensive positions

Mediterranean Sea

Marengo Campaign 1800

0	20	40 Miles
0	30	60 Kilometres

SWITZERLAND

St Gotthard Pass

Lausanne

Villeneuve

Alps

Lake Geneva

Simplon

Lake Maggiore

Lake Como

Aosta

Fort Bard

St Bernard Pass

Adda

Ivrea

Ticino

Novara

Milan

Crema

Mont Cenis Pass

Pavia

Po

Turin

Alessandria

Piacenza

Tanaro

Varreggio

Marengo

Desaix's march

Austrian offensive April

Bonaparte's advance May–June

Other French forces

Cadibona Pass

Genoa

Savona

Mediterranean Sea

Austrians

Adige

Arcola

Austrians

15 November

French

Ronco

Battle of Arcola 15–16 November 1796

0	1	2	3 Miles
0	1	2 Kilometres

Alpone

16 November

Albaredo

Austrians

Monte Baldo

Gorge of R. Adige

Battle of Rivoli 14–15 January 1797

0	5	10 Miles
0	5 Kilometres

Rivoli

Lake Garda

French

Adige

Verona

Peschiera

Main French communications

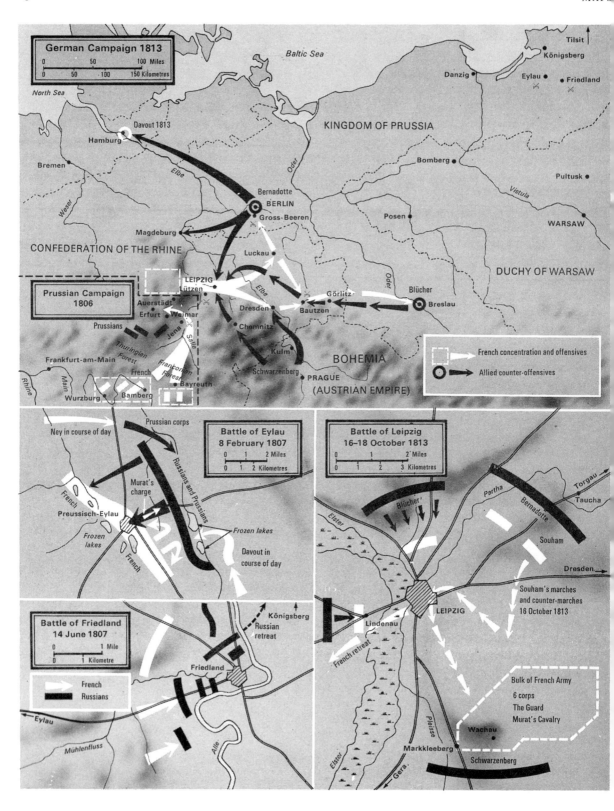

German Campaign 1813

0 — 50 — 100 Miles
0 — 50 — 100 — 150 Kilometres

North Sea

Baltic Sea

Tilsit

Königsberg

Eylau ● ● Friedland

Danzig ●

KINGDOM OF PRUSSIA

Davout 1813
Hamburg ●

Bremen ●

Bomberg ●

Pultusk ●

Elbe

Oder

Weser

Vistula

WARSAW

Posen ●

Bernadotte
BERLIN ◉
Gross-Beeren

Magdeburg ●

DUCHY OF WARSAW

CONFEDERATION OF THE RHINE

Luckau ●

Prussian Campaign 1806

LEIPZIG
Lützen

Auerstädt
Erfurt ● Weimar

Prussians

Jena

Thuringian Forest

Saale

Elbe

Oder

Görlitz ●

Blücher ◉

Breslau ●

Dresden ●

Bautzen

Chemnitz ●

Kulm ●

BOHEMIA

Frankfurt-am-Main ●

Franconian Forest

French

Rhine

Main

Bayreuth ●

Wurzburg ● Bamberg ●

Schwarzenberg ●

PRAGUE ●

(AUSTRIAN EMPIRE)

French concentration and offensives

Allied counter-offensives

Ney in course of day

Prussian corps

Battle of Eylau
8 February 1807

0 — 1 — 2 Miles
0 — 1 — 2 Kilometres

Russians and Prussians

French

Murat's charge

Preussisch-Eylau

Frozen lakes

Frozen lakes

French

Davout in course of day

Battle of Leipzig
16–18 October 1813

0 — 1 — 2 Miles
0 — 1 — 2 — 3 Kilometres

Elster

Blücher

Partha

Bernadotte

Torgau

Taucha

Souham

Dresden

Lindenau

LEIPZIG

Souham's marches and counter-marches 16 October 1813

French retreat

Battle of Friedland
14 June 1807

0 — 1 Mile
0 — 1 Kilometre

Königsberg
Russian retreat

Friedland

French

Russians

Eylau

Mühlenfluss

Alle

Elster

Pleisse

Gera

Bulk of French Army
6 corps
The Guard
Murat's Cavalry

Wachau

Markkleeberg

Schwarzenberg

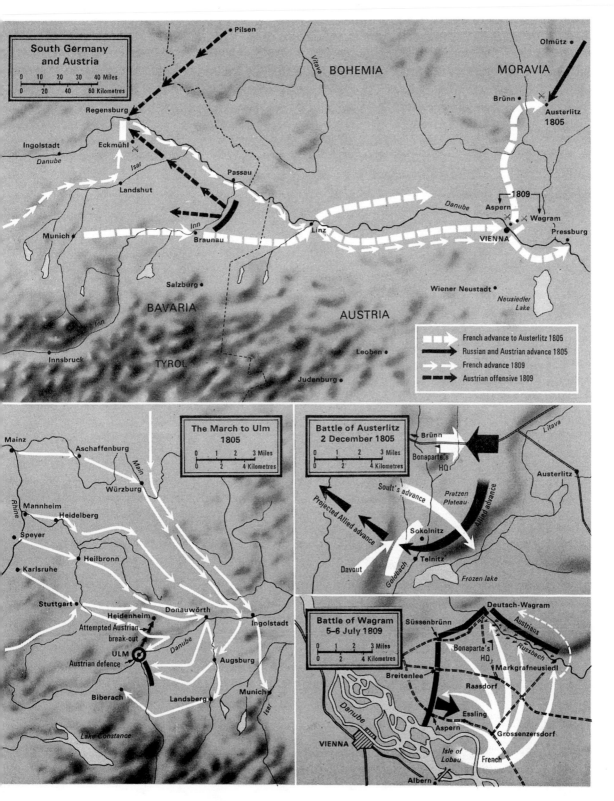

South Germany and Austria

0	10	20	30	40 Miles
0	20	40		60 Kilometres

Pilsen

BOHEMIA

Vltava

MORAVIA

Olmütz

Brünn

Austerlitz 1805

Regensburg

Ingolstadt

Eckmühl

Danube

Isar

Passau

Landshut

1809

Aspern

Wagram

Munich

Inn

Braunau

Linz

Danube

VIENNA

Pressburg

Salzburg

BAVARIA

AUSTRIA

Wiener Neustadt

Neusiedler Lake

Innsbruck

TYROL

Leoben

Judenburg

French advance to Austerlitz 1805
Russian and Austrian advance 1805
French advance 1809
Austrian offensive 1809

The March to Ulm 1805

0	1	2	3 Miles
0	2		4 Kilometres

Mainz

Aschaffenburg

Main

Würzburg

Rhine

Mannheim

Heidelberg

Speyer

Heilbronn

Karlsruhe

Stuttgart

Heidenheim

Donauwörth

Attempted Austrian break-out

ULM

Danube

Ingolstadt

Austrian defence

Augsburg

Biberach

Landsberg

Munich

Isar

Lake Constance

Battle of Austerlitz 2 December 1805

0	1	2	3 Miles
0	2		4 Kilometres

Brünn

Litava

Bonaparte's HQ

Austerlitz

Soult's advance

Pratzen Plateau

Projected Allied advance

Allied advance

Sokolnitz

Davout

Telnitz

Goldbach

Frozen lake

Battle of Wagram 5–6 July 1809

0	1	2	3 Miles
0	2		4 Kilometres

Deutsch-Wagram

Süssenbrünn

Austrians

Bonaparte's HQ

Russbach

Markgrafneusiedl

Breitenlee

Raasdorf

Danube

Essling

Aspern

Grossenzersdorf

VIENNA

Isle of Lobau

French

Albern

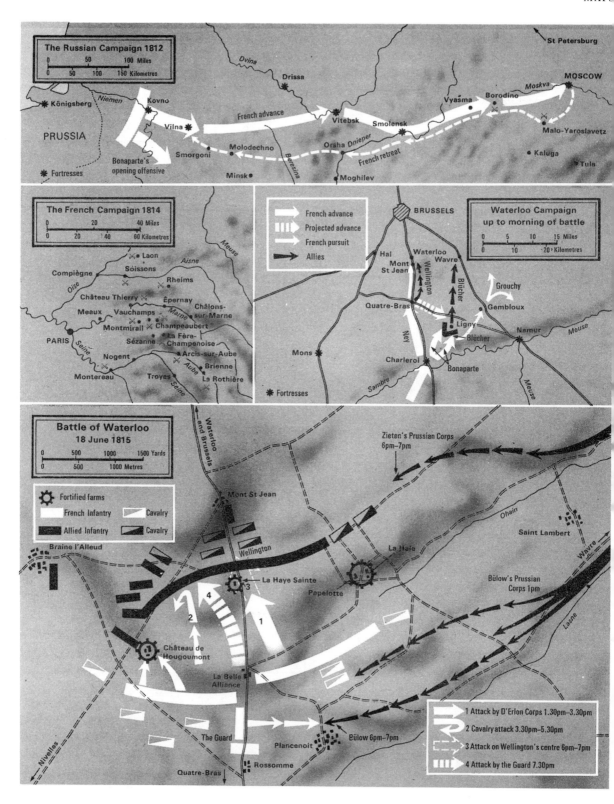

The Russian Campaign 1812

0   50   100 Miles
0   50   100   150 Kilometres

St Petersburg

MOSCOW

Dvina

Drissa

Moskva

Königsberg   Niemen   Kovno

Vyasma   Borodino

PRUSSIA   Vilna   Vitebsk   Smolensk

French advance

Malo-Yaroslavetz

Molodechno   Orsha Dnieper

Smorgoni   Bereśina   French retreat   Kaluga

Bonaparte's   Minsk   Tula
opening offensive   Moghilev

Fortresses

The French Campaign 1814

0   20   40 Miles
0   20   40   60 Kilometres

Meuse

Laon
Soissons   Aisne

Compiègne
Rheims
Oise
Château Thierry   Épernay
Meaux   Vauchamps   Châlons-
    Marne   sur-Marne
Montmirail   Champeaubert
La Fère-
Sézanne   Champenoise
PARIS   Seine
Nogent   Arcis-sur-Aube
Aube   Brienne
Montereau   Troyes   La Rothière

Fortresses

French advance
Projected advance
French pursuit
Allies

BRUSSELS

Waterloo Campaign
up to morning of battle

0   5   10   15 Miles
0   10   20 Kilometres

Hal   Waterloo
Mont   Wavre
St Jean

Wellington   Blücher   Grouchy

Quatre-Bras   Gembloux

Ligny   Meuse
Ney   Blücher   Namur
Mons   Charleroi   Meuse
Bonaparte

Sambre

Fortresses

Battle of Waterloo
18 June 1815

0   500   1000   1500 Yards
0   500   1000 Metres

Waterloo
and Brussels

Zieten's Prussian Corps
6pm–7pm

Fortified farms
French Infantry   Cavalry
Allied Infantry   Cavalry

Mont St Jean   Ohein

Saint Lambert

Braine l'Alleud
Wellington   La Haie   Wavre

La Haye Sainte
Château de   Papelotte   Bülow's Prussian
Hougoumont   Corps 1pm

Lasne
La Belle
Alliance

The Guard   Plancenoit   Bülow 6pm–7pm

1 Attack by D'Erlon Corps 1.30pm–3.30pm
2 Cavalry attack 3.30pm–5.30pm
Nivelles   3 Attack on Wellington's centre 6pm–7pm
Rossomme   4 Attack by the Guard 7.30pm
Quatre-Bras

PROLOGUE

At about 5 p.m. on 8 April 1792, Easter Day, Lieutenant-Colonel Napoleone Buonaparte, second-in-command of a battalion of republican volunteers on duty in the Corsican city of Ajaccio, heard sudden yells and shots from the nearby Rue de la Cathédrale. Ordering half a dozen of his officers to follow him, he ran towards the Cathedral. It being Easter Day, this was packed with the devout and therefore, in the opinion of Lieutenant-Colonel Buonaparte, who was a fervent Jacobin and hater of religion, the reactionary. In front of the Cathedral he found a hostile mob, some of whose members were brandishing muskets they had just seized from a platoon of his volunteers. Buonaparte was not yet twenty-three: about five foot six and a half inches in height, lean but thick-shouldered; a fine roman head, straggly brown hair, olive skin, pale blue-grey eyes, a curled lip above a jutting chin. Without hesitation he stepped up to the crowd and demanded the muskets back. An animated argument in the local Italian patios ensued. Then more anti-republican townsfolk poured out of the Cathedral, their hostility to the volunteers newly fortified by their devotions. Anger crackled into fresh violence, and a musket-shot dropped one of Buonaparte's officers dead. Buonaparte and his remaining companions bolted for safety into a nearby house, later to make their circumspect way back to battalion headquarters in the Séminaire.

By now Ajaccio was swarming with townspeople equipped with knives and pistols and loudly proclaiming their keen wish to employ them on the volunteers. There was much random firing, both by republicans and anti-republicans; more casualties. A local civil war had thus got under way. And Lieutenant-Colonel Buonaparte himself bore much responsibility for the tension which had led to it. His opportunity arose from a decree of the National Assembly in Paris that monastic houses and religious orders were to be dissolved. The Directory (or administration) of Corsica, itself fervently republican, had made haste to carry out the Assembly's decree. But in March 1792 after a public meeting the leading civic bodies of Ajaccio petitioned the Directory that the Capucins, one of the banned orders, should not be dissolved. The Directory refused, and in the cause of the revolutionary ideals of liberty and the rights of man, informed the petitioners that their public meeting was an illegal assembly.

To Jean Christophe Saliceti, the chief official of the Directory, and especially to Lieutenant-Colonel Buonaparte, here was a splendid opportunity for crushing the supporters of the *ancien régime* in Ajaccio, those 'enemies of the nation', and turning the city into a republican fief. Buonaparte had therefore urged that the presence of four companies of republican volunteers in Ajaccio was 'very urgent and necessary'. The volunteers, most of them country people, were duly sent into the city, with the hardly surprising consequence that ill-feeling between them and the intensely religious townsfolk had swiftly festered. On Easter Day itself 'unconstitutional' priests (those who, in obedience to papal edict, refused to swear a first loyalty to the new French constitution) conducted a service at the Convent of St Francis; their supporters announced that they would hold a religious procession on the morrow. 'They declare schism,' said Buonaparte. 'Those people are ready for any madness.' The brawl in the Rue de la Cathédrale had done the rest.

And now that open conflict had begun Lieutenant-Colonel Buonaparte proposed to exploit it in order to gain his and his associates' political aims in Ajaccio. In particular he meant to gain control of the Citadel, then held in the name of King Louis XVI by Colonel Maillard, commanding the 42nd Regiment of Infantry. For the husk of royal authority, of the old order, still survived in France and French possessions, even though it was nearly a year now since the King and his Queen, Marie-Antoinette, had failed in their attempt to flee the country and been brought back to the Tuileries as virtual prisoners. Without possession of the Citadel republican domination of Ajaccio could not be complete. The key to Buonaparte's *putsch*[1] lay therefore in Colonel Maillard and his four hundred regular soldiers.

Unfortunately for Buonaparte's purposes Colonel Maillard was an officer of Wellingtonian mould, solid and straightforward, imbued with a simple loyalty to the King and the law, and resolved to do his duty. As he saw it, his duty did not include allowing a rabble of armed political thugs to take over the Citadel. Nevertheless, Buonaparte, for his part, brought notable qualities – tactical adroitness, and a driving urge to impose his will on others – to the task of bluffing, bustling and browbeating Maillard and the municipal authorities into defeat.

His offensive began on the very evening of Easter Day. He and his colonel, one Quenza, visited Maillard and informed him that their volunteers were now in great, but of course entirely unprovoked, danger from the malignant townspeople. They pleaded that Maillard should therefore accord the volunteers asylum within the Citadel. Maillard refused: he would, he told them, allow no armed men in the Citadel except on the orders of the King, his ministers, or his generals. Nor did he accede to their request for ammunition.

Next day, while the narrow, dusty thoroughfares resounded to sporadic firing, Buonaparte and Quenza consoled themselves for their rebuff by arresting the justice of the peace charged with investigating the violence. The justice later made his escape through a back window of the volunteers' quarters with the connivance of other, more squeamish, republican officers who feared for his life.

At the request of the municipality of Ajaccio, Maillard now ordered the volunteers to withdraw from the streets and their present quarters to the Convent of St Francis, outside the city. Buonaparte and Quenza were warned that they must obey this order according to the law, or be pronounced rebels. Buonaparte, however, obtained from the procureur-syndic of the district, a family friend, a counter-order overruling the instructions of the municipality. Moreover, after a fruitless day of secret negotiations between all the interested parties, the Buonaparte family friend ordered Maillard to protect the volunteers as well as the townspeople.

But Maillard would not be outflanked or imposed upon; he flatly refused to do other than carry out the legal order already given him by the municipality.

Buonaparte, however, equally refused to withdraw the volunteers, on the specious grounds that, despite the moderation of their conduct and a flag of truce, they were being fired on by 'rebels', and could not quit their present posts without great personal danger. He and Quenza assured Maillard that tranquillity was their keenest desire; their men, they promised, would refrain from all acts of hostility should the townspeople agree to do likewise. If the municipality would only rescind its order to withdraw from the city to the Convent of St Francis, they for their part would send back to the countryside those peasant volunteers whose habits most upset the inhabitants of Ajaccio.

This time Maillard, a good man wishing to conciliate and avert bloodshed, allowed himself to be taken in. He accepted the offered compromise, and informed the local justice of the peace accordingly. During the night, however, Buonaparte responded to his gesture by seizing various houses by surprise and so extending the area under the volunteers' control to an entire city quarter.

On the following day Buonaparte, Quenza and Maillard patched up another truce; a respite which the contending parties employed in fortifying the houses they occupied. It also enabled Buonaparte himself, exhilarated by the drug of action and conflict, to ride round on his horse haranguing his posts of volunteers on the need to punish the enemies of liberty. Later a picket of the 42nd Regiment with a white flag brought a fresh order to the volunteers to quit Ajaccio, and this time signed by both the municipal and the district authorities. This order too went without effect. Buonaparte was still determined to get his men into the Citadel. One of his officers suggested that Maillard should be seized the next time he left the Citadel to go into the town. Buonaparte himself put forward a more subtle plan – that of inciting Maillard's troops to mutiny. At Buonaparte's instigation a letter was therefore sent to the non-commissioned officers and soldiers of the garrison warning them against Maillard, an aristocrat, and pointing out that their officers did not merit their trust.

Unfortunately the 42nd Regiment proved so blind to these republican truths as merely to hand the letter to Colonel Maillard, and to swear to obey him and the municipality and to defend Ajaccio to the end.

By now food and bread were running short in the city owing to a blockade by republican peasantry. The municipality reluctantly decided to run a cannon out of the Citadel and fire a blank shot to warn the volunteers to quit the city or be expelled by force. On learning of this intention, Buonaparte immediately wrote to Maillard that he held *Maillard* responsible for all the disorders; the volunteers, he claimed, only desired a peaceful settlement.

On the morning of 12 April two cannon were trained on the volunteers' principal strongholds. Buonaparte thereupon promptly sent the municipality a letter drafted by him and signed by all his officers falsely alleging that his battalion had been authorized by the Directory of the department of Corsica to stand fast in its present posts, and to bring in more national guards from the countryside. The municipality, this highly characteristic document asserted, would be responsible for any consequent damage to the city. If the guns were not withdrawn within the hour, the countryside would be summoned to suppress 'the enemies of the Constitution' by force. By way of rasping the municipality's nerves still further, the letter added that the officers were already finding it difficult to keep their volunteers in hand.

The municipality of Ajaccio proved not so staunch as Colonel Maillard. Fearful for their city, they sent a deputation to Buonaparte's headquarters, where a 'peace' was agreed. But when the municipality asked Maillard to approve and guarantee the deal, he refused. His soldiers, he said, were only agents of the law; he could not accept the arrangement made with Buonaparte without breaking the law. He thereupon simply withdrew his guns and his men into the Citadel. Buonaparte was left to save his battalion's face by hanging on in his posts until two commissioners arrived from the island's Directory to sort out the whole question of the conflict in Ajaccio.

Yet the arrival of these commissioners was also a fruit of Buonaparte's fertile tactical invention, for they had been dispatched because of his urgent private letters to Saliceti and to his brother Joseph, were themselves republicans and proceeded now to apply republican justice by arresting prominent Ajaccio citizens.

In the course of a wordy and self-excusing report Buonaparte later justified his defence of a legal order from Maillard and the municipality on the grounds that in 'a terrible crisis' like this 'a man was needed who, if he had been asked after the event to swear that he had broken no laws, would have replied instead like Cicero or Mirabeau: "I swear I have saved the Republic!"' He explained how he, Buonaparte, had acted throughout in a 'consciousness of right', so enabling him to defeat 'the most cunningly woven plots and calumnies'. As for his volunteers, the Directory would, he averred, 'praise their moderation.'[2]

Buonaparte's tactics against Maillard and the municipal authorities of Ajaccio could hardly be bettered by any modern political militant, least of all in the unhesitating assertion of the moral initiative by means of loading his opponents with the blame for conflict he himself had provoked.

There is indeed much more that is revealing of Buonaparte in this abortive Corsican *putsch* as an obscure provincial Jacobin than in some of the grand episodes of his later career. For here, displayed in miniature, are all his essential characteristics as a politician and a soldier.

At the hands of Colonel Maillard he had sustained his first defeat. Before he suffered his last, he was to enjoy a striking succession of victories. But the pattern was to remain the same.

'May it never be drawn except for the defence of the Republic . . .': sabre given to Bonaparte in Egypt. *Bulloz*

I

ALONE IN THE MIDST OF MEN

NAPOLEONE BUONAPARTE was born in Ajaccio on 15 August 1769 even less of a Frenchman than a contemporary American or Irishman was English. For Corsica was Italian by language, culture and historical connection; only ceded to France by the Republic of Genoa in 1768. So little did the Corsicans relish becoming French subjects that they rose in a war of independence under their national hero Paoli. Napoleone's own father, Carlo-Maria, had been one of the Corsican leaders in this war; his mother Letizia had endured all the hardships of guerrilla warfare in the mountains while pregnant with him. The French army only extinguished Corsican resistance a few months before Napoleone was born.

He therefore grew up a passionate Corsican patriot who nourished a no less passionate hatred of the French as alien oppressors. But if he in no sense felt himself to be French, the French for their part in no way regarded the Corsicans as other than newly-conquered foreigners with outlandish customs and institutions. Moreover in French terms Napoleone's social status was as ambiguous as his national identity. His father diligently proved the four quarters of nobility required to win Napoleone a free place at a royal *école militaire*; and yet after the Revolution Napoleone was easily able to avoid the fatal stigma of '*Ci-devant*' aristocrat; nobody was to dispute it when in 1794 he declared himself non-noble.

For the Buonaparte family property hardly amounted to a French seigneurial estate, being a typical Mediterranean assortment of vineyards, olive groves and other lands scattered over the countryside, a house in Ajaccio and another in the country. Nobility in Corsica did not imply the privileged status enjoyed by the French noblesse but rather leadership of a clan, as in the Scotland of the day. And just as in Scotland clan rivalries were ferocious and clan memories long; the Corsicans cherished the institution of the vendetta. Napoleone himself much admired the vendetta, possibly because it chimed so well with his own attitude towards those who crossed him. Vengeance, he once remarked to a friend, was according to Corsican tradition 'a duty imposed by heaven and nature'.[1] He became no less imbued with the Corsican sense of clan solidarity. As Emperor of the French he was to find his brothers and in-laws good kingdoms much as his ancestors might have found their relatives plum jobs in the local administration.

About Napoleone's childhood there are many legend-embellishing fictions, few accredited facts. The noisy, extrovert and free-and-easy life of a provincial Italian family provided its setting – an elder and a younger brother, a sister (more were to follow after he had left home), grandparents, aunts, cousins and uncles. His father, an amateur of letters in the eighteenth-century style, was more preoccupied with his books and writings than with disciplining his turbulent brood. That was a task for the real head of the family, Napoleone's mother Letizia, handsome, of formidable authority both physically and morally. Although Napoleone's father learned passable French, his mother clung to her native Italian, which therefore remained the language of the Buonaparte household, and, since his wet-nurse spoke it too, in every sense Napoleone's mother-tongue.

Such reliable anecdotes as exist about him as a child portray an egotistic and aggressive little boy with a precocious talent for mathematics. He himself was to acknowledge on St Helena that 'I was a quarreller, full of mischief', and much given to thumping other children and having tantrums.[2] In particular he relentlessly bullied his easy-going elder brother Giuseppe (later Joseph, in the French spelling), making it his wily custom to run to his mother in order to accuse Giuseppe of tormenting *him*. Dissembling came easy to him; one of his uncles is supposed to have predicted a great future for him because he had such a habit of lying.[3] Sometimes his tantrums – screamed abuse and flaring nostrils – were genuine enough; sometimes put on in order to gain an end, a ploy he was to find useful throughout his life.[4] Often he was restless and destructive, a scorer of marks on tables, a breaker of plants, a puller of stuffing out of chairs.

(left) '. . . an amateur of letters in the eighteenth-century style . . .': Carlo-Maria Buonaparte, Napoleon's father (1746–85). *Radio Times Hulton Picture Library*

(right) '. . . of formidable authority both physically and morally': Napoleon's mother, Letizia (1750–1836). *Mansell Collection*

This combative Napoleone decided that he wanted to be a soldier when he grew up. His mother was to recall that when she gave her children a large empty room to play in:

> Jerome and the three others busied themselves with jumping and painting puppets on the walls. Napoleon, for whom I had brought a drum and a wooden sword, painted nothing but soldiers drawn up on parade . . .[5]

His brother Joseph has an anecdote which casts some light on Napoleone's nascent self-will and love of domination. At their school:

> . . . the children were placed opposite each other on either side of the classroom under huge flags, one of which bore the initials 's.p.q.r.', the Roman flag, the other being that of Carthage. As the elder of the two I had been placed by the teacher on his side under the Roman flag; Napoleone, impatient at finding himself under the Carthaginian flag, which was not that of the conquerors, would not rest until he obtained permission for us to change places . . .[6]

This assertive little boy already showed remarkable mental capacity. His mother recounted in old age how a lean-to room had to be built on the terrace of the house so that he could study undisturbed by his brothers; how clever he was at mathematics; how he would only go out in the evening, 'and walk absent-mindedly about the streets, without having tidied himself up and always forgetting to pull up his fallen stockings.'[7] Since he was supposed to be in love with a little girl called Giacominetta, the local urchins would prance after him shrieking:

> *Napoleone de mezza calzetta*
> *Fa l'amore a Giacominetta.*[8]

In 1778, when this somewhat solitary and introspective child was still only nine years old, he found himself abruptly wrenched from the rowdy life of the Ajaccio alleys and the enfolding affection of a Latin family, from the brilliant thyme-scented

landscapes of his homeland and sent into distant exile in the bleak plains of northern France.

AFTER THE COLLAPSE of Corsican independence, Napoleone's father decided to make the most of his new status as a member of the French noblesse. He employed his charm and diplomatic skill in wheedling favours out of the local French administration, and in particular out of the Comte de Marbeuf, the governor. Thanks to Marbeuf, whose brother was Bishop of Autun, Joseph Buonaparte was to enter the Church, while Napoleone himself was found a free place at the *Ecole Militaire* at Brienne in Champagne, his father having first successfully proved that he enjoyed the qualifying noble ancestry.[9] Next to Napoleone's name on the list of admissions to *écoles militaires* appears a terse reference to his father's finances: 'three children, no fortune.'[10]

On 1 January 1779 Napoleone and his brother were delivered by their father to the college at Autun where Joseph was to prepare for the priesthood and Napoleone was to spend three months learning basic French. Five years were to elapse before Napoleone saw his father again; eight years before he saw his mother. When the time came for the brothers to part as well, Joseph, according to his own account, was 'all in tears, Napoleone only shed one tear which he tried in vain to conceal.'[11]

At the *Ecole Militaire* of Brienne the nine-year-old Napoleone confronted the existence virtually of an orphan in an institution, and, moreover, one in a foreign country whose language he at first only spoke haltingly. No pupil was allowed to leave the premises except on communal Sunday walks during their entire five or six year stay, let alone go home. Nor could Napoleone hope for visits *from* his family, like the French boys. The regime of the *école* was harsh to the point of inhumanity – sparsely furnished sleeping cubicles locked at night; only one blanket even in the icy winters of Champagne; a studying and praying day that began at 6 a.m. and ended at 8 p.m. The *école* – like the other twelve *écoles militaires* – was run by a religious order, in this case the Minimes of the Order of St Benedict. Religion coloured the whole of school-life, transforming Napoleone, hitherto a pious child, into a lifelong despiser of the Church and the professionally religious. Since the Minimes were poor and ignorant, Brienne rated among the lowest of the *écoles militaires* in quality of education. The purpose of these schools was to prepare sons of the nobility for the *Ecole Militaire* in Paris; however, except for a course in fortification in the senior year, they were not really military schools at all, but colleges dispensing an eighteenth-century gentleman's primary education – French language and literature, Latin, geography, history, mathematics and those essential genteel accomplishments of fencing, dancing and good manners. The ablest pupils were selected later for the artillery, engineers or the navy; those too stupid even for the cavalry were sent back to their families.

Napoleone seems to have reacted to Brienne as a natural rebel reacts to a reform school – the more so as an exiled Corsican surrounded by the hated conquerors of his homeland. His schoolfellows mocked his French, with its Italianisms and Italian accent, dubbing him *la paille au nez* ('straw in the nose') because he pronounced his name 'Napahl-yonay'. He for his part clung to his Corsican identity, an ambiguous posture for a pupil on a French royal bursary granted to him as a French noble. But he hated this dependence on French charity. As one of his fellow pupils wrote later:

> The idea of dependence had for him something demeaning about it and, when often offended by his comrades' jokes on the union of Corsica and the French monarchy, he would reply indignantly, 'I hope one day to be able to restore her to freedom.'[12]

At the same time the sneers of boys of distinguished lineage and connections at Court taught him that in the scales of French society the Buonapartes barely counted among the noblesse at all. So at Brienne Napoleone was constantly reminded that both socially and nationally he was a misfit, a mongrel creature. Quarrelsome and introverted even at home, he responded in the classic pattern of the problem-child: outbursts of violence, verbal and otherwise; withdrawal from the communal life of the school. According to the fellow pupil already quoted, he was 'gloomy and savage, almost always shut up in himself, one would have said like a creature recently emerged from some forest . . .'[13] Such behaviour only worsened things, making him even more unpopular with the boys and the monks. For one misdemeanour he was condemned to eat his dinner on his knees alone at the refectory door, a humiliation so disturbing to him that he suffered some kind of nervous seizure, rolled about the floor and vomited. It was little wonder that his younger brother Lucien, who spent some months with him at Brienne in 1784, found him hard and withdrawn, greeting Lucien 'without the least sign of tenderness, and I owe to these first impressions the repugnance I have always felt in bowing before him.'[14]

'Napoleon Blowing Up His Comrades' – an English lampoon, by George Cruikshank, on his behaviour at the *Ecole Militaire* of Brienne. Though this incident is fictitious, he was a lonely misfit, noted for his 'gloomy and savage' nature. *British Museum*

NAPOLEON BLOWING UP HIS COMRADES.

Yet if Brienne did little to soften his natural egotism or develop his social or moral sense, it forced on the growth of his mental powers. For reading provided his refuge. He became the school library's best customer. He shone at history and mathematics. The second of all his letters to survive, written at the age of fifteen to an uncle on the topic of his brother Joseph's wish to exchange the Church for the army, exhibits the true Napoleonic incisiveness. Even the paragraphs were numbered like a military order:

1. . . . he [Joseph] has not the courage to face the perils of an action. His poor health does not permit him to support the hardship of a campaign, and my brother only envisages military life from the point of view of garrison life; yes, my dear brother would make a fine garrison officer, elegant, gay . . .

2. He has received an education suitable for the Church. The bishop of Autun would have given him a very large benefice, and he would have been sure of becoming a bishop. What advantages for the family! . . .

3. He wishes to find a place in a military corps; very well, but in which corps? In the Navy? He knows nothing of mathematics . . . The Engineers, where he will need four or five years to learn his profession? . . . to be hard at work all day is not compatible with his lightness of character . . .[15]

Brienne, Buonaparte was to say in later years, was 'the homeland of my thought; it is there that I experienced my first impressions as a man' – a comment that may be read in more than one way.[16]

On 30 October 1784 Napoleone left Brienne for the *Ecole Militaire* in Paris, guided there by the kind of lucky chances which later were to seduce him into believing in his 'star'. For his first wish to join the navy was thwarted by a new inspector-general of *écoles militaires* who pointed out that his time at Brienne had not been long enough to qualify him for that service. So he opted for the artillery instead, fearing, however, that being weak in classics he would fail to get a place at the *Ecole Militaire*. But the Minister of War authorized a special intake of candidates outstanding in mathematics; and a letter of 22 October informed Napoleone that King Louis XVI had awarded him a (free) place as a gentleman cadet.

In the *Ecole Militaire*, he had joined one of the elite institutions of the *ancien régime*, founded in 1751 to prepare sons of the noblesse for the armed forces. Housed in an austerely grand building by Gabriel overlooking the Champ de Mars, its classes changed to beat of drum; the cadets paraded on feast days in uniform of blue and silver with their band at their head; and the entire ambiance was one of military elegance. Napoleone loved it, even though he did not always love his fellow cadets. Yet it was not a military academy in the modern sense, with courses in tactics and the art of command. It existed to supply a broad education for future officers and to polish future gentlemen of the world. In this latter purpose the *Ecole Militaire* wholly failed with Napoleone, who was never to lose a certain provincial *gaucherie*. The curriculum was exacting, with extra classes in mathematics for cadets studying for the artillery and the engineers. None the less Napoleone kept up his habit of lonely reading, becoming the school bookworm just as at Brienne.

In the congenial military atmosphere, with a staff of officers instead of monks,

Napoleone ceased to be quite such an embattled and embittered outsider. He made a few close friends. With other non-paying 'king's cadets' he waged war on the haughty sons of great families, yet still felt, as victims of snobbery will, an unacknowledged envy and deference towards his 'betters'; in fact a snobbery of his own which was to become all too manifest later in his career. His Corsican patriotism still blazed out in defiance of the alien conquerors of his country about him. For this he was mocked as much as he had been at Brienne. When so teased he would get out a fencing foil and, amid howls of laughter, try to fight all his tormentors. Yet what *was* his true country? His national identity remained as ambiguous as ever; more so indeed, as a member of the school staff once reminded him: 'Sir, you are a king's cadet; you must remember this and moderate your love for Corsica, which is after all part of France.'[17]

At the beginning of March 1785 he learned that his father had died at Montpellier, in Languedoc, of cancer of the stomach. It is hard to gauge how deeply this loss distressed him, since he had seen his father only once since the beginning of

'. . . one of the elite institutions of the *ancien régime* . . .' The *Ecole Militaire* in Paris, founded in 1751 to prepare sons of the noblesse for the armed forces. Napoleon was a King's cadet during 1784–5. *Bulloz*

1779, and since his letters of condolence to his mother and other relatives are stilted exercises in appropriate eighteenth-century cliché on the death of a dear one. Perhaps his references to 'the first transports of my grief' and 'the incalculable loss of this dear husband' were polished under the eye of the school staff. Or perhaps they offer an early example of his ability to assume different roles, different personalities, according to the occasion.

In any case the approach of the competitive entrance examination for places in artillery schools diverted his mind from sorrow to mathematics, geometry and trigonometry. He swotted harder than ever, passed in September 1785, and was posted to the regiment of his choice, La Fère-Artillerie, stationed at the artillery school of Valence in the Dauphiné. With the end of nearly seven years of unremitting confinement, Napoleone suddenly entered upon the status of an adult, riding in the *diligence* down the Lyon road a free man.

He donned the uniform of La Fère-Artillerie with pride – blue breeches, blue waistcoat; royal blue coat with red facings and pockets braided in red; epaulette with gold and silk fringe. 'I know nothing more beautiful than my gunner's uniform,' he was to remark as First Consul when trying on a new uniform as colonel of grenadiers.[18] And the regiment taught him well: practical training as simple gunner, corporal, sergeant and officer; theoretical study in chemistry, physics, engineering drawing and his favourite subject, mathematics.

In Valence, a town of the Midi whose pot tiles must have made him feel halfway home, the harsh routine of Brienne and Paris gave way to the social round. He lived in lodgings in a big, square old house where the crooked alley of the Rue du Croissant meets the hardly wider Grande Rue. His landlord, a moving spirit in Valence's life of the mind and culture, took him up as a protégé. The landlord's charming but unmarried fifty-year-old daughter, Marie-Claudine, mothered their awkward sixteen-year-old lodger. Another understanding middle-aged lady, a Madame Colombier, invited him to stay at her country house, prompting him to judge, like Rousseau in his *Confessions* (which young Buonaparte read with rather undiscriminating enthusiasm), that the conversation of such an older woman was worth more than whole tomes of philosophy. And then there were the quite other charms of Madame Colombier's teenage daughter Caroline, with whom, so he said on St Helena, he once picked cherries at dawn. Under all these happy influences Buonaparte seems to have softened and relaxed, as if after all he might settle down to a steady career as a regimental officer and marry some suitable woman of sense and character.

On 1 September 1786 he left for Corsica on leave. 'I have arrived in my homeland,' he wrote on arriving in Ajaccio, 'aged seventeen years and one month, seven years nine months after leaving it.'[19] All the family, including his wet-nurse, was there to welcome him. His brother Joseph was to say wistfully twenty years later, 'Ah! The glorious emperor will never make up for the Napoleon whom I so much loved and whom I wish I could find again just as I knew him in 1786.'[20]

But he had come home to trouble. His late father had left the family virtually broke. Their influential French friends in Corsica had all died or been posted. In particular, there was the affair of the mulberry trees. In 1782 Buonaparte's father had obtained a government concession to start a nursery of mulberry trees. Unfortunately the government gave up the scheme, leaving the Buonapartes with the trees and no compensation. Buonaparte tackled the bureaucracy with energy and aggression; the bureaucracy fought a skilled delaying action. Eventually he decided he would have to go to Paris to settle the matter, and applied for an extension of leave on medical grounds (he had in fact been suffering from a fever). He was to be absent from his regiment for twenty-one months in all; but that was nothing unusual in the French army of the period.

In Paris he displayed the same spirit of attack, hammering on every bureaucrat's door, soliciting at Court, even obtaining an audience with the King's chief minister. He swallowed his jagged pride and wrote grovelling letters – useful practice for a future careerist. Yet his time in Paris was not only spent in ministerial anti-rooms; he went often to the theatre, and, a young man so long shut up in celibate institutions, strolled among the whores of the Palais-Royal in a mixture of repulsion and fascination. One freezing night in November 1787 he took one of them back to his lodgings, hesitations overcome because instead of the usual 'sergeant-major' manner, she had an air of frailty and softness. He later wrote up their brief communion, probably his first sexual experience, into a trite and rather priggish autobiographical fragment.

In January 1788, still without success over the mulberries, he was back in Corsica, only to find his mother now desperately hard-up, with five children at school and Joseph at the university of Pisa, and not a servant in the house. 'The sorry condition of our family,' he wrote to an uncle that summer, 'afflicts me all the more because I can see no remedy for it.'[21] It was perhaps the grimmest period of his youth; serving like Brienne and the *Ecole Militaire* in Paris to wind tighter the spring of his resentments and ambition.

When at last he rejoined his regiment in June 1788, it had changed its station to Auxonne, where the bastions and ramparts of the fortress look out over lush Burgundian water-meadows and the broad, slow Saône. Here, broke except for money spent on books, alone in his room in one of the bastions, he plunged back into solitary reading. Although he caught a fever from the stagnant water in the moat beneath his window, he was soon hard at it again in the new year. 'I have no resource here but to work,' he wrote. 'I go to bed at ten and rise at four. I have only one meal a day.'[22] His fifteen months at Auxonne in 1788–9 therefore mark the climax, though not the end, of all the intense private studying of his youth. And his notebooks – including his experiments at writing – reveal much more about him as a young man than the scant reminiscences of those who knew him at the time. They reveal indeed not one character, but two, and those discordant to the point of paradox.

IN LATER YEARS he prided himself on being a scientist *manqué*, and there was some substance in the claim, since in his artillery school he had received as good an education in general science and engineering as to be found anywhere in the Europe of the period. Its foundation was mathematics, a subject Buonaparte had always found deeply congenial because it was, in his own words, 'where all is resolved by logic and where all is rational.'[23] Since the calculating mind needs data, Buonaparte's notebooks manifest a voracious appetite for facts and figures of every kind, plundered out of all the standard works of the epoch. He summarized the constitutions and administrative systems of leading states from Britain to China, their histories, natural resources, trade statistics, revenues. He studied natural history, noting such topics as life expectancy in different countries at different periods. He amassed geographical facts as if compiling a world gazetteer, from climatic zones to the languages, customs and skin colours of the races. He completed a dossier on British possessions in the East, not omitting an analysis of the revenues of Bengal.

This mathematical, factual Buonaparte took a poor view of human passion, always excepting patriotic fervour. He considered it a 'precipice' from which we are guarded 'by the eyes of reason'. Ambition seemed to him particularly dangerous: a madness; a fire which, he wrote, only comes to an end when it has consumed everything. Ambition was also bad for the character: 'Crimes are no more to it than games; the cabal no more than a means; calumny and slander mere figures of speech.'[24] Moreover, ambition 'is never content, even on the summit of greatness.'[25] Sexual love was another passion Buonaparte condemned – 'harmful to society and to the individual happiness of men . . .'[26] It was a product of weakness and loneliness. It shut our ears to reason. It deprived us of command over ourselves and our actions. Therefore, in order to fulfil one's patriotic duty, one must know how to master one's soul and close it to love.

Yet cohabiting uneasily in the notebooks with this Buonaparte of data and calculation is a very different creature – given up to romantic fantasy and dreams of glory, emotional, fascinated by strife and violence. This second Buonaparte recorded the histories of nations as chronicles of war, murder, usurpation and revolt. He thrilled to the exploits of great patriotic heroes, more especially as represented in tragic drama. Corneille's *Cinna* brought him to tears. At home he loved to declaim such heroic parts himself in company with his brother Joseph. He admired Rousseau, the outstanding figure in the new romantic movement in literature and ideas, and his own romanticism vented itself in attempts at historical or adventure novels, love stories; all highly coloured in language and far-fetched in plot.

His views on politics and society, owing much to Rousseau's *Du Contrat Social*, display Buonaparte the egotist and Buonaparte the mathematician–engineer in uneasy collaboration. For society is conceived of as one great machine, constructed according to correct calculations which in turn are based on the right data. There is little sense of free association between individuals or groups, little sense of any natural community larger than the Corsican-style family or clan; no sense of organic social growth. Instead there are the competing egotisms of individuals, bridled or organized by the higher egotism of the State, whose will impels and directs the whole national apparatus. Buonaparte's ideal State enjoyed this untrammelled power because it was the organ of the people's will. Naïvely he believed that only hereditary monarchies could be tyrants. He scorned the *ancien régime* in France, with its agglomeration of different societies, partly regional, partly aristocratic, guild or religious; this is what constitutes the 'privilege' which he and other progressives wished to sweep away. Buonaparte's chief complaint against the Catholic Church, for instance, lay in the very fact that it was independent of the State:

> Christianity forbids men to obey any command contrary to its laws . . . it thus contradicts the first article of the social contract, the basis of government, because it substitutes its private trust for the general will constituting sovereignty . . . it totally breaks the unity of the State . . .[27]

Lieutenant Buonaparte's political ideas thus point straight towards the tyranny of the Consulate and the Empire; indeed towards every modern tyranny where the State bosses the entire life of the people in the people's name.

Repeatedly in his writings he holds up 'energy' and 'strength' as virtues worthy of admiration, rather than adherence to principle or integrity of character. He displays little conception of duty, in the sense of sacrifice of self. On the contrary he more than once states that the purpose of human existence is the fulfilment of egotism: 'What is happiness? It is the object for which we are on earth . . .' And how is happiness achieved? 'Happiness is nothing else but the enjoyment of life in a way best suited to our nature . . .'[28]

Egotism then, self-will, was what drove that ill-matched team, Buonaparte the romantic and Buonaparte the calculator, on their way.

Yet apart from this fundamental split into two characters, his youthful writings also display him searching for a true identity amid a whole wardrobe of possible personalities: the philosopher, the sentimental novelist, the hero, the politician, the scientist, the administrator, the soldier. The search mirrored the ambiguities underlying his life: a nobleman scorned by the noblesse; a Corsican patriot in a French uniform; a man without a place. Even during the friendships and social round of Valence he had written:

> Always alone in the midst of men, I return to dream with myself and give myself up to all the force of my melancholy. What madness makes me desire my own destruction? Without doubt, the problem of what to do in this world . . . Life is a burden to me because I feel no pleasure and because everything is affliction to me. It is a burden to me because the men with whom I have to live and will probably always live have ways as different from mine as the light of the moon from that of the sun. I cannot then pursue the only manner of living which could enable me to put up with existence, whence follows a disgust for everything.[29]

Two months after Buonaparte rejoined his regiment at Auxonne in June 1788, Louis XVI, under the pressure of France's worsening financial and political crisis, convoked the States-General, or parliament, which had last met in 1614. It was the move which eventually opened the way for all the forces seeking to bring down the *ancien régime*. Within a year the Bastille had fallen, an event at once a symbol and a trigger. For Europe the Revolution was to mean the destruction of a civilization; for Lieutenant Buonaparte, unimaginable opportunity.

II

THE ATTRIBUTES OF A TYRANT

IN THE AFTERNOON OF 19 JULY 1789 Auxonne followed at five days' delay the new Parisian fashion of clanging tocsin and rioting populace. Like most risings in the provinces, Auxonne's revolution stemmed from resentment at feudal dues and obligations of the kind abolished in England by the end of the Middle Ages, and by sheer misery at high unemployment and high food prices. On 16 August – it was less than a week after the new National Assembly in Paris finally abolished all such privileges and feudal dues – La Fère-Artillerie mutinied. The mutineers' first revolutionary demand, loudly voiced outside the colonel's house, was for the contents of the regimental strongbox. The colonel, his loyal personnel being outnumbered, gave way, and the mutineers celebrated the people's victory by getting drunk and dancing the farandole. It was decided to disperse the regiment in detachments along the Saône. Baron du Teil groaned that 'the troops no longer recognize authority and yet they are supposed to maintain it.'[1] It was true of much of the royal army, and it spelled the doom of the *ancien régime*.

Lieutenant Buonaparte's attitude to the happenings in Auxonne and Paris was equivocal. As a soldier he could not approve of civil disorder, let alone mutiny. Yet he was convinced that the tide of revolution was going to sweep over whatever obstacles might be placed in its way. Moreover, as anti-monarchist, anti-cleric and anti-noble, and a believer in rule by the sovereign people, he sympathized with its objectives. He applied therefore in September 1789 to go to Corsica on leave – in order to ride the tide himself, as a faster mode of progress than waiting for promotion in a dying military hierarchy. And in Corsica the wand of revolution touched Lieutenant Buonaparte, that morose, studious officer of La Fère-Artillerie, and changed him into a mob leader.

It was Napoleone himself who drafted a public letter from the revolutionaries of Corsica to the National Assembly in Paris warning it that reactionary forces still remained in control of the island, and who placed his name at the head of all the signatories. This letter was instrumental in the Assembly's decision in January 1790 to declare Corsica an integral part of France instead of a form of colony. Buonaparte's Corsican patriotism had thus been swallowed by his revolutionary ardour; he now believed that Corsica would find her freedom as part of the ideal new French state now under construction. His personal dream of one day leading his homeland back to independence yielded to the ambition of becoming a leader in French revolutionary politics, albeit with a Corsican power base. But such a swift and drastic switch in attitude must cast doubt on the depth of his earlier love of Corsica. Had the Corsican cause merely served as a banner of defiance against his French schoolfellows, a rallying point for himself in time of adversity? Or had it even simply acted as a vehicle of his own egotism until discarded in favour of a better one?

Thanks to extended leave and to storms in the Mediterranean which twice drove him back to Corsica, he did not rejoin his regiment until the beginning of 1791. The whole of 1790 saw him engrossed in his new career as revolutionary politician – and revolutionary politics in Corsica, complicated and enlivened as they were with clan rivalries, called for cunning, sharp elbows, and a not too fastidious sense of honesty. Brother Joseph was elected to the Ajaccio municipal council even though his opponents produced his birth certificate to prove that he was under age. The elections once over, Napoleone advocated that the new republican-dominated municipality should intimidate those citizens ill-judged enough to be of other opinion, or as he termed them, 'the arrogant, the proud and the prejudiced'. They now learned, in his words, 'even if trembling', to obey the magistracy 'as representing the people'.[2]

The years of submission and constriction fell away, the pleasures of conflict and the pursuit of domination grew upon him. In seeking to crush rivals of the Buonaparte clan on the general council of the department of Corsica, Napoleone urged that they should be sacked, on the grounds that they had fomented rumours and discontent; a charge that came particularly well from him. That such sackings would be illegal did not bother him. He merely quoted Montesquieu to the effect that there were causes in which a veil had to be cast over liberty just as one hid the statues of the gods. The safety of the people, averred Buonaparte, took precedent over principle. In January 1791, he joined the Ajaccio Jacobin Club at its foundation and thereafter never missed a meeting. With hungry features and pale-eyed stare projecting conviction, decision and sheer personal force, he quickly became its dominating member; the inspirer, and often the author, of pamphleteering attacks against political rivals and the husk of royal authority.

But even in these extraordinary times professional soldiers had eventually to rejoin their regiments, and in February 1791 Buonaparte found himself imprisoned again in the stale routine of Auxonne. The royalist officers of the regiment moreover offered only a cool welcome back to their notoriously Jacobin confrère. So he took up his studies again. As from 1 June, however, Lieutenant Buonaparte found himself posted to the 4th Artillery regiment at Valence, his old station. Only four days after he joined his new regiment on 16 June 1791, Louis XVI and Marie-Antoinette made the attempt to escape from France which ended in their discovery and apprehension at Varennes. As one consequence of this disastrously unlucky adventure, the National Assembly imposed a new oath on officers of the army, whereby they were to swear to maintain the constitution and only to obey orders arising from decrees of the National Assembly. This requirement completed the sundering of loyalties within the army. Revolutionary sympathizers like Buonaparte were quick to swear the new oath, while officers loyal to the king and royal authority resigned their commissions in great numbers; many of them to emigrate. These resignations proved as good as a war in opening up promotion for those who remained.

By now the ever-quickening pace of revolution in Paris, spurred on by economic distress and the power of the mob, was carrying change far beyond the limited aims of moderate reformers two years earlier. In 1789 the Abbé Sieyès had asserted that the 'nation exists before all things . . . Its will is always legal, it is the law itself . . .'³ But 'the nation' was swiftly becoming no more than a self-appointed elite of Parisian politicians. What this could mean in terms of tyranny grew more evident month by month, as all institutions which stood in the way of 'the nation' were trampled flat.

In the case of the Church the revolutionary attack was not only motivated by anti-religious bigotry and a desire to destroy independent centres of power, but also by pressing economic reasons. Since 1789 the revolutionary regime had confiscated all Church property and sold it in order to provide backing for the new paper currency, or *assignats*. For the nation's financial plight had given birth to a novel process of stripping capital assets so as to provide cash-flow. However, if bankruptcy were to go on being postponed in this fashion, it required the acquisition of more and more assets to be stripped. Economically as well as politically, the Revolution had entered upon a course of unstoppable dynamism.

Lieutenant Buonaparte, in his new *persona* of revolutionary agitator and Jacobin officer, was not at all out of sympathy with unstoppable dynamism. Eschewing the 'good society' in Valence he had enjoyed during his earlier posting, he joined the local republican club, where he harangued his fellow members and became secretary and librarian. 'This part of the country,' he enthused to a friend, 'is full of fire and zeal.'⁴ On 3 July 1791 a vast gathering took place in Valence to celebrate the bringing back of the King and Queen from Varennes to the Tuileries. Mass oaths of loyalty to the Constitution were sworn amid the fraternal joy of soldiers and populace. Buonaparte, intoxicated by such events, informed a friend that the 'southern blood runs in my vein with the speed of the Rhône; forgive me therefore if you find it hard to read my scrawl.'⁵ This was the period and the mood in which he wrote *Le Discours de Lyon*, an essay entered for a literary prize but justifiably rejected by the judges, being a rambling, pretentious disquisition on man and society full of echoes of modish claptrap by such intellectuals as Rousseau and the Abbé Sieyès.

But Corsica remained for him the land of revolutionary opportunity. In October, with a fresh grant of leave, he plunged back into the island's politics for another eight months. He was now the acknowledged manager of the Buonaparte family, although Joseph, as the eldest brother, remained its formal head. Napoleone's natural bossiness manifested itself by meddling in all family affairs large and small. Meekly his brothers and sisters acquiesced. 'We did not argue with him,' Lucien wrote later, 'he got nettled at the slightest criticism and became enraged at the slightest opposition.'⁶ His immediate ambition lay in getting himself elected to a commission in the local volunteers, for even though they were military rubbish, such a commission might enable him to remain in Corsica while at the same time conferring political leverage. Since ranks of lieutenant-colonel and upwards were exempt from a new regulation requiring regular officers to rejoin their regiments by 1 April 1792, Buonaparte decided to run for lieutenant-colonel, with one Quenza as running-mate for colonel. The climax of all the pressures and fiddles of an ingeniously crooked election was provided by the kidnapping by the Buonaparte clan of one of the three commissioners sent to Ajaccio to supervise the poll. It happened that the commissioners' choice of lodgings was politically important, because it would indicate to the voter which faction they favoured. One commissioner was ill-judged enough to lodge with enemies of the Buonapartes. After agonizingly considering how best to get him out of that house and into theirs, the Buonapartes decided to send round a strong-arm party and remove him by force. Napoleone explained to the victim, 'I wanted you to be free; you were not so at the Peraldis; here you are at home.'[7] When, the following day at the election, a prominent opponent of the Buonapartes attempted to object to this action, he was hooted down by Buonaparte supporters and dragged by the legs from the platform. Quenza and Buonaparte were then duly pronounced elected, to the great joy of the Buonaparte clan.

Although Lieutenant-Colonel Buonaparte now set about introducing some military order and efficiency into his volunteers, he was principally concerned with exploiting the tension between the Jacobins and the religious townsfolk of Ajaccio; a concern which bore fruit in the streetfighting of April 1792 and his abortive attempt to bluff or badger Colonel Maillard, commandant of the Citadel, into accepting his volunteers within its walls.

Meanwhile the Buonapartes, who at first had been staunch supporters of the returned Corsican leader Paoli, were steadily falling out with him, partly because Paoli still wished to restore Corsica's independence, partly because he regarded them as pushing young nuisances with Jacobin views, and instead favoured clients of his own. In May 1792 Paoli informed Joseph that a new battalion of volunteers (the colonelcy of which he had promised Napoleone) was not after all to be raised. That was one setback for Napoleone; another that his name had now been placed on a list of regular officers not present with their units. And without his regular soldier's pay, he was destitute. In passing on Paoli's bad news about the new battalion of volunteers, brother Joseph remarked to Napoleone that it 'seems to me that it would be the moment for you to return to France.'[8] So it seemed to Napoleone himself. His second career as a Jacobin politician in Corsica was at an end.

But already he had demonstrated that he interpreted the republican ideals of *liberté* and *fraternité* in practice as the rooting out of dissent and the exercise of domination over others. Already too he had transgressed against the convictions expressed less than a year earlier in *Le Discours de Lyon* about the evils of ambition and the unprincipled nature of the ambitious. Only a month after his return to France, his younger brother Lucien gave vent to a fear that in Napoleone ambition was stronger than love of the public weal. 'I believe,' he wrote with remarkable prescience, 'that in a free society he is a dangerous man; he seems to me to have the attributes of a tyrant, and I believe he would be one, if he were king, and that his would be a name of horror to posterity and to the sensitive patriot.'[9] Lucien discerned moreover a void in his brother where there ought to have been that core of human character, integrity: '. . . no men are more detested in history than those who change with the wind; I perceive, and it is not only as of today, that in the case of a [fresh] revolution, Napoleone would seek to keep himself at the top and, even for the sake of his material interests, I believe him to be capable of acting the turncoat.'[10]

At the end of May 1792 Buonaparte arrived in Paris to solicit reinstatement to the strength of the 4th Artillery from the Committee of Artillery, producing specious certificates from the Corsican authorities to excuse his absence from duty. He found Paris in vast turmoil. In April the National Assembly, undismayed by hovering national bankruptcy and the near dissolution of the army (out of some 9,000 officers, some 6,000 were, like Buonaparte, no longer with their units for one reason or another), had declared war on Austria; the first step towards twenty years of general European strife. Already a panic rout at Tournai had exposed France to invasion by an allied army under the Duke of Brunswick. The paper *assignat* had fallen to less than half its face value. Buonaparte reported the Parisian scene to Joseph in terse, perfunctory letters like reports from a battlefield:

Paris is in the greatest convulsions, [he wrote the day after his arrival]. It is flooded with outsiders and the malcontents are very numerous. The National Guard guarding the King at the Tuileries has been doubled. The corps of the Maison du Roi [once crack household troops] is to be broken up, being said to be in a very poor state . . .
I have not yet seen Marianna [his sister, still at school in the convent of St Cyr], I will go

The attack on the Tuileries by the Paris mob on 10 August 1792, followed by a massacre of nobles and Swiss Guards. Bonaparte was a disgusted eyewitness, writing: 'If Louis XVI had mounted his horse, the victory would have been his . . .'. *Musée Carnavalet, Paris. Photo: Lauros-Giraudon*

the day after tomorrow . . . Give my news to the family. Write to me promptly. I embrace you.[11]

On 10 August he was an eyewitness of the second, and more serious, of the summer's two attacks on the Tuileries by the Paris mob, when some eight hundred nobles and Swiss Guards were killed in the fighting or in the massacre that followed. On seeing a Marseillais about to slaughter a *garde du corps*, he said to him: 'Man of the Midi; let us spare this unfortunate! – Are you from the Midi? – Yes. – Ah well! Let us spare him.'[12] The conduct of the mob left him with a lifelong disgust with and contempt for the common man in action; a disgust which nevertheless accorded ill with his own recent exploitation of mob passion in Ajaccio. Perhaps even more revealing of his response to the mob in action was a letter he wrote to Joseph on the very day of the assault on the Tuileries: 'if Louis XVI had mounted his horse, the victory would have been his . . .'[13]

The violence of 10 August made his mind up to remove his sister from St Cyr, while the need to conduct her safely home provided a fine excuse for asking yet more leave from his regiment so that he could re-enter Corsican politics. For such was the dire shortage of officers that he had been restored to the strength of his artillery regiment despite his absences, and even promoted to captain. Back in Corsica and once more commanding his battalion of volunteers, he took part in a campaign to get Joseph elected as a Corsican representative to the new National Convention. Yet he did not display his old political zest. He asked himself whether the opposition might not prove too strong for him to achieve success in Corsica; he pondered whether he might not do better to enter the English army in Bengal; he even went so far as to wonder whether the best career prospect of all might not lie in returning to duty with his regular regiment.

For the Revolution was no longer a purely French affair, but beginning to involve all Europe, and in a struggle on such a scale Corsica dwindled to a backwater. In September the Duke of Brunswick's invading army was turned back at Valmy by Dumouriez, who in turn, two months later, invaded the Austrian Netherlands. Another French army under Custine swept through the Rhineland. This march of French armies beyond the national frontiers was inspired not only by revolutionary idealism but also by a pressing need for more assets that could be stripped to supply cash, such assets now only existing outside France's own territory. In November the new Convention offered aid to all peoples who wished to recover their freedom; and annexed Savoy. In January 1793 Danton proclaimed the doctrine of France's 'natural frontiers', the most controversial of which lay along the entire course of the Rhine from Basle to the sea. In February the Convention declared war on England and in March on Spain. So the twin dynamics of revolution and economic need gathered momentum, propelling France into limitless wars of expansion. There was a third dynamic force at work as well, however – that of terror and violence, shattering the ordered calm of eighteenth-century civilization, where even war had been brought within a restricting code, and breeding yet more terror and violence in turn. Fear, not *liberté* or *fraternité* or *egalité*, was revolutionary France's first gift to Europe. On 21 January 1793 the head of Louis XVI dropped into the sawdust under the guillotine. Between February and

April 1793 the machinery of 'the Terror' itself, that frenzied decapitation of French citizens, was constructed and put to work in the name of the Republic, One and Indivisible. The sovereign people shrank to the Committee of Public Safety, a collective dictatorship which controlled the lives and thoughts of the nation with a completeness and a ruthlessness undreamed of by the monarchs of the *ancien régime*.

Captain (or Lieutenant-Colonel) Buonaparte's own role in the Republic's wide selection of new wars was limited to taking part in February 1793 in a minor amphibious operation against the neighbouring Sardinian island of La Maddalena. His debut as a soldier in action thus came two and a half years later than his debut as a

'Fear, not *liberté* or *fraternité* or *egalité*, was revolutionary France's first gift to Europe.' Contemporary illustration. *Mansell Collection*

politician. As the young Arthur Wellesley serving in the British army in the Netherlands at this same period learned how not to do things, so did Buonaparte on the Maddalena expedition. The ships were manned with the mutinous sweepings of local ports, the troops were raw volunteers, the entire expedition conceived and executed in muddle. Only Buonaparte displayed the qualities of a professional, planting his batteries and silencing the enemy forts just as he had been taught at Valence and Auxonne. To add to his chagrin, he was forced to abandon his guns on the beach during the precipitous evacuation which concluded the venture.

The Buonapartes' political ventures in 1793 ended just as disastrously, thanks largely to brother Lucien's pure devotion to his republican principles. For in a speech to the Republican Club in Toulon, where he was then living, he denounced

Paoli as a tyrant who ought to be submitted to the rigours of republican justice. The denunciation impressed the Convention in Paris, who ordered Paoli's arrest and dispatched three commissioners to carry it out. In spite of his slights at Paoli's hands, Napoleone did not welcome these developments. What would happen to the Buonaparte family properties if, as now seemed certain, there should be a civil war in Corsica between Paolists and republicans? He addressed a cogent letter and a petition to the Convention requesting them to withdraw the decree against Paoli. This they did, but it was too late: Paoli had already begun an armed revolt against French republican rule with the aim of restoring Corsica's independence at last. Napoleone himself figured on Paoli's wanted list, and in the course of a hazardous journey from Ajaccio to safety with republicans in Bastia, had to escape through the cellar of a cousin's house when it was searched by a Paolist gendarme. His mother and the rest of the family fled to friends at Calvi, and the family house abandoned to pillage. By the end of June the whole family of refugees was reunited in France, at La Valette near Toulon.

In Buonaparte's own later words, 'Everything had collapsed; my presence was pointless; I quit Corsica.'[14] Except for a brief visit in 1799 on his voyage back from Egypt, he was never to see Corsica again, this homeland he had appeared to love so deeply. French historians glibly assure us that henceforward France became his *patrie*, the focus of his love and duty. But this is too easily to pass over an episode crucial to an understanding of his life and character. For he did not really 'choose' France; it was the collapse of his ambitions in Corsica which took him there. And soon afterwards a combination of luck and personal influence launched him on a fresh career in France, this time as a soldier rather than a politician. Passing through Nice on 16 September on his way from one routine assignment near Avignon to another with the Army of Italy, he called upon Jean-Christophe Saliceti, a fellow Corsican, an old friend and political patron and now one of two 'representatives of the people' (or political commissars) with the army besieging Toulon, which was then in the hands of royalists and British and Spanish forces. As it happened, a replacement was urgently needed for the commander of the army artillery, who had been seriously wounded. So, in the words of Saliceti's report to the Committee of Public Safety, 'chance served us marvellously; we stopped Citizen Buonaparte, a highly-trained officer who was on his way to the Army of Italy, and we ordered him to take Dommartin's place.'[15]

It was not then a new-born love of France or a new-found sense of being a Frenchman, but a chance opening up of a new avenue for his ambition which led Buonaparte finally to swap *patries*; an act which he performed with all the emotional upheaval of a man changing his hat.

WHEN BUONAPARTE reached the army's headquarters at Ollioules, a few miles inland from Toulon, on 18 September 1793, he found a shambles of amateurism and unpreparedness typical of the military forces of the Republic. The emigration of royalist officers had left the French army as denuded of trained leaders as the Soviet army in 1918–19, and, as with the Soviet army, the right political views constituted as important a qualification for command as military capacity.

The republican pedigree of General Carteaux, commanding the army in front of Toulon, was unimpeachable; he had been aide-de-camp to the commanding officer of the volunteers at the taking of the Bastille on 14 July 1789. Unfortunately his single military quality lay in his sweeping black hussar moustache, while his staff matched his own incompetence. The minority of old royal regulars in his 10,000 soldiers was swamped with republican volunteers, as yet ill-trained, ill-disciplined and soft. As for the artillery itself, Buonaparte found a few field guns, two 24-pounders, two 16-pounders and two mortars, little ammunition and no organization. With this exiguous military junk yard he was expected to breach the defences of a first-class fortress.

Yet the very decrepitude of Carteaux's army offered an able, energetic officer a matchless chance to display his talents. Captain Buonaparte was in fact virtually the only officer in a key position in that army who knew his job. Moreover, as a Jacobin agitator, his own political pedigree was as unimpeachable as Carteaux's. And even though because of his junior rank and acting appointment he had to struggle against the obstruction offered by Carteaux and his staff, he enjoyed decisive leverage because of his existing close friendship with Saliceti, one of the two all-powerful representatives of the people, and the new friendship he made with Saliceti's colleague, Citizen Gasparin. No wonder Carteaux was to moan that 'to attack the chief of artillery is to attack the representatives themselves.'[16] Buonaparte nevertheless recognized that if the voice of the artillery was to carry the weight it ought, the appointment of a more senior officer as its chief was needed. He suggested an old professional colleague of his now with the Army of the Eastern Pyrenees. Luck again blessed Buonaparte because the letter was misdirected to the Army of Italy and the designated officer only arrived after the end of the siege. Although another officer, General du Teil (brother of the commander of the Auxonne artillery school), was appointed later in the siege, he was old and sick, happy to leave everything to his subordinate. There was no one, therefore, to dim or share Buonaparte's credit.

Toulon, France's principal Mediterranean naval base, lay on the eastern shore of the inner of two roadsteads. A narrow gut of water led between hilly peninsulas from this inner roadstead to the outer, which was itself embraced by two more arms of pine-covered hillside. Beyond again lay the open sea, with the humped shapes of the Iles d'Hyères strewn eastwards like gigantic stepping stones. From the French positions near Ollioules the rigging of Admiral Hood's English fleet could be seen bristling thickly above the turquoise surface of the inner roadstead; and on this fleet the survival of the enemy garrison of Toulon utterly depended.

Buonaparte's ruthlessly analytical mind cut to the heart of the problem immediately; he saw that if Hood's ships could be forced to withdraw, Toulon must fall, and without costly direct assaults. And the key to forcing out Hood lay in establishing French batteries firing red-hot shot on one or other of the two peninsulas which commanded the narrow entrance to the inner roadstead. The western peninsula, Le Caire, lay within a short march of the present French positions, and, furthermore, was so far less strongly defended than the rest of the Toulon perimeter. Buonaparte therefore urged that they should attack and capture

the Le Caire peninsula and its two forts without delay. But Carteaux, who was
ignorant even of the ranges of different cannon, wanted to scatter the limited French
firepower on the town itself, on its forts and on the English fleet; after which, in his
view, Toulon would fall to cold steel and republican ardour. He was overruled by
Saliceti and Gasparin. On 21 September the French successfully occupied part of the
Le Caire peninsula, but failed to capture the two forts at its tip because Carteaux had
only allotted four hundred men as reinforcements. The one opportunity of evicting
the enemy from Toulon quickly and easily had been thrown away. The English
now greatly strengthened their defences on Le Caire, constructing a new redoubt,
Fort Mulgrave, on its commanding height.

   In Buonaparte's conviction, however, Le Caire remained the key to Toulon,
even though its recapture would now demand long and thorough preparation. As
he wrote to the Minister of War on 14 November 1793, 'the plan of attack . . .
which I have presented to the generals and the representatives of the people is, I
believe, the only one practicable; if it had been pursued from the beginning with a
little more energy, it is likely that we should now be in Toulon.'[17] And in a long
appendix, he tactfully drew the minister's attention to all the measures taken by
Major Buonaparte (he was promoted on 18 October) since assuming command of
the artillery: the guns he had concentrated; the wood for gun platforms he had
commandeered; the engineering gear he had organized; the repair shops. It was a
document salted with imperious phrases – 'I have required . . .'; 'I have established . . .';
'I have had fetched . . .'; 'I have taken measures . . .'. Yet there was no exaggeration.
In all he did he exemplified those qualities of energy and force which he had once
held up for admiration in his writings, and which he had equally demonstrated as a
Jacobin agitator in Corsica. Considering perhaps that loyalty need not extend to
fools, Buonaparte ceaselessly denounced Carteaux behind his back to the
representatives of the people, so materially contributing to Carteaux's dismissal on
23 October and his final departure from the army on 7 November.

The inner roadstead of
Toulon after the naval
base's recapture from the
English and Spaniards in
December 1793, looking
across at the town from
Le Caire peninsula.
Gouache by Honoré de
Balzac. *Musée de la
Marine, Paris*

   On 25 November 1793 a council of war under the new army commander,
Dugommier, aged seventy-five but able and intelligent, accepted Buonaparte's
plan for a renewed attempt to capture the Le Caire peninsula. Not until the third
week of December were preparations completed to Buonaparte's satisfaction.
Making skilful use of the rolling terrain of low, rocky hills to the west of Fort
Mulgrave, the key to the English defence, he steadily constructed fresh batteries,
until he was able to bring down an overwhelming weight of converging fire. On
the night of the planned attack, 17 December, the weather – low cloud trailing
gouts of rain over the streaming hillsides – was so bad that Dugommier and the
people's representatives succumbed to an urge to postpone the operation. It was
Buonaparte who decisively tilted the moral balance back again in favour of action
by arguing that the weather would provide cover to the attackers. Nevertheless, as
Dugommier feared, it was a night of black confusion and setbacks that could have
been disastrous. But the courage and persistence of the assaulting troops, led by
Buonaparte and old Dugommier in person, finally carried the log ramparts of Fort
Mulgrave at about three o'clock in the morning. Buonaparte himself had his horse
shot during the advance and a bayonet stuck in his thigh during the final wild

struggle. At first light the attackers moved on to assault the forts at the tip of the Le Caire peninsula, only to find that the enemy had already evacuated them.

As Buonaparte had always predicted, the loss of the Le Caire peninsula doomed the allied occupation of Toulon. That day the triumphant French on Le Caire saw the English fleet make sail in great haste and head out past them towards the open sea, for fear of being trapped by French batteries commanding the narrow exit with red-hot shot. The ships carried as many men of the allied garrison as could be embarked in panic rush. On 19 December Toulon was reunited with the French Republic amid the slaughter of local royalists and other celebrations of liberty and fraternity.

Luck and influence had provided Buonaparte with a unique opportunity to found a military reputation; he, clearminded, professional and energetic in an army where these qualities were lacking, had exploited the opportunity to the utmost. Dugommier reported glowingly upon him, and du Teil, his titular chief, informed the Minister of War: 'I lack words to convey Buonaparte's merit to you; much knowledge, equal intelligence and too much bravery; that is but a feeble sketch of this rare officer's virtues . . .'[18]

On 22 December 1793 the two representatives of the people demonstrated their own appreciation of Buonaparte's role by naming him a brigadier at the age of only twenty-four. But it was perhaps more important for his own future that he should have attracted the admiring notice of Citizen Paul Barras, who arrived from Paris in November as an extra representative *en mission* with the army, and who within two years would be one of the most powerful men in France.

III

FORTUNE IS A WOMAN

IN 1795 BUONAPARTE seemed to feel under him the firm stride of a successful career. Appointed artillery commander to the Army of Italy, then fighting a mountain war against the Austrians and Piedmontese in the Maritime Alps and Apennines, he became the army's principal fount of operational plans, just as at Toulon. His friend and patron Saliceti was also with the army as representative *en mission*, while Buonaparte acquired a valuable new friend in Saliceti's colleague, Augustin Robespierre, brother of Maximilien Robespierre, the outstanding figure in the Committee of Public Safety. His careerist flair for cultivating useful contacts nevertheless displeased General Schérer, who assumed command of the army in November 1794. While acknowledging in a confidential report on Buonaparte that he possessed 'real knowledge' of artillery, Schérer added the rider: 'but he has a little too much ambition, and intrigues for his own advancement.'[1]

In July 1794, however, the fall of Robespierre senior and the subsequent guillotining of both Robespierre brothers exposed all their associates and hangers-on to suspicion, and on 8 August Buonaparte found himself under arrest in the Fort Carré in Antibes; a reminder of the precarious, even perilous, nature of useful contacts in a revolutionary age. Fortunately his friend Saliceti was able to report to Paris that no evidence could be found against him and that the army urgently needed his talents. He was set free on 20 August. The flow of plans resumed; he played a major part in organizing a successful minor offensive; and so another brick was laid in the rising edifice of Brigadier Buonaparte's reputation. But within only eight months of his release this renewed fabric of success collapsed, leaving him an unemployed officer with scant prospects.

In March 1795 he sailed as artillery commander with an expedition to reconquer Corsica from the Paolists. The expedition ran into the Royal Navy and returned to France sadly knocked about. Buonaparte's old post with the Army of Italy being now filled, he journeyed to Paris in order to solicit another. Unfortunately he was only offered a job as an infantry brigadier with the army engaged in putting down the rebels of the Vendée. Since this assignment promised obscurity rather than fame, Buonaparte refused the posting and went on extended sick leave – but in Paris, just in case anything should turn up.

The abrupt cessation of forward motion in his life, plunged him back into the old anguished searchings for an identity and a future. Perhaps as a sign of how hard a knock he had taken, he fell in love. Had he not once written that love was the product of weakness and loneliness? The object of this novel emotion, Desirée Clary, of Marseille, the sixteen-year-old sister of his brother Joseph's wife, gave herself a new name for her lover alone, Eugénie, in the romantic style of the time:

Oh! my friend, take care of your days so as to preserve those of your Eugénie, who will not know how to live without you. Keep the vow you have made me as faithfully as I will keep the one I have made to you.[2]

All through that summer of stalled ambition Buonaparte consoled himself by playing his part in this romance. He did better: he used it as material for a novel, *Clisson et Eugénie*, an escapist fantasy reminiscent of Rousseau's *La Nouvelle Hélöïse*, in which he, the hero Clisson, a brilliant young warrior, dies gloriously in battle after learning that his wife, the gentle Eugénie, has fallen in love with his friend.

A letter to his brother Joseph, one of the relatively few in all his vast lifetime's correspondence that seems to speak straight from the heart, reveals how deeply the blighting of his budding career had affected him:

> Desirée asks me for my portrait, so I am going to have it painted; you must give it to her if she still wants it, otherwise keep it for yourself. In whatever circumstances fortune places you, you know well that you cannot have a better friend, who holds you more dear or who desires your happiness more sincerely. Life is a trifling dream which fades away. If you depart, and if you think this could be for some considerable time, send me your portrait. We have lived so many years together, so closely united, that our hearts are as one, and you know better than anybody how much mine is entirely yours. In writing these lines I feel an emotion such as I have seldom experienced in my life . . .[3]

Thrashing about for some new avenue of advancement, Buonaparte proposed to the Committee of Public Safety that he should be seconded to the service of the Sultan of Turkey in order to reorganize the Turkish artillery; further evidence that essentially he was a rootless soldier of fortune. He crawled to the influential in Paris with a skill and persistence worthy of his father. In particular he sought out Paul Barras, who had been so impressed by him at the siege of Toulon, and who was now a prominent figure in the regime that had replaced Robespierre and his colleagues.

And in August 1795 Buonaparte's lobbying was rewarded. Influence plucked him from the abyss and attached him to the *bureau topographique* of the Committee of Public Safety, which, once a simple map section, now fulfilled the intelligence and planning functions of a modern general staff. Buonaparte in effect had become chief military adviser to the government. But at the same time he took care to ensure that he would not be endangered by an all-too-probable further political convulsion. On 6 September, in a letter breathing renewed confidence and thrustfulness, he told Joseph that whatever happened, 'you need have no fear on my behalf; I have all the right people as friends, whatever their party or opinion . . .'[4]

So it proved. On 5 October (13 Vendémiaire, in the new republican calendar), the chronic political instability in France since the destruction of the monarchy manifested itself in yet another rising in Paris, this time largely of royalist sympathizers. Paul Barras, now Commander-in-Chief of the Army of the Interior, delegated to his protégé Buonaparte the task of smashing the expected revolt. Buonaparte had once led a *putsch* himself in Ajaccio and had witnessed two others in Paris; and he had long since formed his own opinion as to how such manifestations should be dealt with. Now he acted without hesitation. He ordered troops and guns to be brought into Paris in utmost haste. He posted one cannon so as to rake the Rue St Honoré, the route that would be taken by the rebels in a march on the

Convention; 8-pounders at all exits from the street; more guns in reserve to take the rebel column in flank should it succeed in forcing a way through.

At five in the afternoon the rebels began their expected march. By two the next morning Buonaparte was reporting to Joseph in phrases like the crash of cannon what had happened:

> We deployed the troops; the enemy came to attack us at the Tuileries; we killed plenty of them; they killed thirty men of ours and wounded sixty. We have disarmed the [rebel] districts and all is calm. As usual with me, I was not wounded.
>
> PS: Happiness is mine; my heart to Eugénie and Julie.[5]

In '13 Vendémiaire' Buonaparte gained one of the most important of all his victories, both for the course of French history and his own career. The Paris mob, since 1789 the ultimate arbiter of governments, had yielded to military force, henceforward the ultimate arbiter instead. Buonaparte himself was appointed Commander-in-Chief of the Army of the Interior and of the Paris Military District. Here was real success, real power. That autumn, money in his pockets at last, he moved with relish through a Parisian society miraculously restored to pleasure after the austerities and terrors of Robespierre's republican virtue. For France enjoyed a new regime – for the time being – in the Directory, and Buonaparte's patron Barras figured as the principal among the five Directors. *Arrivistes* of every kind, hard-faced profiteers who looked as if they had done well out of the Revolution and their decolletée women, aped as best they could the departed elegance of the court of Louis XVI. Perhaps the most fashionable event of the season was provided by the Ball of the Victims, subscribed to by all who had lost relatives under the Terror, and where in gaining admittance the death certificate of a decapitated dear-one supplied the place of the usual invitation.

(left) The new Republican calendar, symbol of a romantic optimism which believed that mankind had entered a new era when tyranny would be unknown. Year One began on 22 September 1792. The ten equal months of the year were poetically named after the nature of the season, and divided into three ten-day weeks. The five days left over were devoted to Republican *fêtes. Giraudon*

(below) '. . . a Parisian society miraculously restored to pleasure . . .' French fashions under the Revolution: left, 1789; centre, 1796; right, 1801. *Mansell Collection*

This was the time and this was the society in which General Buonaparte met Josephine Tascher de la Pagerie, the widowed Viscountess de Beauharnais, and the charm of Desirée Clary's simple sincerity faded quickly from his attention.

T HE LADY, having been recently discarded by Paul Barras and lacking a fortune, was living on appearances and her wits in an apartment in the Rue Chantereine. Her husband, the late Viscount, had been guillotined during the Terror, and she herself was only released from the Carmes prison in July. At thirty-two, with teenage son and daughter to keep, her only assets lay in what remained of the Beauharnais furniture and of her own sexual allure. This, like the furniture, was carefully preserved and displayed. Makeup smoothed out the lines on a sweet, soft face with tip-tilted nose; the wistful smile which played so seductively on the delicate lips was never allowed to reveal the already darkening and eroded teeth. Thick clusters of chestnut curls enhanced her prettiness and feminity. Her body was *en suite*, softly fleshed, slender, pliant, with the sun-warmed grace of the Creole. For Josephine had been born and bred on the French Caribbean island of Martinique. Unfortunately neither her mind nor her character matched her charm, for she was shallow, easily bored and spendthrift. She offered little as a wife to a man of sense and accomplishment.

It seems therefore the more remarkable that Buonaparte, that mathematical, calculating mind, that ruthless penetrator to the heart of questions, should have chosen her. But Josephine was really courted by that other Buonaparte, the fiery romantic, the author of *Clisson et Eugénie*; and for him the sweet face, the tragic personal history, the beguiling voice with the creole lisp, the elegance and the randiness, were enough. Then again, there was yet a third Buonaparte promoting the courtship: the prototype middle-class snob, flattered to be taken up by a member of the old aristocracy he claimed to despise, seduced by the easy manners of good breeding.

The lady for her part, somewhat flattered by Buonaparte's romantic devotions and much impressed with his prospects, decided that she could do worse than marry this strange little Corsican.

So it was entirely appropriate that the match was solemnized in mutual deceit. The lady did not reveal that far from being a fortune, she was in poverty, and she gave her age as twenty-nine instead of thirty-two. The general, not wishing to appear more young and gauche than necessary, produced his brother Joseph's birth certificate (Joseph's second name was also Napoleone), which made him out to be twenty-eight instead of twenty-six. None of his family was present at the ceremony, a civil one, on 8 March 1796, nor was his mother consulted about the match beforehand.

It had not hindered Buonaparte's courtship and marriage that he had entered into a prior engagement with Desirée Clary. He did not share that sense of honourable obligation which was to impel Arthur Wellesley unhesitatingly to renew his proposal to Kitty Pakenham despite nine years of separation. 'You have made me unhappy for the rest of my life', wrote Desirée to Buonaparte on hearing of his marriage, 'and yet I am weak enough to forgive you completely. So you are married! Poor Eugénie is no longer allowed to love you . . .'[6] However, Buonaparte later made some amends by marrying her off to one of his generals, Bernadotte.

Two days after the wedding Buonaparte bid farewell to his bride and set out for Nice, there to take up a new post as general commanding the Army of Italy; Clisson off to the wars, but parted from the wrong Eugénie.

S OLDIERS, you are naked, ill-fed; though the Government owes you much, it can give you nothing. Your patience, the courage you have shown amidst these rocks, are admirable; but they procure you no glory, no fame shines upon you. I want to lead you into the most fertile plains in the world. Rich provinces, great cities will lie in your power; you will find there honour, glory and riches. Soldiers of the Army of Italy, will you lack courage or steadfastness?[7]

This order of the day from Buonaparte to his new command epitomizes in more ways than one the romantic legend of his Italian campaigns of 1796 and 1797; a legend which in turn served as the foundation for the grander legend of Buonaparte as hero and genius. For the order is in fact spurious, dictated by Buonaparte more than twenty years later on St Helena, which became after 1815 the main centre of production in the Napoleonic myth industry. But Buonaparte began propagating his own legend just as soon as the Army of Italy marched, feeding Paris with

Mariage de Napoléon B. à paris.

grandiloquent accounts of his successes, exaggerating enemy losses and defeats. Yet the wide acceptance of Buonaparte's own version of the Italian campaigns of 1796–7 as a series of dazzling victories over old and slow opponents, leading to a brilliant peace treaty which ratified astonishing conquests, owes itself to other factors too. Firstly, there is the grovelling disposition of men, especially in the romantic nineteenth century, to hunt about for 'geniuses' and 'heroes' to admire. Secondly, military historians have praised Buonaparte as the man who fulfilled the theories of contemporary writers on war, in particular Guibert. Guibert had argued that armies should live on the resources of the country, so breaking free from the limitations of eighteenth-century warfare, with its elaborate wagon-trains and magazines, its consequently slow marches and its preoccupation with besieging fortresses. This would permit a new kind of warfare, free-ranging and fast-moving. As Guibert put it, 'The enemy must see me march when he believes me shackled by calculations of subsistence; this new type of war must astonish him, leave him no time to draw breath anywhere . . .'[8]

However, Guibert and the military historians who have admired Buonaparte's Italian campaigns commit the error of divorcing the operational conduct of war from its political context. They treat war as a kind of game, in which the footwork and strokeplay of the players is to be admired for its own sake, forgetting that in point of fact war is an aspect of the business of states. And considered in *that* light, the grey light of realism, the Italian campaigns of 1796–7 lose their glitter.

The unleashing of the first of these campaigns followed nearly two years of strategic debate about the scope and purpose of the general European war being waged by the French republic. That debate in turn reflected the growing dilemmas and contradictions of the republican regime at home, as a gulf opened between the small cliques of revolutionary politicians in Paris and the nation as a whole. For with the abolition of the privileged orders and feudal obligations and the passing of the land to the peasant, the Revolution had long since fulfilled its purpose for the French masses. By 1795 the republican regime, far from representing the will of the sovereign people, rested on no more legitimate a foundation than a wish to keep itself in power and a claim to be a truer voice of the nation than the nation itself. This precarious ruling minority was also facing the imminent economic collapse of the country. The time bought by stripping assets for cash had run out. In August 1795 government expenditure amounted to some eighty million francs, income to between six and eight million. The hundred-franc *assignat* was worth fifteen sous.

The true interests of France and her people lay in a compromise peace, abandoning the extravagant claim to the Rhine frontier, and in retrenchment and stability at home – possibly even a political deal with the royalists. But the interests – the survival indeed – of the republican regime itself lay, as Robespierre had seen, in the opposite course of sharpening the struggle against 'reaction' both at home and abroad; in keeping the revolutionary dynamic going. And that necessarily meant exporting the cost of war. In the summer and autumn of 1795 Buonaparte and other mettlesome young officers therefore urged a bold offensive strategy on the Directory, not least so that the French armies could 'support themselves by making war at the expense of other countries . . . if the Army of Italy does not change its theatre of war very quickly, it will become an extremely heavy burden on the public exchequer . . .'[9]

The object of the projected offensive was no less than to traverse the whole of northern Italy in the teeth of hostile armies, enter Austria via the Tyrol, and then, in conjunction with the Army of the Rhine, 'set out to dictate a glorious peace . . . in the heart of the hereditary lands of the house of Austria.'[10] It was, then, a German rather than an Italian strategy; its aim to secure for the republic the coveted 'natural frontier' of the Rhine.

Orthodox eighteenth-century statecraft would have regarded such a project as a fantasy. France was verging on economic collapse; Austria an empire of vast resources. The military risks were immense; no less so the logistical problems; and all to be incurred for the sake of a territorial ambition little related to France's crying real needs. Like the Schlieffen Plan of 1914, the Italian offensive of 1796 was, in terms of overall national interest, a seductive folly. No responsible, legitimate government of the day would have sanctioned such a gamble. But the Directory was a self-appointed rump facing political and financial bankruptcy. It clutched at this gamble as the way out of all its troubles. And who better to carry it out than its principal advocate, General Buonaparte? Nevertheless, in its directive to him as the new Commander-in-Chief of the Army of Italy on 6 March 1796, the Directory did not for the moment look beyond the driving of the Austrians out of Italy; itself an aim ambitious enough by conventional standards.[11]

Buonaparte's first task on taking up his new command lay in asserting his leadership over officers older and more experienced than he. That savageness which had so daunted his schoolfellows had now matured into a force of personality before which even the toughest quailed. In the words of a close subordinate:

> . . . although he lacked a certain dignity and was even gauche in his bearing and gestures, he had the quality of command in his attitude, his gaze, his manner of talking; and everyone, sensing this, found himself ready to obey . . .[12]

It was at this time that he deleted the 'u' from 'Buonaparte', so rendering his surname less blatantly Italian.

His second task lay in preparing the army for an offensive in utmost haste. He set about it with the same crackling energy he had displayed at Toulon. Yet despite artillery limited to twenty-four mountain-guns and an exiguous supply system, the Army of Italy was a formidable force; its soldiers young, fit and intelligent; its formations hardened and trained by more than two years of mountain warfare. Its 41,000 effectives faced a Piedmontese army of 25,000 and an Austrian army of 38,000 posted along the crestline of the Apennines from north of Genoa westwards to Cuneo. The junction point between the Piedmontese and the Austrians lay to the north of the Cadibona Pass, which cuts through the Apennines from Savona on the Mediterranean coast.

According to the Directory's instructions Bonaparte was to attack and beat the Piedmontese first, taking their fortified camp at Ceva and advancing on their capital, Turin; and then turn east against the Austrians. But while Bonaparte was still preparing his offensive, the Austrians moved a strong force to Montenotte, just northeast of the Cadibona Pass, so threatening the right flank of his projected advance. This forced him to abandon the Directory's instructions and deal with the Austrians first in order to clear his flank. For this strategically defensive operation he typically chose an offensive tactical plan: a fixing attack against the Austrian front near Montenotte coupled with a flank march against their rear. Outfought and outmanoeuvred, the Austrians fell back northeastward on Acqui. This scramble in the mountains round Montenotte figures first in the litany of Bonaparte's victories; sold to history as a brilliant *offensive* move designed to split the Austrians from the Piedmontese. The Austrians, according to this mythical version, now retreated away from the Piedmontese on Alessandria. In fact, they turned *northwestwards* from Acqui through Nizza Monferrato in order to link up again with their ally.

Bonaparte now reverted to his original instructions and attacked the Piedmontese, winning another local action at Millesimo and driving them back on their entrenched camp at Ceva. The new Guibertian or Bonapartian way of warfare did not of course believe in wasting time over the pedantic siege of fortresses, and so Bonaparte, having no siege train, simply ordered his troops to take Ceva by assault on 16 April. They were repulsed with heavy losses, thus presenting the French commander with an unwelcome conundrum. Fortunately for Bonaparte, the Piedmontese commander, Colli, abandoned Ceva next day and fell back towards Turin, probably in order to concentrate all the Piedmontese forces and link up with the Austrians. A delay at Ceva would have proved fatal to Bonaparte, for his troops were hungry, his supply arrangements ramshackle. Now, advancing into the rich plains of Piedmont, his army could live by organized pillage. On 21 April, for example, he ordered the municipality of Mondovi to supply 39,500 rations of biscuit, 16,000 rations of meat, 8,000 rations of bread and 8,000 bottles of wine before the next morning.[13] The process of stripping other countries' assets to ward off the bankruptcy of the French exchequer was also put in hand, and he reported to the Directory that, 'This fine country . . . will offer us considerable resources; the single province of Mondovi will give us a million in contributions . . .'[14] Nevertheless, pillage could not provide him with the field artillery he desperately lacked,[15] or replenish his nearly exhausted stocks of ammunition. With his already grossly inadequate supply lines lengthening as he continued to advance on Turin, and with the still undefeated main bodies of the Piedmontese and Austrian armies concentrating ahead of him, his position was not so much triumphant as precarious – as he himself acknowledged to the Directory on 24 April, when he reported that the enemy numbered 100,000 men as against his own 37,500, was strong in artillery, fighting well, and knew all about his, Bonaparte's, shortages.[16]

From this unpromising situation – from the inevitability of an early retreat in fact – Bonaparte was fortunate enough to be rescued on 28 April, when Piedmont concluded an armistice with him at Cherasco. According to Napoleonic legend, and despite the military realities, this armistice is supposed to be the fruit of Bonaparte's 'brilliant' victories. In fact, defeatist sentiment and a desire for peace had been gaining ascendancy at the Piedmontese court since as long ago as January, before Bonaparte was even appointed to command of the Army of Italy. Bonaparte's apparent successes merely supplied this powerful peace party with the means of panicking the court into asking for an armistice.

The armistice of Cherasco offered Bonaparte the occasion of issuing one of the first of many rhetorical orders of the day to his troops, and at the same time launching a legend on its way: 'Soldiers, you have won six victories in five days, taken twenty-one colours, fifty-five pieces of cannon, several fortresses, conquered the richest part of Piedmont . . .'[17]

With Piedmont out of the war, Bonaparte turned eagerly against Beaulieu, the Austrian commander, reporting to the Directory of 28 April that within a month, having crossed the Po and conquered Lombardy, 'I hope to be in the mountains of the Tyrol, meet the Army of the Rhine and together carry the war into Bavaria. This project is worthy of you, of the army and of the destinies of the Republic.'[18] First, however, he had to defeat Beaulieu, now posted in depth behind three parallel tributaries of the Po, with the Po itself protecting his left flank; an immensely strong position. Bonaparte's solution, which has been much admired since, was to avoid attacking Beaulieu's position frontally and instead march along the south bank of the Po and cross at Piacenza, so turning all three of Beaulieu's river lines and threatening his lines of communication with Austria. But this flank march violated the neutrality of the Duchy of Parma, whose city Piacenza was. Moreover, Bonaparte first took the governor of Piacenza hostage for the city's good behaviour, having tricked him by an invitation to meet and discuss matters 'of the greatest importance'; an echo of the tactics he had employed against the election commissioner in Ajaccio in 1792.[19]

In a purely military sense the plan to manoeuvre Beaulieu out of an otherwise almost impregnable position was successful, although the Austrian commander made good his escape without difficulty; an unnecessary and costly French attack over the narrow bridge at Lodi on his rearguard taking its due place in Napoleonic myth. Yet the plan succeeded only because Buonaparte had broken those eighteenth-century rules which limited the scope and destructiveness of war. As he went on to break these rules again and again, so his opponents too would learn to fight without rules (Beaulieu secured his line of retreat by occupying Peschiera, belonging to neutral Venice); and war would cease to be a regulated affair of state business, with minimum social and political side-effects. Violence – moral as well as physical – would breed hatred and fear; they in turn would breed countervailing violence; trickery would destroy all trust, so reducing treaties to worthless parchment; and relations between the states of Europe would regress to the level of a Corsican blood feud.

But to Europe at that moment, to France, to Bonaparte and his army, it was like living some heroic adventure out of an ancient fable, so rapid and so great were the conquests. Bonaparte himself, the romantic Bonaparte, was only too conscious of playing the part of a new Alexander. After the triumphal entry into Milan on 15 May 1796 which consummated his conquest of Lombardy, he confided to a subordinate, Colonel Marmont:

> They haven't seen anything yet, and the future holds successes for us far beyond what we have so far accomplished. Fortune . . . is a woman, and the more she does for me, the more I will demand from her . . . In our day no one has conceived anything great; it is for me to give an example.[20]

The same romantic Bonaparte – but in the role of Clisson the warrior lover – dispatched frequent love-lorn letters to Josephine, who refused to leave the gaieties of Paris and join him amid the rigours of the campaign, and who was finally to take refuge in the lie that she was pregnant and could not travel. In April he had implored her to return with Junot, his aide-de-camp, whom he had sent to Paris with captured enemy colours:

> You must come back with him, do you understand? . . . unhappiness without cure, inconsolable anguish, sorrow without end, should I be unhappy enough to see him return alone. My adorable sweetheart, he will see you, he will breathe upon your temple; perhaps you will even grant him the unique and priceless favour of kissing your cheek, and I myself will be alone, and far, far away. But you are coming, aren't you? You are going to be here at my side, on my heart, in my arms, on my mouth. Take wing, come, come! . . .
>
> A kiss on your heart, and then one a little lower down, much lower down![21]

Though Emma Hamilton would have relished such letters worthy of a character in a novel, they were wasted on the unromantic Josephine. 'He's funny, Bonaparte', she would say with her creole lisp.

While hanging those of his soldiers caught helping themselves to the occasional gold or silver chalice from a church, General Bonaparte carried out with his usual energy the Directory's instructions to levy immense contributions on the Italian states and on the property of the Church, half to support the army, half to go back to the French treasury. The neutral Duke of Parma, for example, was relieved of two million French livres in ten days, and told that 'he will hand over twenty pictures, to the choice of the general in chief . . .'[22] On 18 May Bonaparte sent the Directory a positive shopping list of the pictures and *objets d'art* lifted from various towns, including Leonardos, Raphaels and Titians. At the same time he proclaimed to the people of Lombardy that whereas a monarchical army spreads terror in its advance, a republican army 'vows friendship to the peoples whom its victories free from tyranny'; and assured the Lombards of his army's 'respect for property, for persons; for the religion of the people.'[23]

The question of loot caused the only major disagreement between the Directory and its obedient general, for in May the Directory called a temporary halt to his plans for entering the Tyrol, and ordered him to undertake a round tour to Leghorn, harvesting the treasures of Italy as he went, while the pursuit of the Austrians was to be entrusted to General Kellerman. Bonaparte protested vigorously and successfully against this division of command, but otherwise obeyed. By mid-July, the harvest home, he was back in Milan.

Yet thus far his triumphs had all been too easy; obtained, as it were, on credit, and still to be paid for. He had not yet fought, let alone beaten, the main body of the Austrian army, and Austria, recovering from the defection of her ally Piedmont, now began to put forth her immense reserves of military strength. From July 1796 to January 1797 General Bonaparte had to fight a sometimes desperate defensive campaign against three major Austrian offensives aimed at recovering Lombardy. And the key to this campaign lay in the fortress of Mantua and its Austrian garrison.

'. . . stripping other countries' assets to ward off the bankruptcy of the French exchequer': Bonaparte in Italy, as seen by the English cartoonist, George Cruikshank, in 1814. *British Museum*

For while Mantua held out in Bonaparte's rear, it was impossible for him to implement his strategy of invading Austria by the Tyrol. It is a remarkable fact that the Po valley campaigns of 1796 and 1797, so often regarded as masterpieces of a new kind of mobile warfare that dispensed with such clogging eighteenth-century formalities as the siege of fortresses, revolved round Bonaparte's persistent failure to take Mantua, despite an ample siege train plundered from Italian arsenals. Whereas Marlborough had taken Lille, the premier fortress of France, in three months, it was to be eight before Mantua fell.

During this period Bonaparte was also having to contend with the unexpected consequences of levying contributions at the point of a bayonet, of violating neutrality and of outraging the susceptibilities of a religious people. For as early as May revolt had begun to flare in the area of French occupation. Faced with this sudden unlooked-for menace to his overstretched army, Bonaparte reverted to his 1790–2 form as Corsican politician. The people of the Milanais were told on 28 May, for instance, that 'The French army, magnanimous as it is strong, will treat peaceable and tranquil inhabitants as brothers; it will be as terrible as the fire of heaven towards rebels and the villages which harbour them . . .'[24] He ordered ringleaders to be summarily shot, hostages to be taken, villages to be burned. These ruthless measures crushed the immediate outbreaks. But the outbreaks marked only the beginning of the political and social dissolution of northern Italy; and hence of Bonaparte's very base of operations. By autumn 1796 he had become profoundly alarmed at the tide of Italian hostility lapping his small army at a time when he was at grips with the Austrians. '. . . our position in Italy,' he wrote to the Directory on 8 October, 'is uncertain and our political system very bad . . .'[25] Far from setting out to revolutionize Italy, Bonaparte and his masters were at pains to dampen the hopes of local republicans. Nor was the creation of the Cispadane Republic in October 1796 and later of the Cisalpine Republic the consequence of some noble vision of a free and democratic Italy, but of his and the Directory's need for puppet administrations to fill a political void. The Guibertian – or Bonapartian – military short-cut was proving, and not for the last time, a quicksand without apparent end.

On 29 July 1796 the first of the Austrian counter-offensives opened, when Field-Marshal Count Wurmser and 47,000 men advanced to the relief of Mantua in four columns: three in the valleys east and west of Lake Garda leading south from the mountains into the Venetian plain; one moving westward across the plain from Vicenza. The columns were to unite south of Lake Garda and march on Mantua. Wurmser's offensive caught Bonaparte with his forces widely scattered along a seventy-five-mile-wide covering front, drove in his centre, cut his communications with Verona and Milan, and threatened to split his army in two. It was an entirely successful exercise in that *manoeuvre sur les derrières* which Bonaparte's admirers see as his speciality rather than that of his enemies. To save himself from catastrophe demanded all Bonaparte's qualities of furious speed and energy, his mathematician's ability to solve the complex problem of combining in space and time the operations of different formations. He ordered General Serrurier to raise the siege of Mantua, bury his siege artillery, and throw stocks of ball into the marshes and gun carriages into the river; a measure of the degree of emergency. Indeed Bonaparte was contemplating the possibility of a general retreat. The scattered French forces converged pell-mell on the decisive sector south of Lake Garda – all except for Serrurier, whom Bonaparte unaccountably left for four days without orders twenty-five miles away at Marcaria. On 5 August Bonaparte attacked Wurmser before he could unite with the most westerly Austrian column. Wurmser, with the Austrian main body, was holding the village of Castiglione, standing on one of the vine-clad hills that rise from the Venetian plain. As at Montenotte, Bonaparte launched a fixing attack in front coupled with a swing round the Austrian flank. The Austrians, peasants drilled in the rigid tactics of the eighteenth century, were outfought by the agile, intelligent and ferociously aggressive soldiers of the Army of Italy. Wurmser retreated northwards with the loss of 6,000 killed and wounded.

The victory of Castiglione set Bonaparte's self-confidence abounding again, and he gave vent to hopes of crossing into the Tyrol before the end of August. Unfortunately for him an attempt to take Mantua by surprise assault failed with heavy loss, and a pause for the army's recuperation became essential. Unfortunately too the supply services were, in Bonaparte's own words, 'in absolute confusion.'[26] Indeed, so far as supplying his army was concerned, Bonaparte's performance in 1796–7 wholly failed to better Lord Raglan's in the Crimea, although he has escaped the relentless criticism directed against that unlucky English commander.

Early in September Wurmser made a fresh attempt to reach Mantua, this time via Bassano and Vicenza. Chased by Bonaparte down the valley of the Brenta, he was brought to battle at Bassano on 8 September; only a partial French success, however, for Wurmser succeeded in carrying the greater part of his army onwards into Mantua. Whereas the Austrian commander had certainly failed in his main object of driving the French out of Italy he had at least managed to re-victual and reinforce that key fortress, even at the cost of getting bottled up in it himself.

In October the Austrians launched their second counter-offensive, under the command of Field-Marshal Count Alvinzi. This time they marched westwards with their main body over the Venetian plain through Vicenza on Verona, while a subsidiary force distracted the French by advancing from the north down the Adige valley. Once again the Austrians caught Bonaparte with his army dispersed: Vaubois with 8,000 men blocking the Adige near Rivoli, Kilmaine with 9,000 besieging Mantua, and only Masséna's and Augereau's divisions, with 10,000 men, actually available to meet Alvinzi. Moreover, Bonaparte now had no fewer than 14,000 sick. This was the period, too, when the political and social consequences of French conduct in Italy were coming to their crisis. No wonder he was sunk in gloom, indeed despair, writing to the Directory on 13 November 1796 that the inferiority of his army and the exhaustion of even its bravest men 'make me fear the worst. Perhaps,' he went on, 'we are on the verge of losing Italy.'[27] Later in the same report comes a cry that hardly accords with the legendary picture of a triumphant conqueror sweeping irresistibly from success to success: 'We are abandoned in the heart of Italy . . .' And once again he contemplated general retreat.

On 14 November Alvinzi turned away south from the Verona road, intending to cross the River Adige by a pontoon bridge near the village of Zevio, and then march straight to the relief of Mantua. Bonaparte thereupon decided to repeat his favourite manoeuvre to a flank by crossing the Adige from south to north, and attacking Alvinzi's left and rear by surprise. If all went well, this manoeuvre would cut Alvinzi's communications and take his army in reverse.

The countryside where the coming battle was fought resembles the English fens: flat fields and marshes cut up by ditches and by streams dyked between high embankments. Unfortunately for Bonaparte, he chose to throw his pontoon bridge over the Adige at Ronco, rather than a few miles further downstream at Albaredo, with the result that his troops found themselves boxed up in marshy ground on the wrong side of the Alpone stream, a tributary of the Adige running between raised banks and passable only by a narrow wooden bridge at Arcola, now resolutely defended by the Austrians. Had Bonaparte crossed at Albaredo, beyond this tributary, he would have enjoyed firm going and open ground all the way into the Austrian rear. Now desperate attempts to carry the bridge at Arcola failed in the face of the Austrian fire, even despite such heroics as Bonaparte himself seizing a regimental colour and leading his soldiers to the attack in person; heroics which turned to comedy when an officer, wishing to preserve him from apparently certain death, tried to pull him back, with the result that, in the course of tuggings this way and that, General Bonaparte fell in the dyke and had to be fished out.

His attempt to take Alvinzi in the flank had thus totally failed: he now faced an alerted and fully deployed enemy, while his own troops, cramped in by dyke and marsh, were milling in confusion. It was only when after two days of stalemated fighting he threw a pontoon bridge over the Adige at Albaredo and attacked along the firm, open ground on the far side of the Alpone that the enemy fell back northwards.

Yet there was no real necessity for this Austrian retreat, for the French army, ragged, shoeless, hungry, had suffered heavy casualties and could call on fewer reserves than Alvinzi himself, while Alvinzi's other force, advancing from the north, was about to debouch on to Bonaparte's communications. Not for the only occasion in Bonaparte's career, want of doggedness on the part of an enemy commander handed him a victory when mere continuance of the fighting might have brought him to disaster.

Now Bonaparte again bounced back from despair to overconfidence, telling the Directory on 19 November 1796 in his report on the Battle of Arcola that the fall of Mantua 'ought not to be delayed beyond fifteen days', and promising them that if they sent him the reinforcements he asked for, 'I promise you to force the (Austrian) Emperor to make peace within six weeks . . .'[28] But Mantua did not fall; nor was the French army in any condition to march into Austria. According to a general order issued by Bonaparte later that month, 'the army's state of destitution imperiously demands that all resources at present existing in Italy be promptly realised.'[29]

It was the enemy instead who launched the next major offensive, in mid-January 1797, and again under Alvinzi's command. In order to confuse Bonaparte as to the direction of his main thrust, Alvinzi divided his army into three groups: one advancing westward on Verona, another from Padua on Mantua itself, and the third, the main body under his personal command, coming out of the northern snows, down the valleys in between the Alpine foothills that finger out into the North Italian Plain. And yet again Bonaparte was caught with his forces dispersed, from Legnago on his right to the western shore of Lake Garda on his left; and this time paralysed by uncertainty as to which Austrian thrusts were the feints, and which was the real attack. On 12 January the Austrian forces east of Verona attacked the French positions, but were repulsed. That same day Alvinzi and the main body, 20,000 strong, advancing from the north, forced the local French commander, Joubert, back on the village of Rivoli, between Lake Garda and the Adige, so threatening Bonaparte's communications with Milan. Urgently Bonaparte signalled Joubert to ask 'if you think the enemy has more than 9,000 men in front of you. It is vital that I know whether the attack he is making on you is a real attack . . . or if it is secondary . . .'[30] By the following afternoon, however, Bonaparte was able to inform his commanders that 'the enemy has revealed his movements, and all (sic) his forces are directed against the Rivoli position . . .'[31] Once more the French concentration was a last-minute, pell-mell, touch-and-go affair. In fact some of Bonaparte's formations only arrived in the course of the battle itself.

The battlefield of Rivoli lies hemmed in between Lake Garda to the west and the River Adige to the east. North of the French position looms the huge, humped shape of Monte Baldo, a mountain which forced the Austrians to divide themselves into three columns, one advancing to the west of it along the shore of Lake Garda, the second to the east, and the third further eastwards still, down in the gorge of the Adige. At the southern exit of this gorge the road winds up a steep and narrow pass by a series of dog-legs. Bonaparte arrived in the small hours of 14 January just in time himself to save Joubert from losing command of this vital exit. He rode forward with Joubert in the moonlight to reconnoitre, observing the twinkle of the enemy's watch fires along the foot of Monte Baldo's snow-softened bulk. As soon as it was light a French counter-stroke drove back the heads of the Austrian columns and established a firm grip on the head of the pass. But meanwhile the westernmost

Austrian column had swung round well to the south of Monte Baldo across the French communications. One of Bonaparte's subordinates, Colonel Marmont, later recalled that he was 'one of the last to enter the circle, and I only penetrated into it at the very instant when it was completed and under musket fire . . .'[32] Bonaparte's army was now penned into a saucer of land round the village of Rivoli, with Austrians on high ground to the north, west and south, and with the broad Adige to the east. The Austrian strategy, another *manoeuvre sur les derrières*, could hardly have succeeded more brilliantly.

But Bonaparte and his army saved themselves yet once again by their superiority in sheer pugilism: by pace, nimbleness and hard-punching; by will to win. While Masséna's division smashed away the Austrian force holding the west and the south of the ring, assisted by another French division arriving on the outside from the south, the bulk of the army flung itself on the Austrians lining the heights to the north, and tumbled them backwards towards Monte Baldo. The third Austrian column remaining bottled up in the Adige gorge throughout the battle. This time there was no doubt about the nature of Bonaparte's victory, for the Austrians broke up in rout and fled northwards by mountain tracks.

Next day, however, Bonaparte learned that a fresh danger had developed at the other end of his long front, thirty miles away at Mantua, where an Austrian force had slipped past his screening troops and got to within two miles of the besieged fortress. Bonaparte instantly dispatched troops already tired by twenty-four hours of fighting at Rivoli on a forced march to Mantua. They arrived at dawn on 16 January. The Austrian commander, trapped by superior forces, surrendered. By his speed in switching forces from one end of his front to the other, Bonaparte had doubled the effective power of his army.

This total defeat of the third Austrian counter-offensive in Italy spelled the end for the garrison of Mantua. On 2 February 1797, starving and almost out of ammunition, it surrendered, and at long, long last the way was clear for Bonaparte to invade Austria, as the Directory freshly instructed him to do by their letters of 12 and 20 February 1797.[33] Towards the end of March Bonaparte was riding among those mountains which for so many months had tantalizingly bounded his northern horizon; far-off pale ghosts turned now to rock, snowfield, torrent and precipice. The traversing of mountain landscapes was to provide a recurrent theme in his career, and one all too apt for thrilling the imagination of a romantic age.

While Joubert away to the west crossed into the Tyrol by the Brixen Pass, Bonaparte and the main body entered by the Tarvis, the most direct route to Vienna, marching by Villach, Klagenfurt, Scheifling and Judenburg up the long winding corridor of the Mur valley. On 7 April the Austrians asked him for an armistice; on 18 April a preliminary peace treaty was signed at Leoben.

It looked like the triumphant finale to an astounding campaign – had not Bonaparte exacted peace from a vanquished Austria when only a few days' march from Vienna? So runs the legend. But the truth was very different. The armistice and the preliminaries of peace, like the armistice of Cherasco at the very beginning

'So the legend was successfully established of a "glorious" peace "dictated" to Austria at the gates of Vienna by a young military genius . . .': the signing of the Treaty of Leoben on 18 April 1797, after a painting by G. Lethière. *Bibliothèque Nationale, Paris. Photo: Lauros-Giraudon*

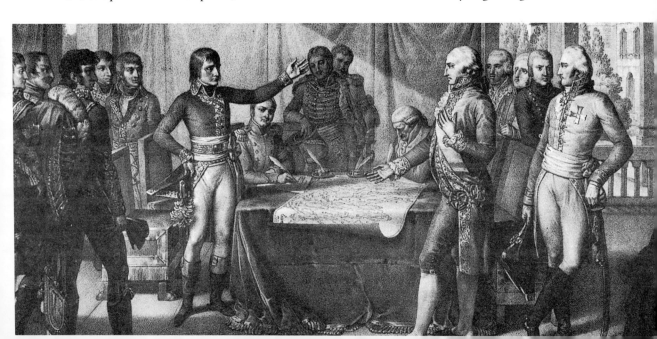

of the Italian adventure, came just in time to save Bonaparte from an inevitable retreat. For his strategic position, far from being one of ascendancy, was precarious in the extreme, as he virtually admitted to the Directory.[34] In front of him lay the Archduke Charles, the most able Austrian general, and all the resources of the Austrian heartlands; on his left flank lay the Tyrol with its ferociously hostile peasantry, a potential base for an Austrian thrust against his rear. He could count on no help from the Army of the Rhine, which had not yet begun its forward march. His own army, strewn amid mountains offering poor prospects for living by pillage, was desperately short of supplies. And his immensely extended line of communications, running all the way back over the Alps to Milan and on to France, was now imperilled by a general revolt of the peasantry of the Veneto and by widespread insurgency in other Italian states.

It was true that at first his advance on Vienna threw the Austrian court into a panic, resulting in the Austrian request for an armistice. But then the Austrians became aware of his true weakness. In the negotiation of the peace preliminaries at Leoben, it was Bonaparte who was in haste to reach an agreement; and the terms, public and secret, showed the price he was prepared to pay in order to get it. For by them France waived, instead of enforcing, her claim to the 'natural' frontier of the Rhine, while Austria was to gain the entire mainland territory of Venice, an immense prize, as compensation for her far-off and indefensible Belgian territories, which, already in French occupation, passed to France. Austria would now possess a solid block of territory from the Danube to the Adriatic. France's only other gain, if it were a gain rather than an entanglement, was Lombardy, which became an 'independent' republic, geographically cut off, however, from its French protector. While the Austrians could hardly credit their fortune, Bonaparte himself was at pains to excuse the terms to the Directory.[35]

But good public relations have sold worse products. After Leoben, Bonaparte sent his generals home in relays so that the French public could see their new heroes in the flesh one by one. And after the final terms were signed at Campoformio on 17 October 1797, with terms slightly but not materially more favourable to France, Bonaparte returned to Paris to hand over in person to the Directory in a public ceremony at the Luxembourg the treaty signed by the Emperor of Austria. The Councils of the Ancients and the Five Hundred (the fancifully named legislative houses under the current constitution) entertained him to a banquet in the great gallery of the Louvre. The street where he resided was renamed the 'Rue de la Victoire'. He was nominated as a member of the *Institut de France*, section of mathematics, an honour which so gratified him that he placed the title '*Membre de l'Institut*' at the top of his letter heading. Throughout all these splendid celebrations, Bonaparte himself feigned a simplicity and a modesty worthy of a republican hero, so swelling the general admiration.

So the legend was successfully established of a 'glorious' peace 'dictated' to Austria at the gates of Vienna by a young military genius in the climax of one of the most brilliant campaigns of history. Europe was dazzled, France was dazzled, Bonaparte's future opponents were dazzled, and, perhaps most fateful of all, Bonaparte was dazzled too.

IV

EVERYTHING I UNDERTAKE MUST SUCCEED

BETWEEN THE PRELIMINARY PEACE of Leoben, in April 1797, and the final Treaty of Campoformio in October, the young conqueror and his companions-in-arms enjoyed a summer's idyll interrupted only by the need to put down sundry Italian revolts with fire and sword, and annex Venice in order to hand her over to Austria under the secret articles of the peace terms. One member of Bonaparte's entourage was to remember their stay in the Villa Manin at Passeriano during the Campoformio negotiations for 'its altogether unique spell; it had a character of its own which no circumstance afterwards was able to re-create. We were all very young, from the supreme chief down to the most junior officers, all bright with strength and health, and consumed by love of glory . . .' True adventurers, they also felt a 'complete security in regard to our future, a confidence without limit in our destinies . . .'[1]

Bonaparte, enjoying the magnificence of the Villa Manin and the marble and gilt of the Crivellis' vast palazzo at Mombello, outside Milan, which he made his vice-regal seat, carried his new stature with aplomb. According to a young French diplomat who stayed with him at Mombello:

> The appearance of the General-in-Chief is very imposing. Although he is affable and cheerful, his officers never fail to approach him with respect, since he is severe and does not allow familiarity. With him are his wife, his sister and a younger brother, and he seems like the father of a family, whom everyone reveres . . . Not a day passes without envoys from the Powers coming to see him, and it is easy to see that with them he upholds perfectly the dignity of the nation on which his exploits have so often shed lustre . . .[2]

Bonaparte, averred this young admirer, towered above his colleagues 'by his genius and by the grandeur and power of his ideas.'

Bonaparte's wife, running out of excuses, had finally reached Milan in July 1796, when he was at Verona at grips with Wurmser. He returned to Milan for two days of rapturous reunion with Josephine, and thereafter wrote her daily love letters in his romantic novelist's style even amid the most pressing emergencies of the campaign:

> Ah! I pray you, let me see some of your faults; be less beautiful, less gracious, less tender, less good above all; above all, never be jealous; never cry; your tears take away my reason, burn my blood . . . Come and join me again, and at least before dying we could say to ourselves: We were happy so many days![3]

His wish that Josephine should show herself less good was soon granted. She had made her reluctant journey to Italy in the company of a young Monsieur Hippolyte Charles, who possessed all those talents of amusing conversation and amorous skill which Bonaparte lacked. When Bonaparte took the field from time to time to engage the Austrians, Monsieur Charles took to Bonaparte's bed to engage Josephine. Long suspicious and finally aware, Bonaparte suffered an anguish of jealousy. Against his own strongly argued views, he had succumbed to a woman, and been betrayed: a fresh experience to harden him in his solitariness and egotism; another moral bond snapped, even though for all her frailties Josephine's physical spell was to hold him still.

So Monsieur Charles returned to Paris, Josephine writing soon after to an aunt: 'I am very bored.'[4]

During 1797 Bonaparte the political sage, student of Rousseau and author of *Le Discours de Lyon,* was much occupied in devising, in accordance with the Directory's detailed instructions, a constitution for the new Cisalpine Republic in northern Italy. As with the current French constitution, sovereignty was to be vested in the people according to the best revolutionary principles. Unfortunately the Italian people still remained wedded to the institutions and beliefs of the *ancien régime*, and it was all too likely that they would exercise their newly granted sovereignty in directions contrary to French interests. Bonaparte was therefore instructed that 'so long as we are there the legislative will must be exercised by you alone.'[5] A foreign general was then to act as stand-in for the sovereign people: a grotesque sham. The sham arose from the contradictions between revolutionary idealogy and the revolutionaries' own love of power. And in France also those same contradictions were beginning to point towards a similar outcome, for the French people were demonstrating by their votes in elections a mounting hostility towards republican rule, a yearning for the *ancien régime*. The opposition press thrived. There was even criticism of General Bonaparte – suggestions that his triumphs were no more than hollow bluff. Could the sovereignty of the people be allowed to go as far as this? In July 1797 Bonaparte recommended to the Directory:

> You can save the republic at one blow . . .: have the *émigrés* arrested; destroy the influence of foreigners. If you have need of force, call on the armies. Break the presses belonging to the journals in English pay . . .[6]

At the end of the month he sent a hatchetman, General Augereau, to Paris to lend support to those of the Directors who wished to maintain the republican regime by force. On 4 September Paris awoke to a military occupation. The elections in forty-nine departments were quashed; the opposition press was muzzled; and seventeen prominent members of the opposition were exiled to Guiana. By these means, so reminiscent of Germany in 1933 and Czechoslovakia in 1948 and 1968, the Republic was saved, and with it the career of its thus far studiously obedient instrument, General Bonaparte.

WITH THE SIGNING of the Treaty of Campoformio, the French republic had made peace with all its enemies in Continental Europe. But with England war still went on. This was the Directory's doing, not England's, for the English Cabinet had offered to recognize France's claim to the 'natural' frontiers and restore all the colonies England had captured – far better terms than England had ever

offered the old French monarchy. They were not, however, good enough for
Barras and the other Jacobins who since the military coup of 3–4 September 1797
had come to dominate the Directory. They asked for more: compensation for
French ships lost at Toulon in 1793; the return of Dutch colonies to the French
puppet Batavian republic. English mistrust hardened, not least because of the
Directory's evident desire to dominate both Italy and Germany. The peace talks
collapsed. Puffed up by the outward success of the Italian gamble, the Directory had
provoked the obdurate resistance of the one European power immune from the
march of French armies. But in any case Barras and company no more wished for a
dim compromise peace with England now than with Austria two years earlier.
They again meant to gather up every chip on the table, which they believed would
only require one more strategic throw.

This took the form of an invasion of Egypt; a project mulled over even under the
ancien régime, and now put forward by Talleyrand. But Bonaparte himself had
written to the Directory in August 1797 that soon 'we will come to the conclusion
that, in order really to destroy England, we must seize Egypt.'[7]

The final decision to invade Egypt was taken by the Directory at meetings on
1 and 2 March 1798, whereupon Bonaparte, appointed General-in-Chief of the
Army of the Orient, plunged with zest into the immense task of preparing the
expedition in the customary utmost haste. According to his instructions of 12 April
from the Directory the strategic purpose was to bring England to peace by
destroying those supposed foundations of her wealth, her commerce and
possessions in India and the East. Egypt itself was to be at once the stepping stone to
India and a new colony for France in its own right.[8] In this grandiose strategy may
be detected the fruits of young Bonaparte's cramming of the trade statistics of the
British Empire and of the history of the Arabs. But Bonaparte also intended the
expedition to divert English seapower to the East and so expose England itself to
invasion in the coming autumn.[9] The entire strategy rested on his assumption that,
thanks to nine Venetian ships of the line now in French hands, France would, in his
words, 'always retain the mastery of the Mediterranean.'[10]

The expedition sailed in four separate squadrons, the largest from Toulon and the
others from Marseille, Genoa and Civita-Vecchia, and joined up at sea. Bonaparte
himself left Toulon in the fleet flagship *L'Orient* on 19 May 1798. Such a moment
called for an order of the day:

> Soldiers! You are one of the wings of the Army of England. You have waged war in the
> mountains, in the plains . . . it remains for you to wage war at sea . . .
>   Soldiers, Europe has its eyes on you . . .[11]

Bonaparte was taking even greater risks than at the outset of the Italian campaign.
His three hundred transport vessels were slow and ill-armed, their crews ill-trained;
they and their escorting fleet (fourteen ships of the line, thirteen frigates) were
stuffed with 29,000 soldiers and all their stores. Nor was the enterprise a secret, the
preparations having been reported in *The Times*, although its destination was
guessed to be Naples and Sicily. By the end of May Nelson was cruising in the
Mediterranean with a powerful squadron; if he succeeded in intercepting

MAY 7.

Letters from Peterſburgh inform us, that PAUL I. is extremely deſirous of interfering in the affairs of Germany, but that the ferment which prevails in his dominions, and eſpecially at Peterſburgh and Moſcow, prevents him from ſatisfying his wiſh.

We learn by letters from Turin, that the inſurgents in Piedmont have been defeated in ſeveral engagements, and that tranquillity is likely to be ſoon reſtored in that country.

Buonaparte poſitively left Paris early on the morning of the 5th inſt. It is underſtood that he is gone to Toulon, and the intended expedition againſt Egypt is entirely laid aſide. His great object is ſtated to be, the effecting a junction between the Toulon and Spaniſh ſquadrons.

The flotilla under the command of *Muſkein*, has effected a junction with that of Cherbourg. The former ſuſtained the enemy's fire for 3 days without ſuffering any damage.

Sir SYDNEY SMITH has found means to eſcape from the Temple. Several armed perſons went ſome days ſince to that priſon with a counterfeit order from the Miniſter of Police, under the pretence of transferring him to Mélun. He was delivered to them by the keepers, and it was only ſome days after that the government was informed of his eſcape.

(left) '. . . the preparations having been reported in detail in *The Times* . . .': a paragraph from the issue of Wednesday, 16 May 1798. *Photo: Derrick Witty*

(right) 'A check here, with Nelson on the roam, could lead to catastrophe. But after three days' hesitation the Knights capitulated.' Bonaparte takes the surrender of Malta from the Knights of St John on 12 June 1798. Engraving by Nodet. *Bibliothèque Nationale, Paris*

Bonaparte's armada, he would destroy it as easily as trawling for herring.

On 9 June Bonaparte appeared off Malta, his first objective, an island then in the possession of the Knights of St John. Valetta, the capital, was a powerful fortress, with batteries barring the entrance to the Grand Harbour. A check here, with Nelson on the roam, could lead to catastrophe. But after three days' hesitation the Knights capitulated. Once more Bonaparte found himself delivered from the consequences of an inherently unsound strategic situation by the faint heart of an enemy. Pausing for less than a week in order to abolish all religious orders, set up totally new systems of administration, taxation and education, and arrange for street lighting to be introduced, he set sail on 19 June for Egypt.

On 22 June his outlying frigates were spotted by Nelson's squadron. But Nelson, misled by information from a Genoese vessel that Bonaparte had left Malta on the 16th, believed that by now the French fleet must have reached Alexandria, and thither he was sailing at utmost speed. Lacking frigates to dispatch on reconnaissance (they had parted from him in a storm), he chose not to halt his pursuit in order to investigate the mysterious sails on the horizon. The alarmed French sheered away towards Crete; Nelson sped for Alexandria, only to find it empty of enemy ships. Unable to believe that the French could be still on passage, he sailed again on 29 June for the Syrian coast. Three days later the French armada dropped anchor off Marabout, just west of Alexandria. Luck, and luck only, had brought Bonaparte unscathed from France to Egypt.

That same day he carried the dilapidated defences of Alexandria against feeble resistance. The French were disillusioned to find that this celebrated city was now no more than a nest of stinking and pest-ridden hovels. Next day Bonaparte issued a proclamation to the inhabitants of Egypt, which they were able to read in their own language thanks to his agents' seizure of an Arabic press from the Vatican propaganda department in Rome before the expedition sailed. It was a wordy and rambling disquisition in his '*Discours de Lyon*' style, in which he promised to respect 'God, his prophet and the Koran.'[12] He blamed the woes of the Egyptian people on their rulers, the Mamelukes: 'Is there a fine piece of land? It belongs to the Mamelukes. Is there a fine slave, a fine horse, a fine house? They belong to the Mamelukes . . .' The Mamelukes were therefore cast for a role of villain similar to that of the 'privileged orders' and the Church in Italy in 1796–7. By a neat double, he even made use of his record in Italy in order to prove that the French were friends of true mussulmans. 'Is it not we,' he asked, 'who have destroyed the power of the Pope who said that war ought to be waged on Mussulmans?'[13]

Uniforms of the French Republican Navy. Left: Commodore; right: Captain. Engraved by Labrousse after Grasset de Saint Sauveur. Bonaparte' fleet was destroyed by the superior seamanship and gunnery of Nelson's fleet at the Battle of the Nile on 1 August 1798. *Bibliothèque Nationale, Paris*

Later in his proclamation, however, he reverted to one of his favourite political themes:

> Three times happy those who will be on our side. They will prosper in their fortune and their rank . . . But woe, three times woe, to those who take up arms for the Mamelukes and fight against us! There will be no hope for them; they will perish.[14]

This paragraph fairly summarized what was to be Bonaparte's civil policy in Egypt: blandishments and the bludgeon; in fact, Italy over again. But there was an important difference. In Italy Bonaparte had remained in close communication with his political masters in Paris; obedient to their instructions and careful to do nothing without their sanction. Here in Egypt he was on his own, enjoying supreme authority for the first time.

Militarily the campaign was a walk-over compared with Italy. Far from equalling the Austrians, the Mamelukes, a gorgeous medieval array of brave but ill-disciplined horsemen, were nothing like so formidable even as the native Indian armies in India defeated during this period by the greatly outnumbered English commanders Wellesley and Lake. With each of his divisions deployed in a square, Bonaparte easily smashed the Mameluke charges at Shubra Kit on 13 July and at the Battle of the Pyramids outside Cairo on the 21st; musketry and case-shot proving on both occasions mightier than the sword. Only in the matter of supply were there resemblances to the 1796–7 campaigns. Egyptian towns and villages yielded little in the way of sustenance to the pillager, and, in the absence of vast convoys of carts of the kind organized by the British in India, the French army went even hungrier than in Italy and this time thirsty too.

Eleven days after Bonaparte entered Cairo his fleet was destroyed by Nelson in Aboukir Bay, so marooning the French in their new possession. In a report to the Directory, Bonaparte made haste to blame the catastrophe on his admiral, Brueys, killed in the battle, alleging that he had ordered him to shelter without delay within the harbour of Alexandria or sail to Crete. This was grossly to distort the purport of his instructions to Brueys. On 30 July, two days before the Battle of Aboukir, Bonaparte informed Brueys that 'the whole conduct of the British leads one to believe that they are inferior in numbers, and that they are contenting themselves with blockading Malta . . .'[15] He wanted Brueys to go to Crete not in order to

escape the English, but so that he might be well placed to exert pressure on the Sultan of Turkey.[16]

The severing of communications with France and the loss of the ships raised urgent problems of supply while at the same time plunging the French soldiery into the glooms of homesickness. Confronted by this double crisis, moral and material, Bonaparte put forth his formidable powers of leadership. As he told his subordinates, character must rise above circumstance. He quietened the army's apprehensions by the example of his own calm, confidence and resolve. He threw himself with all his resourcefulness and energy, his executive ability, into the task of transforming Egypt into a self-supporting base. The distinguished scientists who had accompanied the expedition were put to work on such problems as investigating local resources for making gunpowder, brewing beer without hops and purifying Nile water. Indeed Nelson's victory served as a sharp spur to the work of organizing and exploiting Egypt as a French colony. What the British were doing generation by generation in India, Bonaparte sought to accomplish in Egypt in the span of a few months. New systems of administration, finance and taxation were created; new land registration; a divan, or consultative committee of native leaders, set up; surveys of land and resources put in hand; hospitals; streetlighting; organized rubbish disposal; French-style cafés and pleasure gardens. Bonaparte resembled a latter-day tycoon reconstructing some newly taken-over and hitherto moribund company. He reported to the Directory on 8 September 1798 that 'All goes perfectly well here. The country has submitted and begins to get used to us. The rest is the work of time . . .' And he went on: 'Never did a colony offer more advantages . . . Mistress of Egypt, France will in the long run be mistress of India. The Cabinet in London is perfectly aware of it. I do not doubt then that this is at least the guarantee of a general peace . . .'[17]

Yet this remarkable exercise in instant empire rested on no firm foundations of consent or even acquiescence on the part of Egyptians, but on the shifting sand of outright hostility – largely stirred up, just as in Italy, by the Bonapartian system of supporting his army off the country it occupied. From start to finish the central theme, the determining factor, in the French occupation of Egypt was shortage of ready cash, and the ever more drastic expedients adopted in search of a remedy.[18] At first only the Mamelukes – the 'privileged' – or those who openly resisted French rule were pillaged by the seizure and forced sale of their property and valuables. But soon this limited source proved insufficient. Extraordinary levies were then made on the merchant communities of the major cities, which in turn impinged on the Egyptian consumer. Finally Bonaparte instituted a new tax upon all transactions in real estate; a tax which from its novel nature and its universal application incensed the population at large.

Moreover, despite the Egyptians' apparent submission to French force, despite also Bonaparte's hypocritical assurances about his love of Islam, they continued to look upon their conquerors as infidels – just as the Italians had looked upon the French army as atheists come to destroy the Church. Soon after the occupation of Cairo, local revolts broke out; attacks on isolated French garrisons or troops on the move. Bonaparte had to balance his policy of winning Arab hearts by one of

Bonaparte pardoning the insurgents of Cairo, by Antoine-Jean Baron Gros. In reality he ordered the throats of all prisoners taken in arms to be cut and the beheaded corpses to be thrown into the Nile. *Bulloz*

chopping off Arab heads and burning Arab villages. He wrote to a subordinate in July: '. . . I am having three heads cut off here every day and carried round Cairo; it is the only way to break the resistance of these people.'[19]

On 21 October 1798 Cairo rose in general revolt, the igniting spark being the new property tax, and the rebels' stronghold being the El Azhar mosque. Bonaparte reacted in standard form, ordering that all those encountered in the streets with arms in their hands be put to the sword: '. . . Exterminate everyone in the mosque . . .'[20] He crushed the revolt in the course of two days' butchery in the streets. On 23 October he ordered Berthier, his chief-of-staff: 'You will please give orders, Citizen General . . . to cut the throats of all prisoners taken with arms in hand. They will be conducted to the banks of the Nile . . . their corpses without heads will be thrown into the Nile.'[21]

Force having prevailed once more, Bonaparte now renewed his efforts to win the goodwill of the Egyptians. But the French henceforward remained on the *qui vive*, always aware that they were an alien army of occupation amid a potentially hostile people.

According to the Directory's strategy, Egypt was supposed to serve as a stepping stone to India; as a base for destroying the eastern foundations of England's wealth. Unfortunately Egypt was surrounded by deserts and seas and even though Desaix was campaigning in upper Egypt and there were French posts on the Red Sea, Bonaparte now found himself boxed in by geography and the Royal Navy. How without seapower did one proceed from Egypt to India, or even the Persian Gulf? Total want of information about events outside Egypt – in France, in Europe, in Turkey – no less walled him in, for in a pique he had ordered his subordinates to break off all communication with his only source of news, Commodore Sir Sidney Smith, commanding the English squadron left to blockade Egypt. In mid-December he was writing to the Directory that he had heard nothing from France since July. The highroad to the Indies had turned out to be a cul-de-sac.

Beyond Egypt fresh enemies were gathering. The Sultan of Turkey declared war on France on 2 September 1798. A Turkish army began to assemble in Syria under its governor, Djezzar ('The Butcher') Pasha. English ships of war might land this or even a further Turkish army on the coast of the Nile Delta. So Bonaparte decided to march across the Sinai Desert and destroy Djezzar's army.

He had made his first preparatory move as far back as August, when he sent an emissary to Djezzar Pasha to point out that the French were his friends and to assure him that he, Bonaparte, had no intention of seizing Jerusalem. On 11 September he ordered the country between the Delta and Gaza to be reconnoitred, and the following day wrote to the Pasha of Aleppo drawing his attention to French goodwill, and informing him that the French recognized the Muslim faith 'to be sublime, we adhere to it, and the moment has arrived when all enlightened Frenchmen will become true believers.'[22] In November similar protestations of friendship were dispatched to the Grand Vizier in Constantinople. No reply was received to any of these missives, so similar in character to those addressed to his adversaries during the Ajaccio *putsch* six years before.

All through November and December military preparations were pushed forward: stocking of magazines; concentration of troops; more reconnaissance; a seaborne siege train. By late January all was ready to Bonaparte's satisfaction. Yet what was his true purpose in undertaking the invasion of Syria? To the Directory he claimed in familiar enough fashion that he had no option, but was provoked into it by Djezzar's warlike preparations and harassment of French citizens. His correspondence suggests nothing more ambitious than a two-months' strategic raid as far as Acre in order to destroy Djezzar's army. But his diplomacy was reaching out to the Persian Gulf – and beyond, for he had just tried to get into written communication with Tippoo Sahib, the ruler of Mysore and the most dangerous of England's opponents in India. Was Syria to be a first stage of an attempt to emulate Alexander the Great and march to India? Or was it Constantinople which beckoned Bonaparte, the city of the sultans and Byzantine emperors that was to fascinate him all through his career? Either objective was more in keeping with Bonaparte's character than Djezzar's ragged army, given that Bonaparte, the eternal fidget, wished to get on the move again. Yet whatever the ultimate motive, the march into Syria still remained an attempt to retrieve the failure of the Egyptian gamble by venturing on another.

The march began in the early days of February 1799; a struggle to get the guns through shifting sand; a diet of dogs and camels and brackish water. Bonaparte had ordered his leading division to build a fort at El Arish, the first town on the Palestinian side of the Sinai. Unfortunately the division found a fort already in existence and garrisoned by resolute Turks, so blocking the army's exit from the Sinai. By the 18th the army found itself in a familiar kind of plight, 'placed', wrote Bonaparte, 'in a situation where the least delays could become disastrous for it.'[23] On 21 February Bonaparte repaired this consequence of his poor reconnaissance by bombarding El Arish into surrender with every available gun.

The army pushed on through countryside much resembling, Bonaparte remarked, that round Béziers in Languedoc – rolling hills, vineyards, citrus groves, windbreaks of cypresses. But this was Palestine in winter: driving rains, the tracks mere sliding bogs of mud and water. On 7 March Bonaparte breached the walls of Jaffa and took the town by storm. Two thousand Turks were put to the sword in the course of the storm, while a further 2,000 were taken to the seashore at Bonaparte's orders and shot.[24] More creditably, the general-in-chief visited a plague hospital and himself carried out the corpse of a victim in order to rally morale; he believed rather unscientifically that only those afraid of the plague could catch it.

Bonaparte now addressed to the sheiks and the cadis of Palestine his customary message to a newly invaded country:

> It is well that you realise that all human efforts are useless against me, because everything I undertake must succeed. Those who declare themselves my friends prosper. Those who declare themselves my enemies perish . . .[25]

Yet there was a slight difference this time: his message spoke of 'I' and 'me' and 'my', whereas earlier examples of the genre had spoken of 'we' and 'us' and 'France' and 'the Republic'.

On 17 March he reached Haifa, whence he could see Acre, his principal immediate objective, across the bay to the north. Though only a ruinous medieval walled fortress, Acre stood on a rocky peninsula and was therefore exposed to siege only on its landward side. It was garrisoned by Turks – at their best in position warfare – and by a sprinkling of bluejackets from Commodore Sir Sidney Smith's squadron. The Turkish commander was ferocious and resolute, while Sir Sidney Smith himself was an officer of high spirit in no way daunted by Bonaparte and the French army; and they drew on the professional skill of a French aristocratic émigré engineer, de Phélippeaux, who had been at the *Ecole Militaire* in Paris with Bonaparte and had even been commissioned on the same date.

Unfortunately for Bonaparte the vessels transporting his siege train from Egypt fell into the hands of the Royal Navy off Acre on the day he reached Haifa. He was later to use this as an excuse for his failure to take Acre despite a siege lasting two months. Certainly he had lost the 18- and 24-pounders necessary to smash thick

masonry; certainly the 8- and 12-pounders to which he was forced to resort could not adequately do the job. Nevertheless, it would have made no decisive difference if his siege train had not been captured, for he had originally ordered his admiral to embark only two hundred rounds per 24-pounder,[26] and in later instructions three hundred rounds per mortar and 24-pounder[27] – grossly inadequate stocks for such a task as breaching the walls of Acre. The standard provision in the British army for breaching was 1,000 rounds per gun and five hundred shells per mortar,[28] while Bonaparte's own orders for the bombardment of Jaffa called for a rate of fire of twenty rounds per gun per hour. Moreover, when at last fresh 18- and 24-pounders arrived at Acre in May, Bonaparte still failed to take the fortress. The truth was that, with his customary slapdash overconfidence, he had counted on Acre falling without much of a fight, and so had neglected to make adequate preparations for a formal siege. Furthermore, in the opinion of Brigadier Marmont, a distinguished gunner present at Acre and later a marshal, the siege could have succeeded even without the heavy guns, if only the available resources had been properly organized and efficiently employed.[29] But to settle down to a systematic and protracted siege, or even await the arrival of fresh siege guns, was of course unthinkable to the impatient Bonaparte; after all, the campaign was supposed to have been brought to a victorious conclusion by the end of March. Instead, confidently predicting all the time that the fortress was about to fall, he launched one hasty and ill-prepared assault after another.

The first took place on 28 March, after only a short bombardment. The toadies in his entourage had encouraged him in his blind refusal to acknowledge that such an assault must fail, given that the alleged breach was no more than a small hole some six feet up the wall from the bottom of the dry moat. General Kléber, however, remained silent, so provoking Bonaparte into demanding his opinion. 'Certainly the breach is practicable, *mon général,*' replied Kléber, 'a cat could get through it.'[30] The event proved at heavy cost that the French army could not.

Once again the master of lightning strokes found himself paralysed by a fortress he could not take: March turned to April; April dragged into May. The sole relief to his fuming frustration before Acre was afforded by the appearance of a Turkish field army from the north, which he easily smashed at the Battle of Mount Tabor on 16 April. On 10 May, after new siege guns had at last arrived and pounded a breach, he launched his final assault; it was thrown back with murderous losses. The siege had failed; it only remained for him to organize the retreat, make private excuses to the Directory, and take steps publicly to represent this decisive strategic defeat as another victory. The retreat involved mobilizing bakers and cooks as stretcher bearers to the wounded, throwing much of his artillery into the sea, and, had Bonaparte had his way, killing all the plague-patients with overdoses of opium. But the army's chief medical officer, Desgenettes, refused. To the Directory Bonaparte reported that having reduced Acre to a heap of stones, there was no point in actually entering the place and incurring the risk of bringing out the plague into his camp. 'The season, moreover, is too advanced; the objective I had proposed for myself has been fulfilled; Egypt calls me . . .'[31] To the army he issued a proclamation:

> Soldiers, you have crossed the desert which separates Africa and Asia faster than an Arab army. The army which was marching on Egypt has been destroyed . . .[32]

Plague-ridden, burdened by wounded, starved by the customary breakdown in the commissariat,[33] the French army straggled back through Palestine. Apprehensive of the effects this inglorious return might have on Egyptian opinion, Bonaparte took great pains over his public-relations arrangements. An officer was sent ahead to display captured Turkish flags in every village along the route; distinguished Turkish prisoners were to be ceremonially locked up in the Cairo citadel. The army was to be met outside Cairo by the garrison and then both were to re-enter the city with palm branches ornamenting helmets and hats, bands playing, and amid salvos of salutes. There were to be victory rejoicings. All this was done. It was not enough. For the truth passed by word of mouth through the villages, and Egypt knew.

Soon after his return to Cairo Bonaparte wrote to the Directory asking for 6,000 men in replacement of his losses and for abundant supplies of arms. If the Directory could send him another 15,000 men on top of that, he 'would be able to go anywhere, even Constantinople.'[34] But without replacements, he added, they

'. . . the quality of command in his attitude, his gaze, his manner of talking': Napoleon Bonaparte at the age of twenty-eight, painted in 1798 on board *L'Orient,* flagship of the expedition to Egypt. Miniature by André Dutertre. *Musée Frédéric Masson, Paris. Photo: Maison Dubout*

Bonaparte, the eastern potentate, in a caricature by De Vinck. As well as wearing Turkish costume, Bonaparte pretended that he and his army were about to embrace Islam. *Bibliothèque Nationale, Paris*

would eventually have to make peace. Such was the military position after a year in Egypt. Shortage of cash had become acute again too, and the French administration had recourse to forced loans, money penalties for infringements of the law and fresh tax devices. Yet the general-in-chief enjoyed his reliefs from these anxieties and the routine burdens of running a country. There was his mistress, Marguerite-Pauline Fourès, née Bellisle (hence her nickname 'la Bellilote'), wife of a lieutenant, and known to the army as Cleopatra, a lively girl who liked to show off her well-sculpted rump and thighs in the tight breeches of an officer's uniform. Though Bonaparte astutely sent her husband home on a special mission, his ship was captured by the English, who returned him to Egypt out of courtesy; another grudge for Bonaparte to hold against England. Then there were the weekly meetings of the *Institut d'Égypte* founded by Bonaparte the previous summer in imitation of the *Institut de France* as a centre of scientific and scholarly research. Bonaparte liked to attend these meetings as a member of the fraternity of science. There were signs after his return from Syria, however, that despite his ill-fortune in that campaign he was becoming too grand to endure the free-for-all of intellectual debate. When Bonaparte launched some sarcasms against medical science, Desgenettes answered him by alluding cryptically to his own refusal to take part in a criminal action (the giving of an overdose of opium to the plague-patients at Acre), and to the danger of transgressing moral principles. Although Bonaparte and the chairman of the meeting tried to silence Desgenettes, the meeting was already in turmoil, with the bandying about of remarks hardly welcome to Bonaparte, such as 'mercenary adulation' and 'oriental despotism' and 'armed guards at the very door of a peaceful literary society' (a reference to the General's escort of Guides). Desgenettes himself refused to retract, and instead charged Bonaparte with 'being something other than a member of the Institute while here' and with 'wanting to be top dog everywhere'.[35]

On 25 July 1799 a Turkish army which had been landed at Aboukir by British and Turkish ships was easily routed. But Egypt, though now secure, had become a dead end both strategically and for Bonaparte personally. How much of a dead end he discovered when Sidney Smith cunningly passed on English newspapers during an exchange of prisoners after Aboukir. For the first time he learned that Austrian and Russian armies had inflicted smashing defeats on France and overrun Italy, Switzerland and Germany; that France itself was heading towards a fresh political crisis.

He thereupon decided to return to France without orders from his government; in other words, to desert his army and his command.

. . . musketry and case-shot proving mightier than the sword . . .': the Battle of the Pyramids on 21 July 1798, when the French army, deployed in divisional squares, routed the Mameluke horsemen. Painting by Louis François Lejeune, 1806. *Musée de Versailles Photo: Musées Nationaux*

V

THE LOYAL ARM OF THE REPUBLIC

BONAPARTE SAILED BY STEALTH at five in the morning of 22 August 1799 accompanied by five chosen generals and two scientists, though not by Bellilote. He arranged his departure in such haste and secrecy that his designated successor, Kléber, only learned of his new appointment from a letter left behind for him. After an anxious voyage and a narrow escape from English ships of the line very near to the French coast, Bonaparte's little squadron of two frigates and escorting vessels made a thankful landfall at Fréjus on 9 October.

Josephine, having accumulated debts and men in his absence, set off in trepidation to meet him *en route* for Paris in order to soothe his anger with the wiles of love. But when she reached Lyons she discovered that in travelling via the Bourbonnais she had chosen the wrong route; Bonaparte had gone via Burgundy, so reaching Paris before her. She hastened back to the capital and laid siege to him with tears and entreaties, supplementing her own with those of her children. Bonaparte, always vulnerable to a woman's tears, indeed flummoxed by any violent display of human feeling (was he, as his early writings suggest, afraid of it?) succumbed, forgave. Her allure resumed its sway. The marriage endured, albeit amid storms of mutual jealousy. Nevertheless, Bonaparte now took the precaution of making sure that Josephine was never left alone with a man. He blended a Latin sense of male sexual proprietorship with a bourgeois concern with the chastity of the family females.

In the capital he was rapturously welcomed as the heroic victor of Italy and the conqueror of Egypt returned to deliver his country. In fact the worst of the crisis was over. General Brune had repulsed the Anglo-Russian invasion forces in Holland; Masséna had swept the Russians and Austrians out of Switzerland again. But in Italy the French army was struggling to hold that very Apennine crest whence Bonaparte had launched his first offensive. It was as if his victories of 1796–7 had never been.

And indeed those victories had been largely responsible for the Second Coalition which was now waging war on France. They had convinced the powers of Europe that the Republic aimed at dominating Europe by the unlimited use of armed force; that the existing social and political order lay in mortal danger; and that the conflict was no traditional limited war but a struggle for survival. The enemies of the French Republic had therefore resolved that she must be forced to give up her extravagant territorial and ideological ambitions. So the Directory's – and Bonaparte's – faith in the efficacy of force had brought its nemesis of force. Instead of achieving the looked-for result of 'a glorious peace', the Italian gamble of 1796–7 had in due time landed France in a fresh war of an incalculably more dangerous nature.

At home too the regime was once again struggling, tottery. Chouan, or royalist, rebels controlled large areas of western France. Public opinion, expressed through elections, was now lurching back to the Left, and the regime faced a virulent and effective group of neo-Jacobins in the Legislature. At the same time an undercurrent of longing for moderation and stability, above all, peace, ran deep and strong in the French people. France was once again verging on bankruptcy. The Directory itself was feeble and discredited.

It was fortunate for Bonaparte that although the Italian adventure had been as much his affair as the Directory's, he was far off in Egypt when its consequences were being reaped; just as, having won kudos from the showy conquest of Egypt, he was to be absent from the scene in 1801 when that gamble too ended in complete failure with the surrender of the Army of the Orient to the English. The personal lustre conferred by Montenotte, Arcola and Rivoli being therefore untarnished, Bonaparte was able scathingly to rebuke the Directory in public for casting away his achievements. That autumn Paris looked to him, talked of him, as the one man who could save the Republic. For the first time since the days of Danton and Robespierre the blur of mediocrity gave place to a name.

Bonaparte acted the required part of austere republican hero with skill and zest; he was Cato, he was Cinna. He professed devotion to the Republic and its principles, on one occasion melodramatically putting his hand on the hilt of his sword and exclaiming, 'May it never be drawn except for the defence of the Republic and its government.'[1] Through attendance at the *Institut de France* (in the role of a returned member with interesting information to impart about Egyptian society and antiquities), he won the trust of the intellectuals, who believed he would put an end to the excesses of the Revolution and finally achieve the fulfilment of eighteenth-century progressive ideals. And Paris at large looked on that stern Roman visage of his and simply saw the leadership and integrity that would save the country.

Even before his return one member of the Directory, Sieyès, had been looking for a soldier who could be used to strike down the enemies of the regime. His first choice, Joubert, had been killed at the Battle of Novi; his second, Moreau, had declined to intervene in politics. Now that Bonaparte was home, however, he had his man. And Bonaparte was willing enough. In the three and a half years since he first assumed command of the Army of Italy, the obedient soldier careful to keep in with his political masters had developed into a man with supreme confidence in his own capacity to rule and corresponding contempt for the kind of politician to whom he had formerly toadied. More than that, his victories, his exercise of virtually sovereign authority in Egypt, his good luck even, had inspired him with a sense of personal destiny; the rootless wanderer of the early years had found his path. In his announcement to the sheiks of Palestine that 'everything I undertake must succeed', there is more than the bombast of propaganda, there is the ring of true conviction. But this sense of destiny meant that Bonaparte the romantic was now finally in the ascendant, subjugating to the service of his egotistical visions Bonaparte the mathematical brain, the man of facts; a fateful combination.

The purpose of Sieyès' proposed *coup d'état* was to limit the powers of the two legislative houses in favour of a much stronger executive. He naïvely believed that Bonaparte would be content to serve as nothing more than his tame military instrument in this venture. The *coup d'état* was prepared with a cunning as skilled as Nazi management of the Reichstag fire.[2] On 7 November (16 Brumaire) the conspirators' parliamentary caucus met privately to draw up a decree transferring the sittings of the two legislative houses to the Palace of St Cloud, outside the capital, where the houses could be more easily intimidated, and appointing Bonaparte commander-in-chief of all troops in the Paris region, or chief intimidator. As the pretext for this decree, the conspirators invented a terrorist plot. An extraordinary session of parliament to approve the decree was called for eight o'clock in the morning of 9 November (18 Brumaire). This approval was secured without difficulty, thanks to the precaution of only delivering notices of the session

(left) 'He thereupon decided to return to France without orders from his government; in other words, to desert his army and his command': Bonaparte's departure from Egypt as seen by a contemporary English cartoonist. *British Museum*

to members' houses three hours beforehand and not at all in the case of the opposition; thanks as well to the atmosphere of crisis evoked by the troops with which Bonaparte had filled the centre of Paris. In the Council of the Ancients, Bonaparte himself swore loyalty to the Constitution he was about to overthrow: 'Misfortune to those who want trouble and disorder! I will arrest them . . . aided by my comrades in arms . . .'[3] It might have been Ajaccio in 1792. Ringingly he lied: 'We want a republic founded on true liberty, on civil liberty, on representation of the nation; we will have it! I swear to it.'[4]

Next day, 10 November (19 Brumaire), parliament met in the Orangery of the Palace of St Cloud; the lower house, the Five Hundred, under its president Lucien Bonaparte. This time the opposition was present in force, asking such pertinent questions as 'Why are we at St Cloud?' and 'Why are we surrounded by an army?', and shouting 'Down with the dictators!' Meanwhile, Bonaparte himself, in an address to the Ancients, was denying that he wished to usurp the government. He

(above) The *coup d'état* of 18–19 Brumaire interpreted by an anonymous English cartoonist. Bonaparte, as a Nile crocodile with a crown already on his head, disperses a Council of Five Hundred composed of frogs. *British Museum*

had indeed, so he claimed, rebuffed such suggestions because 'liberty is dear to me'. He assured his audience that 'I will only be the loyal arm of the Republic.' Darkness had already fallen when, accompanied by the grenadiers of the parliamentary guard, he quit the Ancients to address the Five Hundred. As he entered the chamber with the grenadiers at the door behind him, the opposition members left their seats and crowded forward in the dim candlelight to greet him with angry shouts of 'Down with the tyrant!' 'Down with Cromwell!' 'Outlaw the dictator!'

Under the close impact of this sheer force of personal hatred, Bonaparte, who had not flinched at Lodi or Arcola, lost his nerve completely. White-faced, at first speechless, he tried to stutter out some words of self-justification, his frightened eyes flicking towards the soldiers at the door. In answer to this mute appeal General Lefebvre, his second-in-command, plunged forward at the head of the grenadiers to rescue him, and he withdrew from the chamber under their protection, still shaken. Even when safely outside, his powers of leadership and decision remained entirely paralysed; he could only mutter again and again: 'They wanted to kill me; they wanted to outlaw me.'

Inside the chamber there was tumult; a formal motion to outlaw Bonaparte. Lucien, the President, tried to defend his brother, but he too had to be rescued by the soldiers. The fortunes of the *coup d'état* now hung in the balance. With Bonaparte himself still unstrung and useless, it was Lucien who rallied the troops in the courtyard and ordered them into the chamber to arrest the opposition leaders, on the pretext of delivering the majority of representatives from intimidation. As the troops burst in led by Murat, the representatives rose and cried, 'Long live the Republic!' In vain: they were driven from the building in undignified rout at the point of the bayonet.

With the conclusion of these lurid events, all was over bar the devising of a new constitution. In the following weeks this occasioned lively debates between Bonaparte, who meant to arrogate all powers to himself, and Sieyès, who hoped to shackle him with paper restrictions. Bonaparte, however, had an army at his back, and after a chilling reference to there being blood up to their knees if he failed to get his way, the Constitution finally provided for a First Consul, Bonaparte, responsible for initiating all legislation, appointing all ministers and officials, and declaring war and making peace. The two other consuls were to enjoy only advisory and consultative functions. All three were appointed for ten years. The powers of the new lower house, the Tribunat, were restricted to approving or rejecting legislation without amending it. Of the members of the new upper house, the Senate, half were to be co-opted by the other half – which in turn were to be appointed by the First Consul. Though a façade of universal suffrage was retained, a complicated system of indirect voting ensured that the sovereignty of the people could not be carried as far as choice. The preamble of this constitution declared it to be founded on 'the true principles of representative government, on the sacred rights of property, liberty and equality', and that it guaranteed 'the rights of citizens.'[5] It would have been more honest to declare that it was founded on humbug. In fact it fulfilled the promise of French constitution making in Italy; the promise of Rousseau's original *Contrat Social*; the promise of Lieutenant

Buonaparte's musings on politics and society back in 1788–91 – an all-embracing State whose power was untrammelled by law or any other institutions whatsoever. This was the destination towards which the Revolution had been inevitably, inexorably, travelling ever since it began in 1789; Marat, Danton, Robespierre, the Committee of Public Safety, the Directory, all had signposted the way to Bonaparte.

In a plebiscite on 7 February 1800, an electorate fed up with assemblies and their factious debates, yearning for stability after eight years of revolutionary turmoil, voted 3,011,007 in favour of the new Constitution; 1,562 against. Could it not be said that, in accordance with the best Rousseauesque principles, the general will and General Bonaparte were now synonymous?

ON THE NIGHT OF 19 Brumaire he slept for the last time in his modest dwelling on the Rue de la Victoire, moving next day to the Palais du Luxembourg and in February 1800 into the old royal palace of the Tuileries. The lonely, savage rebel of Brienne, the Corsican patriot, the revolutionary agitator, the soldier of fortune, had become dictator over 30,000,000 French citizens. Ability had carried him there; the drive of ambition too; but again and again luck and the right contacts had proved the decisive factors.

He was the spiritual heir of the Directory, inspired by the same adventurism, the same lack of scruple, the same belief in the efficacy of force, and the same belief in the merits of exporting the cost of waging war. The difference lay in the matter of effectiveness: one able and singleminded man instead of five bickering mediocrities, and a constitution which gave him virtually free rein.

Experience of government and statecraft in Italy and Egypt had matured the crude, impetuous politician of Bonaparte's Corsican career. Although the underlying determination to dominate over everyone still remained – that was in his nature – he now at first proceeded with caution, subtlety and skill, attempting to draw in behind him the support of all those in France not irreconcilably hostile. His fellow consuls were well chosen: one, Lebrun, a former functionary of the royal government; the other, Cambacérès, an old member of the Convention; reassurance here for the Left and the Right. Bonaparte himself continued to play the part of modest chief magistrate of a republic. Among his first acts were the repeal of the law of hostages, under which relatives of royalist émigrés could be held in prison, and the release of many political prisoners. French intellectuals, with that special gullibility of the clever, were as readily taken in by this pose of devotion to republican ideals of liberty as British intellectuals by Hitler's pose as a peace lover in the 1930s.

But against those who could not be won over, who continued to resist him, he displayed the same desire to crush as in Italy and Egypt. He instructed General Hédouville, in command of operations against the Chouan rebels, on 5 January 1800: 'You are invested, my dear General, with all powers, yes, all powers; act as freely as if you were in the heart of Germany . . . The Consuls consider that generals ought to have leading rebels who are captured with arms in their hands shot on the spot.'[6] In the First Consul's judgment 'Weakness alone is inhumanity.'[7]

From the moment of appointment as First Consul, Bonaparte threw his outstanding executive talents into reconstructing his newest and biggest take-over, the French State, and, as always, in utmost haste. The whole of central and local government was reorganized. Regular weekly meetings to keep track of the work of different departments were instituted. Each minister was to submit nightly reports or numerical charts to the First Consul on the state of the armed forces, civil affairs, law and order, security, morale and public opinion.[8]

But over all these questions loomed the supreme questions of peace and war. The Treasury was destitute; the military reserves remaining inside France unorganized and ill-equipped; the Army of Italy in sharpening danger. Like the Directory four years earlier, Bonaparte had the option of serving France's true interest and needs by giving up expansionist war aims and seeking a compromise peace. Instead, again like the Directory, he determined to have peace on his own terms, either by gulling the enemy coalition by artful diplomacy, or, if need be, by dictating peace after a great victory. His personal need for the prestige of fresh success and his own character alike demanded this course. He therefore dispatched highminded appeals for peace to the English king and the Austrian emperor. Being, as he said, 'a stranger to all feelings of vainglory, my first wish is to prevent the effusion of blood which is about to flow . . .'[9] These appeals twanged no chord in the suspicious hearts of his correspondents. Nevertheless, he did not give up all thoughts of peace even when on the march in the following spring. Anticipating a twentieth-century Communist strategy, he instructed Talleyrand, his foreign minister, that 'in order to speed the coming of peace, we must simultaneously carry on the war and the negotiations.'[10] To the French people themselves, whose yearning for peace he recognized, Bonaparte adroitly alleged in March 1800 that England wished to destroy French prosperity, and assured them that 'the First Consul has promised peace; he will go and conquer it at the head of the warriors whom he has led to victory more than once . . .'[11]

By now preparations for the coming campaign were going ahead at breakneck speed. The problem of cash-flow was solved in the customary fashion. Switzerland (now the puppet Helvetic Republic) was milked for money; the Army of Italy performed a similar service on the commerce of Genoa. The Dutch, under the persuasion of *their* occupying French army, made a loan of twelve million francs. On 5 December 1799 Bonaparte had ordered the formation of a new army, the Army of Reserve, out of the military bits and pieces to be found within France. On 25 January 1800 he issued General Berthier, the Minister of War, with instructions for the new army's organization into three corps each of 18,000 men and sixteen guns, with the centre corps at Dijon, the right at Lyons and the left at Châlons-sur-Marne.

As a strategist it was Bonaparte's intellectual strength to pierce through detail and complexity and so reduce the grandest sweeps over the map of Europe to the simplicity of a battalion attack. He perceived now that the conflict with the Austrians from the Rhineland to the Apennines really constituted a single front, of which Switzerland, in the centre, was the key. And Switzerland, thanks to the successful counter-stroke carried out before he returned from Egypt, lay in French hands. On these considerations Bonaparte founded his elegant plan for the coming campaign. While the larger portion of the Army of the Rhine acted as a flank guard against the Austrians in Germany, the smaller portion together with the new Army of Reserve under Bonaparte's own command would march south over the Alpine passes into the Lombardy plain and across the rear of the Austrian army on the Apennines, so taking it in reverse. Masséna's outnumbered Army of Italy would meanwhile act as a bait to the Austrians, focusing their eyes on the south while catastrophe swept down behind them from the north.[12]

Yet to move armies and especially their artillery across high Alpine passes before the melting of the snows presented a formidable operation and an immense risk. Moreover, the Army of Reserve itself had first to be created from scratch. From January to April 1800 Bonaparte grappled with the problems of organizing supplies and transport, finding horses for the artillery, solving the puzzle of getting artillery over the high passes (he had large sledges constructed to replace the gun carriages). As always, the keynote was speed and improvisation.

On 5 April the Austrian commander in Italy, Melas, launched a great offensive against the centre of the heavily outnumbered Army of Italy under Masséna, and split it in two. By the third week of April Melas had tightly besieged Masséna himself in Genoa and driven the rest of his army westward beyond the River Var. The crossing of the Alps by the Army of Reserve was now a matter of desperate urgency. But which pass to choose? Bonaparte finally chose the Great St Bernard in preference to the Simplon or the St Gotthard because it lay nearer to his advanced base at Villeneuve on Lake Geneva, and his communications would be least exposed to an Austrian stroke north of the Alps in the period before Moreau attacked in Germany.[13] Yet another factor influenced Bonaparte's decision: since the Bonapartian or Guibertian system of feeding an army off the country could not work in high Alpine valleys, he was forced to revert to the eighteenth-century system of supply, stocking magazines and arranging for the army to carry its food with it. The shorter the distance where this was necessary the better. By the Great St Bernard, so Bonaparte pointed out to Berthier, now the titular General-in-Chief of the Army of Reserve,[14] 'you will only have to feed yourself from Villeneuve to Aosta', which at first he reckoned as taking four days,[15] but later eight.[16] One division, however, was to cross by the Little St Bernard and join the main body at Aosta.

On 4 May Moreau in Germany beat the Austrians at Stockach, so eliminating any threat to Bonaparte's communications north of the Alps. On the same day Bonaparte informed Berthier that Masséna might have to capitulate, in which case Melas, the Austrian commander in Italy, would only require eight days to transfer his army from the Riviera to Aosta; he could arrive there at a time when only part of the Army of Reserve would have crossed the Great St Bernard. It was essential, Bonaparte told Berthier, that the French advanced guard reached Aosta on 10 May and the remainder of the army on the 13th or 14th.[17] The margin of time was narrowing and narrowing; the margin allowable for the 'friction' of war – unforeseen mishaps and delays – already virtually expended.

On 10 May Bonaparte ordered Lannes, commanding the advanced guard, to

'The most melo-dramatically romantic of all Bonaparte's mountain journeys . . .'; crossing the Alps by the Great St Bernard Pass on a mule led by a peasant at the outset of the Marengo Campaign, 1800. Painting by Paul Delaroche. *Walker Art Gallery, Liverpool*

cross the Great St Bernard on the 16th; the schedule had thus already slipped by six days. Lannes was now to take enough biscuit to see him through till the 19th.

On 12 May Bonaparte himself reached Lausanne, dispatching an encouraging message two days later to Masséna, who was starving on valiantly in Genoa: 'You are in a tight spot; but what reassures me is that it is you in Genoa; it is in cases like these that one man is worth ten thousand.'[18] Bonaparte now expected the army to reach the plains of Piedmont on the 19th or 20th.[19]

Meanwhile, the Army of Reserve was heading along the northern shore of Lake Geneva, creeping antlike over the floor of the gloomy valley that extends southeastwards from the lake like a gigantic cutting, and on into the ever-narrowing defile that leads to the foot of the pass. The most melodramatically romantic of all Bonaparte's mountain journeys was under way. As he excitedly reported to his fellow Consuls on the 16th, 'We struggle against ice, snow, tempests and avalanches . . .'[20] He did not, however, cross the Great St Bernard in the middle of his troops on a rearing and apparently demented charger as in the painting by David, but several days behind the main body and on the back of a mule.

In accordance with the revised timetable, Lannes and the advanced guard crossed the pass – a track only eighteen inches wide in places – without incident on 16 May and descended as far as Aosta, with the rest of the army strung out behind.

The only obstacle ahead lay in the small fort of Bard, high on its own above the road leading down the valley of Aosta to Ivrea. Bonaparte expected it to fall on the 17th. But it did not. Its garrison of some three hundred soldiers of the Kinsky regiment refused to surrender. This presented a problem, for Lannes had no cannon with him heavier than an 8-pounder – the largest calibre that could be transported over the pass, and then only with great difficulty, the barrels finally being dismounted and laid in hollowed-out logs dragged by mules and men. And 8-pounders could make little impression on Bard's solid masonry. Since Bard's own guns commanded the only route leading through the mountains to Ivrea and the plains of Piedmont, the Army of Reserve therefore found itself helplessly corked-up at the very outset of its march.

Thanks to detailed reconnaissance reports Bonaparte at least knew of Bard's existence and indeed its strength, unlike the fort at El Arish which in similar fashion had delayed the advance of the Army of the Orient from the Sinai desert into Palestine the previous year.[21] He merely failed to take sufficient account of Bard in his planning. For the converse of his talent for visualizing strategy on a European scale lay in a carelessness over detail, a slapdash underestimation of potential difficulties. Now, just as on his first arrival before Acre, he ordered an immediate assault on Fort Bard; just as at Acre, the ill-prepared attack failed with heavy loss.

On 18 May, when the fort had so far only imposed one day's delay, Bonaparte signalled the army chief-of-staff: 'Make General Lannes understand that the destiny of Italy, and perhaps of the Republic, depends on the taking of Fort Bard . . .'[22] The language of this signal was a measure of his alarm. For he was facing nothing less than the collapse of his campaign when it had hardly begun, so fine was the margin of time in a plan whose essence lay in speed and surprise. If he were held up much longer, the Austrian commander, Melas, could profit from his paralysis by switching powerful forces from the Riviera in order to block his exit from the mountains at Ivrea. There was another consideration: for the first time in his career Bonaparte was conducting a war as head of state as well as field commander, and, moreover, a head of state only recently – and illegitimately – installed in place. It was the greatest hope of his political enemies in Paris to see him defeated or absent on a prolonged, unglamorous and indecisive struggle. Bonaparte therefore needed a quick victory and an early triumphant return to Paris politically as much as militarily.

Yet there was a question still more urgent than the likely collapse of his strategy: that of imminent and total catastrophe. In Bonaparte's own words to his chief commissary, the army was 'exposed to dying of starvation in the valley of Aosta . . .'[23]

Bonaparte had originally calculated that the troops should carry enough food to see them through till 19 May, when, according to his planned timetable, they would enter the fertile farmlands of Piedmont beyond Ivrea. But on the 19th the guns at Fort Bard were still blocking the road. Nor could supplies come up from the base at Villeneuve because the army itself encumbered the Great St Bernard Pass and its approaches. There was no hope of living off the country because the mountain valley in which the army was jammed up was, in Berthier's words, 'destitute of everything and most of all near Bard . . .'[24] On that same day, the 19th, Berthier, in writing to Bonaparte, went so far as to mention the option of retreat, 'which we must not think of, as much because of the effect on morale as of the difficulties of execution.'[25]

The army's plight at so early a stage in the campaign hardly accords with that legend of Bonaparte's military genius woven by himself and his admirers. For the benefit of the French public, however, the bulletin of the Army of Reserve on 22 May dilated instead upon the brilliant surmounting of all obstacles in crossing the Great St Bernard and thrillingly described how the First Consul had 'descended from the heights of St Bernard by sledging, traversing precipices and sliding above the torrents.'[26]

Day by day Fort Bard resisted stoutly; day by day Bonaparte increased the tempo of his frantic efforts to deliver his army from the trap in which he had placed it. Rearwards went orders to commissaries and prefects to take extraordinary measures to mobilize transport, to switch the army's main line of communication to the Little St Bernard. Forwards went instructions to Berthier to build a road round Fort Bard; to take it by night escalade; to send infantry and cavalry without guns past Bard by mule tracks and on to occupy Ivrea, commanding the exit into the plain of Piedmont. Here battle could be given to the Austrians; equally this position, in Bonaparte's words, 'would enable us to sweep the plain and spread out in order to subsist . . .'[27] On 26 May Bonaparte reached Ivrea, a week later than once so confidently expected. He now decided on even more drastic measures. Since Fort Bard still blocked the road to guns and wagons, he would push on still further with infantry and cavalry alone (except for six guns sneaked past Bard at night) and rendezvous with General Moncey's corps (from Moreau's Army of the Rhine) which he ordered to cross the St Gotthard on the 27th or 28th. The St Gotthard would then form his main line of communications, since, quite apart from Fort Bard, the valley of Aosta was infested with partisans. All in all, and in view of Moreau's success in Germany, Bonaparte might have done better to have stuck to his original intention of taking the Army of Reserve into Italy by the St Gotthard.

Fortunately for him, the Austrians did not begin to re-deploy their forces to meet him until the 29th, three days after he reached Ivrea. Up till then Melas, the Austrian commander in Italy, believed that it was only a small diversionary force that had crossed the Great St Bernard, while the Austrian government had long been convinced that the Army of Reserve was no more than a domestic drafting and training formation. So yet again Bonaparte found himself saved from the consequences of his own errors by the shortcomings of his enemy.

Now, instead of marching straight to the relief of Masséna in Genoa, Bonaparte turned away due eastwards on Milan, the capital of the Cisalpine Republic, the Austrian-occupied French satellite state, which he entered on 3 June. This decision was partly prompted by the need to rendezvous with Moncey and to replenish his supplies from fertile countryside and Austrian magazines, partly by the political need for an early prize. Fort Bard surrendered on the same day, its walls breached by 12-pounders brought over the *Little* St Bernard. Here was the final irony, for these guns had been easily drawn across on their own carriages. All the ingenious devising and constructing of gun sledges and hollowed-out logs to get mere 4- and 8-pounders over the Great St Bernard had been unnecessary. For want of adequate reconnaissance Bonaparte had taken his army over the wrong pass.[28]

Bonaparte had now completed his descent deep into the Austrian rear, although a fortnight later than he had originally planned, catching the Austrians with their forces widely dispersed, as he himself had been caught by them more than once in his first Italian campaigns. But instead of moving on swiftly to destroy these forces in detail before they could unite, and then relieving Genoa, he chose instead to spread his own army out in blocking every possible river-crossing by which the Austrians might try to break out towards home. As a result Melas was able to concentrate most of his scattered formations, and the more easily because the French garrison of Genoa, bereft of food and hope, surrendered on 4 June. By 13 June Melas was at Alessandria at the head of 35,000 men. Yet Bonaparte had optimistically calculated that Melas' numbers by that date could not exceed at the most 22,000.[29]

The retreat westwards of the advanced guard of a detached Austrian corps after an action at Casteggio wrongly convinced Bonaparte that Melas was about to abandon Alessandria and either withdraw to Genoa or try to slip past him over the Po at Valenza. For this reason he dispersed his own army still further, ordering Desaix with a division of 5,300 men southwards to cut the road to Genoa. Out of the total strength of the French field forces in Italy of nearly 50,000 men, there remained under Bonaparte's own hand on 13 June fewer than 22,000.[30] Of the other 28,000 many formations lay – unlike Desaix – quite out of reach: on the north bank of the Po, at Piacenza, at Crema, at Milan, at Turin.[31] These were dispositions unworthy of a commander whom some have considered a master of concentration at the decisive point, and less than adequate as the culmination of a great if ill-managed strategic march.

And Melas was not about to retreat; he was about to fight his way out eastwards. About nine o'clock in the morning of 14 June 1800 the Austrian columns began to advance out of a bridgehead over the River Bormida, just east of Alessandria, and deploy across a countryside as flat as Lincolnshire and not dissimilar in appearance: a patchwork of large fields, rows of pollarded willows, isolated farms standing massively amid clumps of poplar and chestnut. One of these farmsteads, the Villa di Marengo, just off the Alessandria–Tortona road, was to give its name to the coming battle. Except for such farms, for the village of Castel-Ceriolo and for a narrow stream which hindered but did not halt the Austrian advance, the ground is devoid of tactical features: a football pitch of a battlefield, that day clogging wet after a series of immense thunderstorms, the last only the night before.

Bonaparte was taken utterly by surprise at the news of the Austrian attack. Realizing now the full extent of his error in sending off Desaix, he dispatched an urgent message after him: 'Return in the name of God if you still can.'[32] Meanwhile, Bonaparte himself could only hold on and hope. But hour by hour his outnumbered, ragged, often barefoot troops[33] were slowly forced back, their flanks lapped. By late afternoon, and despite desperate French counter-attacks, the

Austrians – white uniforms now foul with mud and sweat – had advanced nearly five miles. Bonaparte's army, exhausted, almost out of ammunition, was beginning to disintegrate. He had no more reserves. Bonaparte had lost the Battle of Marengo; the *first* Battle of Marengo.

But towards five o'clock Desaix at last arrived on the battlefield with his 5,000 men. There was a brief horseback conference under fire in which Desaix seems virtually to have taken over the exercise of command from Bonaparte, as if indeed Bonaparte were suffering from a moral paralysis just as in the crisis in the Orangery at St Cloud on 19 Brumaire. For it was Desaix who, glancing at his watch, cheerfully exclaimed that though one battle had been lost, there was plenty of time to win another; it was under Desaix's orders that Marmont, the army's chief gunner, formed all the remaining cannon into a battery of eighteen pieces and blasted the nearest pursuing Austrian column with case-shot; Desaix himself who, as the Austrians staggered and stopped, launched his own 5,000 infantrymen into the attack, falling mortally wounded at their head. At this moment General Kellerman, seeing the Austrians in disarray, charged home into their flank with his four hundred remaining troopers. Struck by these surprise blows at a moment when they believed the battle already over and won, the enemy suddenly broke up and fled back to Alessandria. Bonaparte's own contribution to this second Battle of Marengo appears to have been limited to haranguing the soldiers before the attack,[34] and making sure that the army bulletin afterwards portrayed him as the man whose leadership had saved the day.[35]

Next day an armistice was concluded by which the Austrians were to retire north of the Po and east of the Mincio; and on 25 June Bonaparte set off on the return journey to Paris, forewarning his fellow Consuls that he would arrive before the *fête nationale* on 14 July, and requesting them to study well how to render the occasion suitably brilliant.

The death of General Desaix at the Battle of Marengo, 14 June 1800, while leading the counter-attack that saved Bonaparte from defeat. Wash painting by Jacques François Fontaine called Swebach. *Copyright Reserved*

Such was the famous victory of Marengo which freshly gilded Bonaparte's military renown while at the same time consolidating his authority as First Consul and dictator; a decisive one for him personally, because if Desaix had not returned in time, the resulting defeat must have put an end to his career. In terms of the war, however, it was not decisive. Only because of want of doggedness on the part of the

Austrians was Bonaparte enabled to return to Paris and enjoy his triumph. For Melas, had he wished, could have called on larger reserves of fresh troops in Italy than Bonaparte, while the French army itself was exhausted and desperately short of field artillery and ammunition.[36] Like Alvinzi after Arcola, Melas accepted too readily the outcome of a single engagement when a prolonged struggle must have been ruinous to Bonaparte. Nor in any case did the armistice following Marengo mark the end of the war. Instead there ensued a summer and an autumn of haggling with Austria over peace terms, a diplomacy of threats and doublecrosses. In November 1800 the armistice broke down, leading to fresh campaigns in Italy and Germany in which Bonaparte played no part. The battle which finally brought Austria to make peace, the truly decisive battle of the War of the Second Coalition, was won by Moreau at Hohenlinden in Austria on 3 December. The 'victory' of Marengo was therefore as much a trick of illusionism as Bonaparte's 'conquest' of Lombardy in 1796, but thanks to its distorting mirror Europe could only see, exaggerated still larger than the human reality, Bonaparte the figure of myth.

By the Treaty of Lunéville in February 1801 the bounds of French dominion in Italy were spread wider yet; the French puppet Helvetic Republic was recognized; and the whole of the Rhineland passed under the tricolour. Lunéville apparently offered an even more impressive tribute to the efficacy of force than Campoformio in 1797. Yet by challenging Austria's traditional supremacy over the German lands as well as humiliating her still further in Italy, Bonaparte ensured that this peace too could never be accepted by Austria as more than a truce after a temporary defeat, to be overturned at the first opportunity.

In October an armistice was concluded with England too, whom Bonaparte had long come to see as the French Republic's most inveterate and dangerous enemy, and he awaited the arrival of Lord Cornwallis to negotiate a final peace treaty. No innkeeper expecting English milords could have taken more trouble than Bonaparte in preparing a suitable welcome for Cornwallis. The Ministers of the Interior and of Finance were ordered to put the Calais–Paris road and its staging arrangements into perfect order; the Minister of War was instructed to have Cornwallis greeted at Calais 'in the most distinguished manner', with a gun salute, a guard of honour, and an escort en route. There followed five months of haggling in which the French government formed the notion that the English were simpletons to be duped and the English that Bonaparte and his entourage were rogues and tricksters, and moreover consumed with, in the English Foreign Secretary's words, 'inordinate ambition'.[37] The treaty with England that was finally signed at Amiens on 25 March 1802 therefore constituted no more of a true and lasting settlement than Lunéville. So the process which had begun under the Revolution still rolled on inexorably under Bonaparte: ever-more ambitious gambles, each of which was designed to provide a short-cut solution to the problems created by its predecessor, but which instead only rendered a yet further gamble inevitable. Bonaparte resembled a juggler balancing an immense stack of objects on his nose who, every time they began to topple, had to take a step forward in order to restore the equilibrium. The peace treaties of Amiens and Lunéville constituted no more than one such illusory moment of equilibrium before the next forward move.

VI

THERE MUST NOT BE ANY OPPOSITION

FOR THE FIRST TIME in ten years the guns of Europe had stopped firing. Bonaparte had won peace for France, peace with glory; and for himself success apparently without a shadow. He was not yet thirty-three. The lean, almost haggard, features of the revolutionary general of 1796 had fleshed out now into a Byronically sensuous face; the shoulder-length straggly locks had given place to hair trimmed close in Roman style. His figure remained slim enough, flattered by his square-cut general's uniform or his First Consul's dress of red velvet and gold. Distinguished English visitors, flocking after the peace to see the new France for themselves, were curious to note the contrast between the martial Bonaparte taking a ceremonial parade, with his young Caesar's head and hard, piercing stare, and the gracious Bonaparte of the *salon*; the grey eyes now thoughtful, sad, faraway; the manner gentle, courteous. But then he had always been a natural actor able to adopt the personality best suited to the play and the audience; likewise a shrewd reader of men's minds and hearts adept at discerning what that particular personality should be.

This psychological insight did not move him to look upon humanity with compassion and charity, but rather with contempt. The only exceptions, from the evidence of his letters, lay in the members of his own family, in Josephine and in a handful of his companions-in-arms, of whom he had lost Desaix at Marengo. When Desaix joined the Army of Reserve, Bonaparte wrote to him vowing a friendship 'which my heart, today so much older and knowing men more profoundly, has for no one else.'[1] And in briefly reporting the success at Marengo to his fellow Consuls the day after the battle, he explained, 'I cannot tell you more about it; I am in the deepest anguish from the death of the man whom I loved and esteemed more than anyone.'[2] Otherwise, Corsican and French life in an era of revolution hardly afforded an encouraging spectacle of human nature, least of all to a man so intelligent, intolerant and egotistical. As a consequence, the calculating realist in Bonaparte came to see his fellow men as mere factors to be assessed and then manipulated accordingly – in order to further the ambition of Bonaparte the romantic. And thirteen years of political and military careerism had turned him into an outstandingly able manipulator of men, as his various instructions to his diplomats on how best to deal with foreign statesmen serve to demonstrate. When the Marengo campaign was in preparation and Austria had reconquered Italy and Germany, for instance, he told Talleyrand to begin a letter to the Austrian Chancellor 'by deploring the fatal process which prevents governments from being moderate in their aims when things are going well for them; demonstrate compassion a bit with regard to the miseries which will result from this campaign, without there being any real purpose on either side. If anyone could profit from it, it would be the English government alone . . .'[3]

But it was in respect of his soldiers that Bonaparte had developed his most elaborate techniques of manipulation. The army, after all, was his essential power-base, the instrument by which he had finally reached the top as a politician; the equivalent of a party organization to political leaders of a later era. On becoming a general-in-chief in 1796 he had recognized that he commanded a novel kind of military force, composed of citizen soldiers, largely young, instead of long-service regulars, often middle-aged; Frenchmen too, quick-witted, emotional, and inspired by a genuine patriotism and ideological fervour. So instead of trying to enforce through harsh punishment the blind obedience of eighteenth-century armies, he sought to awaken loyalty and enthusiasm, to make every soldier feel that he was an important part of a common venture. The techniques were varied. Resounding orders of the day generated a sense of excitement, of a march with history. Stirring personal addresses to each regiment convinced it that it enjoyed Bonaparte's special trust and affection, while the friendly chats with selected individuals gave the humble soldier the sense that the general-in-chief was no remote figure of authority, but really just one of them. Bonaparte was here a pioneer of that calculated chumminess with the rank and file which in the twentieth century became so notable a feature of democratic politics as well as of generalship. By publically praising units for distinguished conduct and publicly disgracing those which had behaved badly, he fostered a spirit of emulation; an awareness that families and villages were watching their men's exploits with pride. By personally distributing colours and battle honours he bonded the army still tighter to himself and his fortunes. All this was imaginatively conceived, brilliantly done and outstandingly successful.

Towards his senior commanders he had so far displayed an easy *cameraderie*, while never letting anyone forget for a moment that he was the chief. During his first Italian campaigns Bonaparte, according to one subordinate, 'loved to joke, and his sallies were without a hint of sarcasm; they were gay and in good taste; he would often join in our games . . .'[4] He was always to manifest a special attachment to the comrades of his earliest successes at Toulon and in Italy – Berthier, his chief-of-staff, Massèna, Marmont, Murat – perhaps because he felt he could trust them; perhaps as living mementos, precious to his ego, of the time when his greatness was in the process of being born. When a commander suffered a reverse through no fault of his own, Bonaparte would offer consolation and encouragement, telling one such unlucky subordinate in 1796, for example, that 'The fortune of war, my dear general, changes from day to day; we will restore tomorrow or later what you have lost today . . . Nothing is lost so long as courage remains.'[5] But the incapable, disobedient or negligent evoked his full savagery. One general was summarily dismissed from his post with the brutal injunction never to appear before him again.

Bonaparte had originally achieved ascendancy over his subordinates by virtue of his own force of personality: daunting, and indeed on occasion terrifying. Now that ascendancy was enormously reinforced by the prestige and authority which attaches to high office even when the incumbent is a hundred times less able than

'Under the close impact of this sheer force of personal hatred, Bonaparte . . . lost his nerve completely': Bonaparte attacked in the Council of Five Hundred by hostile members during the *coup d'état* of 18 Brumaire. A flattering version of the scene painted by François Bouchot. *Louvre. Photo: Musées Nationaux*

Bonaparte. Moreover, his ascendancy was carried still higher by another factor – the mystique of fame and success, the aura of his personal legend. He had become the first hero of the romantic movement, a Byron in field boots; the man in whose honour Beethoven was to compose the Eroica Symphony. He was perhaps the earliest example of that phenomenon of the emerging mass society, the superstar.

But despite all the outward authority and glamour, Bonaparte still remained the social and national misfit of Brienne and the *Ecole Militaire*. As First Consul he was as touchy about his Corsican origin as once he had been defiantly proud of it. He complained to his younger brothers that Joseph ought to tell his mother:

> . . . not to keep on calling me *Napolione*. In the first place it is an Italian name. Let Mama call me, like everyone else, Bonaparte, not *Buonaparte* above all, that would be even worse than *Napolione*. Let her say the first consul or just the consul. Yes, I like that better. But *Napolione*, always *Napolione*, that makes me lose patience![6]

He felt ill at ease living in the old royal palace of the Tuileries, recounts Josephine in her memoirs, because 'he could not help feeling shocked, in a way overawed, on going into the cabinet of the late King . . .'[7] He preferred living at Malmaison, Josephine's country house just west of Paris beside the Seine, small as mansions go, comfortable in almost English fashion, and surrounded by the 'English' informal garden that Josephine took such joy in planting. Here was nothing to remind him that he did not really belong; no heavy presence of real kings; only the gay, even gimcrack, rooms of the fashionable decorator where an *arriviste* might feel at home.

The social assurance which the First Consul displayed in interviewing distinguished personages and moving through grand receptions was deceptive too. In order to achieve such apparent ease the relationships between him and others had to be clearly defined and mutually understood; a play in which all would act predictably according to their allotted roles – Bonaparte's that of the superior, theirs that of lesser beings to be charmed, familiarly teased or otherwise patronized. When – rarely – he found himself in the free society of equals, and most especially when under criticism or contradiction, he became edgy, short-tempered, rude, even temporarily at a loss. There was, for example, the *fracas* in the *Institut d'Égypte* between himself and Desgenettes, the chief physician of the army. There was, above all, the confrontation between himself and the opposition deputies in the Orangery at St Cloud during the *coup d'état* of 18 Brumaire, in which, as on later occasions when under threat from a hostile crowd, he gave way to panic. On meeting Madame de Staël in 1797, one of the most formidable minds in France, he refused to be drawn into a serious argument with her but instead, as she reproached him, treated her like a doll. When she asked what kind of woman he valued most, he answered: 'The one who has had the most children.'[8] Even Josephine, as prettily doll-like a wife as a man could hope to find, drew his ire because of her want of total docility. As she herself put it, '. . . in his presence, no one had the right to hazard the slightest observation.'[9]

Domination was then more than a lifelong urge with Bonaparte; it was, like action, an essential therapy. Whereas the philosopher Descartes had sought to prove his individual existence by arguing 'I think; therefore I am', Bonaparte in his own quest for identity might rather have said: 'I order everybody about; therefore I am.'

'The lean, almost haggard features of the revolutionary general of 1796 had fleshed out now into a Byronically sensuous face': Bonaparte as First Consul. Painting by Jean-Auguste-Dominique Ingres. *Musée de Liège. Photo: Bulloz*

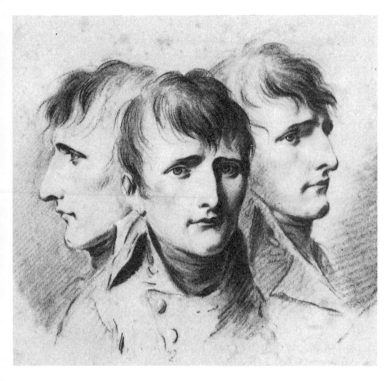

ON BECOMING FIRST CONSUL, Bonaparte wasted no time before exploiting the unprecedented scope for domineering offered by the post. As an idealistic lieutenant, he had believed in 'entire and absolute liberty of thought [and] liberty of speech and writings in so far as it does not injure the social order'.[10] The individual's natural right, he asserted, ought to be limited only by a precise law prohibiting actions directly contrary to society. 'If it were otherwise, the social order would be a calamity, an intolerable slavery.'[11] Unfortunately but hardly surprising his blueprint for French society as First Consul did not fulfil this admirable idealism. Instead it implemented that other, and opposite, strain of thought in his youthful writings, wherein Bonaparte the mathematician and artillery officer well trained in practical physics and engineering had conceived of society essentially as a machine, and Bonaparte the egotist had argued that this machine must be directed by a single will, the State. He began to construct the machine in the winter of 1799–1800, even before the Marengo campaign, and it was completed and clanking away by the end of 1803.

At its centre in Paris stood Bonaparte, himself the boiler providing the steam as well as the engineer in charge. The levers by which he exercised control took the form of a State Secretariat which watched over the doings of every ministry, the ministers themselves, and a Council of State comprising twenty-nine distinguished experts appointed and dismissed at Bonaparte's will. Since the Council of State was purely an advisory study group and since Bonaparte dealt with his ministers individually instead of collectively in a Cabinet, little could challenge his sole grasp on the levers. The primary drive to the machine was transmitted from Bonaparte

(left) '. . . his young Caesar's head . . .': a triple portrait of Bonaparte by Louis-Léopold Boilly. *Count Charles de Salis. Photo: Christie, Manson & Woods Ltd*

(right) '. . . a kind of crowned imprisonment . . .': Josephine as Empress. A sketch by Pierre-Paul Prud'hon. *Collection Malmaison. Photo: Studio Laverton*

through an elaborate bureaucracy in Paris: the ministries of War, Marine, Foreign Affairs, Finance, the Interior and the Police. This bureaucracy in turn drove all the wheels of local administration by means of the prefects, who were appointed by the central government to run the territorial departments into which France had been divided since the Revolution. Their authority was even further enhanced by a 'reform' of 17 February 1800 which abolished what yet remained of elective local government after the earlier efforts of the Committee of Public Safety and the Directory to whittle it away. The prefects were now to appoint all officials down to the mayors of communes, even including members of local councils. By this means, Bonaparte's direction and impulsion reached the tiniest cogs in his social machine.

Not even the prefects themselves were allowed any true responsibility or freedom of decision; even they were no more than larger cogwheels. Bonaparte instructed his Minister of the Interior on 15 February 1801:

> The First Consul is informed, Citizen Minister, that certain prefects believe themselves authorized to interpret the acts of the Government . . . the Consuls desire that prefects be advised by you in writing that it is their duty to conform literally to orders, unless, after making representations to the ministers, they find themselves authorized [otherwise] by precise instructions.[12]

In the same period Bonaparte also engineered new machinery of justice in which judges and presidents of courts too became cogs obeying the levers of appointment and promotion pulled by the First Consul. In 1802 the jury system, with its mechanically inefficient tendency to slow down the judicial apparatus by acquitting prisoners Bonaparte wished to see condemned, was suppressed in a large part of the country.

Bonaparte did not, however, construct his huge bureaucratic engine entirely from scratch, for centralized administration directed from Paris enjoyed a long tradition in France, running back through the Committee of Public Safety to the absolute monarchy of Louis XIV and beyond. But whereas the power of Louis XIV had been limited by the counterpoises offered by ancient custom, by traditions of provincial independence, and by the 'privileges' of church, noblesse and other corporate bodies, no such counterpoises restrained Bonaparte's will, just as nothing previously had equalled the logical completeness of his new administrative system. And so well designed for its purpose was this system that it outlasted Bonaparte himself, outlasted all France's nineteenth-century changes of regime, and survives, even though much modified, to the present day. There are those who consequently admire it as proof of Bonaparte's constructive genius and of his service to France. But in fact it completed the betrayal of the democratic promise of the Revolution; it renewed the destruction of the political, social and cultural independence of the French provinces, so that more than ever France came to live only through the medium of Paris; an imbalance which modern French governments seek with difficulty to put right.

The rule book for Bonaparte's new society was provided by the *Code Civil*, promulgated in 1804 and renamed the *Code Napoléon* in 1807, which reduced the immense jumble of laws inherited from the past into a clear, logically organized code whose 2,281 articles were comprised in a single volume. Exported with

Bonaparte's armies, the *Code Civil* came to form the basis of most modern European systems of civil law, and has been copied all over the world because of its clarity and comprehensiveness. For Bonaparte's admirers the *Code Civil* thus offers further proof of his superhuman breadth of talent, as if he himself had drafted its underlying principles or even as if he had sat down and written all 2,281 articles with his own hand. In fact much preliminary work had already been carried out under the Revolution and the *ancien régime*. Bonaparte's crucial – and characteristic –contribution lay in seeing that the job was at last brought to completion in short order: in August 1800 he appointed a committee of four legal experts and gave them five months to produce a draft.

As might be expected, their draft, with its emphasis on the rights of property and its neglect of the interests of those who owned nothing, closely accorded with his own sentiments. But he himself only took part personally in the discussions on the articles relating to the law of the family. These articles in their final form strongly reflected his Corsican sense of clan solidarity and the prerogatives due to the head of the family, as well as his low opinion of women, whether frivolous like Josephine or formidable like Madame de Staël. For the *Code Civil* invested fathers of families with the authority of miniature First Consuls over their wives and children and family property, while women themselves were not allowed to buy, sell or give away property without their husbands' permission.

Although the *Code* enshrined the revolutionary ideal of equality before the law, at the same time it endangered – like the rest of Bonaparte's reforms – the other revolutionary ideal of liberty by strengthening the hand of State intervention in the private affairs of the citizen. For this reason the *Code* was bitterly fought by the intellectual elite in the Tribunat who had so ingenuously believed earlier that in Bonaparte lay the best hope of preserving republican principles. Such opposition moved Bonaparte to those nostril-flaring rages he had first displayed when thwarted as a child. How could his social machine work smoothly if some of the cogs acted like human beings with opinions of their own? As Bonaparte himself said apropos the draft *Code Civil*, 'There must not be any opposition. What is government? Nothing, if it does not have public opinion on its side. How can it hope to counterbalance the influence of a tribune if it is always under attack?'[13]

So from the beginning of the Consulate Bonaparte busied himself with extinguishing what yet remained of the freedom of expression won during the Revolution and with crushing what yet remained of organized opposition, whether royalist, Jacobin or merely intellectual. On 17 January 1800 he shut down sixty out of seventy-three existing newspapers; by the end of 1800 only nine remained, and those under strict censorship. The theatre was censored from April 1800. With his excessive sensitivity to personal criticism and ridicule, Bonaparte took a direct interest in this censorship, ordering his librarian in July 1801 to prepare for him a weekly summary of contents of all publications whether books, journals, or even placards and announcements, together with a summary of proceedings in all societies and educational institutions.[14] English journals being particularly disrespectful to him, he ordered his Minister of Police in August 1802 to forbid their entry into France; 'above all do not allow them to circulate in public places, nor in reading rooms . . .'[15] If, however, the French minister in London could recommend an English journal more moderate than the rest, then thirty copies might be imported for distribution to reading rooms in their place.

The intellectuals, or as he jeeringly called them because of their undoubted lack of realism, 'the ideologists' or 'metaphysicians', remained his special demons. They were so inconveniently prone to discuss such fundamental questions as liberty, conscience and human values. Who better appreciated the political danger in free intellectual debate than the author of *Le Discours de Lyon*, the man who as a young officer in 1789–93 had watched ideas bring down an ancient monarchy? In the first few months of 1802 he struck at these 'vermin I have on my clothes'[16] by having leading intellectuals purged from the Tribunat, whereupon Madame de Staël prudently left France for Switzerland. In January 1803 Bonaparte even abolished the class of Moral and Political Sciences in the *Institut de France*, and dispersed its members among the remaining four classes, which dealt more safely with factual research. In July 1803 he ordered that bookshops be prohibited from placing new works on sale until seven days after a copy had been submitted to the censor 'so that, as soon as there is an undesirable work, it can be stopped.'[17]

The systematic opening of private correspondence, the ubiquitous police spy, and imprisonment without trial completed Bonaparte's practical interpretation of the 'sacred right' of liberty guaranteed by the Constitution.

With regard to the royalist rebels still in arms in western France Bonaparte pursued in literal truth a Corsican vendetta, shooting one of their leaders, the Comte de Frotté, with six companions in February 1800 despite a safe conduct. But then Frotté in a manifesto had gone so far as personally to insult and ridicule Bonaparte.

In December 1800 it was the turn of Bonaparte's Jacobin opponents. On 24 December he narrowly escaped being blown up in his coach by a mine in the Rue Saint-Niçaise on his way to the Opéra to hear Haydn's *Creation*. Bonaparte and his colleagues attributed the mine to the Jacobins although in point of fact the royalists had planted it. This attempt on his life transported Bonaparte into a tantrum violent even by his own standards. He yelled imprecations against his would-be assassins, and informed the Council of State that 'Blood must run',[18] which it did. Nine Jacobin prisoners were shot or guillotined in January 1801, followed by the royalist bombers themselves in April. One hundred and thirty leading Jacobins were deported to tropical penal settlements, where more than half died in exile. For good measure, a hundred royalists were arrested also and either sent to prison or interned without trial.[19] All this fully realized the promise of Bonaparte's thwarted political career in Corsica a decade earlier.

Yet while Bonaparte the egotist was screwing his heel on those who actively opposed him, Bonaparte the man of calculation recognized that if the mass of the nation were cheerfully to accept their role of cogs in his social machine, their minds needed to be suitably manipulated into acquiescence. A continuous public-relations campaign without rival in its own day sought to sell the merits of glory to the French people, and in particular to convince them that *his* glory was *their* glory. In February 1804, for example, Bonaparte instructed that monuments be erected at

every scene in his march to fame, from the first actions in Italy in 1796 to Marengo; and at the same time ordered three portraits of himself for presentation to the city of Lyon, the city of Rouen, and the appeal court in Paris – the latter picture naturally to be posed with the *Code Civil*.[20] Nevertheless he perceived that the key to the mind of the French nation lay in the Church, for despite all the anti-religious persecution under the atheistic governments of the Revolution, France as a whole remained devoutly Catholic; and, as Bonaparte once wrote, it was religion that directed the human conscience.[21] This was now more true than ever because, under the impulse of the romantic movement, a religious revival had begun to progress among the middle and upper classes. Belief in reason and nostalgia for classical Greece were going out of fashion; faith and the Middle Ages were coming in. Bonaparte reckoned moreover that as things stood at present, the alienated Church lay open to the machinations of *émigré* bishops inspired by England, so serving as a rallying-place for royalist revolt. If the Church could be reconciled with the regime, this would not only dry up the sea in which royalist rebels swam, but would also turn the priesthood into a corps of ready-made political commissars in every village diligently enjoining loyalty and obedience to the First Consul.

When in June 1800 Bonaparte began to woo the Pope, followed in November by formal negotiations for a Concordat (or deal) between the Roman Catholic Church

'On 24 December 1800 he narrowly escaped being blown up in his coach by a mine in the Rue Saint-Niçaise on his way to the Opéra . . .': a lurid contemporary version of the event. Enraged, Bonaparte crushed Jacobins and royalists alike. *Bulloz*

and the French Republic, it therefore did not mark a miraculous conversion from his long-held religious disbelief, but a stroke of policy exactly similar to his attempt to win the support of religious leaders in Egypt in 1798 by professing love for the Muslim faith. Christ or Mahomet, the Bible or the Koran, it was all the same to the political engineer. As he was to say some years later to the Council of State, 'In religion I do not see the mystery of the Incarnation, but the mystery of social order . . .[22] But on the other hand he had always believed that the existence of the Church was politically dangerous because, in his own words in 1786, it 'destroys the unity of the State',[23] being an independent body which 'not only shares the heart of the citizen, but yet can often contradict the views of the government.'[24] He therefore took extreme care to render such independence impossible by the terms of the deal finally signed with Pope Pius VII in July 1801. For the crux of the Concordat lay in the provision by which the First Consul was to choose and nominate the bench of bishops, who then would be canonically instituted in their sees by the Pope. The prelates and priesthood alike would be paid by the State. Bonaparte flattered himself that by these means he had turned the Church into just another of his bureaucratic engines in which the big wheels, the bishops, obeying the operator's hand on the levers, transmitted appropriate motion to the little wheels in every parish. In return Roman Catholicism was officially recognized as the religion of the majority of the French people, including the Consuls, and permission was granted for the re-establishment of cathedral chapters and religious houses (which Bonaparte had been so keen on keeping closed in Ajaccio in 1792).

Since this Concordat was bound to be bitterly fought by republicans as a yet further betrayal of the Revolution, Bonaparte shrewdly delayed passing it into law until after the Treaty of Amiens in March 1802, when the nation's gratitude at the coming of peace made all things possible for him. But the Concordat was only one of a whole series of drastic changes rammed through by Bonaparte in the months following the Peace Treaty, and which consummated his own transformation from the chief executive of a republic, albeit with virtually unlimited powers, into the personal ruler of France.

DURING THE FIRST YEAR of Bonaparte's Consulate there had been those – Josephine for one – who had hoped that he would play the role of General Monck in England in 1660 and restore the old monarchy. In September 1800, however, he informed Louis XVI's brother Louis XVIII, the Bourbon king in exile, that, 'You should not hope to return to France; you would have to walk over 100,000 corpses. Sacrifice your own interest for the quiet and welfare of France . . . History will be grateful to you . . .'[25] For Cromwell rather than Monck offered the more accurate precedent for Bonaparte's actions. In autumn 1801 he emasculated republicanism in the army by selective dismissals and postings, and by dispatching 25,000 men of Moreau's former Army of the Rhine on an expedition to recapture Saint Domingo from revolted Negro slaves, where most of them died of yellow fever. In April 1802 he reorganized the Tribunat by consular decree in order to prevent it from debating his policies; deprived the Council of State of any share in the drafting of laws, so that its sole function became the formal approval of measures drawn up by specialist committees packed with Bonaparte's creatures. On 8 April the Concordat and the so-called 'Organic Articles', by which Bonaparte typically stretched the Concordat's provisions in his favour, were passed into law; on 26 April he granted an amnesty to *émigrés* providing they returned to France before 23 September and swore allegiance to the Constitution. During the spring and summer he carried out the final stages of his *coup d'état* or, perhaps better, his boardroom take-over. By technically unconstitutional manoeuvres a plebiscite was arranged asking the electors to vote on proposals to make Bonaparte consul for life and give him the right to choose his successor. The prefects went to work (producing favourable election results was perhaps their most vital function); the voters, dazzled by the Treaty of Amiens and with no practical alternative in sight, duly voted in favour. The Senate, outmanoeuvred, formally proclaimed Bonaparte Consul for Life on 2 August. On the following day, Bonaparte made an altogether fitting speech of thanks to the Senators: '. . . the life of a citizen belongs to his motherland. The French people wish that mine should be entirely consecrated to it. I obey its will . . .'[26] On 3 August the Senate gave approval to a new constitution, submitted by Bonaparte, which formally invested him not only with unlimited executive powers, but also the authority to make law. The Tribunat was reduced to fifty members constitutionally obliged to remain silent; the Legislative Body was no longer to enjoy the rights to meet regularly or elect its own president.[27]

So the Corsican boy who had vowed revenge on the French for subjugating his native land had subjugated the French in turn, allegedly out of dedication to their welfare; an outcome not lacking in irony.

All the power Bonaparte could want he now possessed. But power itself was not enough for a social misfit on the climb. In March 1803 he ordered that new coins should be struck bearing his effigy and the old monarchical motto, 'God defend France'. Bonaparte's birthday, 15 August, became a new religious holiday, the Feast of St Napoleon. Representatives of France's ancient families began to ornament the regime, and their daughters married into Bonaparte's circle of generals; appropriately symbolic alliances between blue blood and brute force. Bonaparte, overcoming his initial *arriviste*'s uneasiness at living in the royal palace of the Tuileries, began to imitate the manner of a monarch; Josephine now enjoyed the attendance of ladies-in-waiting recruited from the high nobility; a court began to take shape.

Yet these relatively modest pretensions could not satisfy the longings of Bonaparte the romantic, who in his young imagination had marched with Alexander the Great, and who as First Consul was thrilling to the poems, newly published in France, of Ossian, a supposed Celtic bard whose extravagant flights of language recounted the wild adventures of heroes in some early-medieval never-never land.[28] Nor could this half-hearted assumption of the trappings of kingship satisfy Bonaparte the egotist, who measured himself against the greatest figures of history; who would if possible have ruled from a throne set in the sky. There could be only one answer to these combined yearnings of the romantic and the egotist: that he should be Caesar, be Charlemagne, and yet more glorious than either.

How could this imitation monarchy be foisted on a country still a republic in

(right) '. . . as prettily doll-like a wife as a man could hope to find . . .': Josephine in her country house, Malmaison, just west of Paris. Tapestry after the painting by François-Pascal Gérard. *Collection Malmaison. Photo: Studio Laverton*

(overleaf) 'Joseph, if only our father could see us!': Bonaparte crowns himself Emperor of the French in the Cathedral of Notre-Dame on 2 December 1804. Painting by Jacques-Louis David, 1805–7. *Louvre. Photo: Musées Nationaux*

form and which only ten years earlier had conclusively put an end to its centuries-old legitimate monarchy by cutting off the head of its incumbent? Chance again came to Bonaparte's rescue, in the form of the discovery of two plots against him in January 1804; the first one royalist, led by the old Chouan leader, Georges Cadoudal, and the second implicating the staunchly republican soldiers Pichegru and Moreau. Cadoudal and his associates were later shot; Pichegru was conveniently – too conveniently? – found hanged in his cell; Moreau, thanks to the immunity conferred by his victory of Hohenlinden, was to go into exile. But Bonaparte's first reaction to the plot was to wreak a sensational vengeance on the royalists, who he now believed offered a greater menace to his ambitions than the republicans. Reverting to type as Jacobin mob politican, he dispatched an armed party to kidnap the young royal Duc d'Enghien from the neutral territory of Baden. It is possible that he sensed a personal rival in this able Bourbon prince, for his Arch-Treasurer, Lebrun, later remembered that when he, Lebrun, happened to describe Enghien's greatness of mind and character to Bonaparte, and said how much his qualities would appeal to soldiers, 'suddenly one could see in his frozen glance, the tightening of his lips, that this praise of the unfortunate Enghien had made him think deeply . . .'[29] It was soon after this, according to Lebrun, that Bonaparte dispatched the kidnap party. At five o'clock in the evening of 20 March, Enghien was brought back a prisoner to the medieval fortress of Vincennes just east of Paris; at two o'clock the next morning he was shot in the castle ditch beside his already dug grave, after a farce of a trial by a military court on a charge of being an *émigré* in English pay, the entire operation being shrouded in the utmost secrecy.

Under colour of rendering vain the efforts of future assassins by establishing a hereditary succession, Bonaparte now carried out a further *coup d'état*. On 18 May 1804, the same day that the charges against Moreau and Cadoudal were published, the Senate, by a neat formula which ought to have satisfied republicans and monarchists alike, confided 'the Government of the Republic' to a hereditary emperor, Napoleon Bonaparte. No hero's speech in a play could have exceeded the simple nobility of Bonaparte's reply to the Senate:

> Everything that can contribute to the good of the country is essentially bound up with my happiness.
>
> I accept the title which you have thought conducive to the glory of the nation . . .[30]

On this same day too appeared the first orders imperially signed 'Napoleon' – on such weighty topics as having coronets made for the new Arch-Chancellor and Arch-Treasurer of the Empire (lately the Second and Third Consuls), and appointing appropriate styles of address for the various new grades of dignitary.[31] On 19 May fourteen distinguished soldiers found themselves appointed Marshals of the Empire, henceforward to be addressed by Bonaparte in the ceremonial kinship of royalty and nobility as '*mon Cousin*'.

More splendours followed. Brother Joseph became a prince ('His Imperial Highness') and Grand Elector; brother Louis (likewise a prince) High Constable. The new imperial court soon boasted a Grand Almoner, a Grand Master of the Palace, a Master of the Horse, a Master of the Hunt, a Grand Master of Ceremonies and a Great Chamberlain, each with his suite of gorgeously caparisoned flunkeys.

(above) '. . . the English informal garden that Josephine took such joy in planting': The Temple of Love and the island of rhododendrons at Malmaison. One of a series of eight watercolours painted for her by Auguste Garneray.

(below) View of the wooden bridge over the English river at Malmaison. Watercolour in the same series.
*Collection Malmaison
Photos: Studio Laverton*

'. . . a sensational
vengeance on the royalists
. . .': the shooting
of the kidnapped Duc
d'Enghien on 21 March
1804 at Vincennes after a
'trial' by a military court.
A contemporary royalist
engraving. *Bibliothèque
Nationale, Paris*

Beneath all this fancy dress worthy of scenes from a historical novel by Sir Walter Scott, former Jacobins and regicides exchanged bows with returned *émigré* aristocrats and successful profiteers.

Now there was the Coronation to arrange. Bonaparte bent his energies and executive talents to making 'the ceremony of my coronation magnificent and imposing.'[32] Indeed no newly-rich father organizing a society wedding for his daughter could have taken greater pains to see that everything should be just so, or even more so. 'In splendour,' he promised Josephine, 'it shall surpass that of any of the Kings of France.'[33] A long letter to the Grand Master of Ceremonies (the Comte de Ségur, no less!) assessed the comparative advantages of Notre-Dame and the Invalides as the venue for the event. What with the priests and the choir and the military contingents and the distinguished guests, Bonaparte judged that a hall holding 15,000–20,000 people would be necessary. 'It is equally essential that the throne where the Emperor and Empress will be seated surrounded by their households should be set up in a place roomy enough for convenience.'[34] Notre-Dame it had to be therefore. Then there was the procession to organize and schedule. 'If it is indispensable to knock down several houses so that the procession can arrive more easily at Notre-Dame, it would be expedient to draw up appropriate plans for this quickly.'[35]

On the morning of 2 December 1804 Bonaparte and Josephine set out for Notre-Dame, but in the best traditions of a Bonapartian march, two hours late.

Inside the Cathedral, cold as an ice house, the Pope (for who else would do as anointer of the new monarch?) waited with godly patience; the congregation, who were costumed as if by a theatrical designer plundering detail from every epoch for the grand scene of some romantic historical opera, shivered and covertly ate sausage. The guns thundered outside, and two symphony orchestras struck up martial melodies. Bonaparte and Josephine alighted. In front of them the Gothic façade of the Cathedral had been transformed into a triumphal arch bearing the imperial coat of arms and embellished with pyramids. They passed into the Cathedral, Bonaparte attired in layers of velvet, silk, lace and embroidery; the ensemble vaguely late-Roman, Byzantine, Carolingian, but undoubtedly colourful and expensive. The service proceeded. Bonaparte, with his understanding of the importance of symbol, grasped the crown from the Pope's hands and crowned himself. He then crowned Josephine before being enthroned and invested with the ritual emblems of the early-medieval French monarchy: orb and sceptre, and sword. In the midst of these solemnities, the new Charlemagne leaned towards his brother Joseph, standing at his side, and said in a low voice so that none other might hear: 'Joseph, if only our father could see us!'[36]

So the french people had become the supporting cast in Bonaparte's personal drama; the European nations the extras; and Europe itself the stage. What had he written in *Le Discours de Lyon*?

> . . . ambition, which overturns states . . . which fattens on blood and crime, ambition which inspired Charles v, Philip ii, Louis xiv, is, like all unbridled passions, a violent and irrational delirium which only ceases with life; just as a fire, fanned by a relentless blast, only comes to an end when there is nothing left to burn.[37]

The coach, since altered, in which Bonaparte and Josephine rode to Notre-Dame for their Coronation as Emperor and Empress on 2 December 1804. *Musée de Versailles. Photo: Bulloz*

VII

A DITCH WHICH WILL BE LEAPED

AFTER HOLY UNCTION in Notre-Dame there followed a ceremony of communion with his soldiers whose bayonets had opened his road to the throne: on 5 December Bonaparte presented the army with new colours designed by himself on the model of the Roman Legion's eagle standard. This celebration of military pomp and might took place on the Champ-de-Mars, where the long windows of the *Ecole Militaire* reflected back to Bonaparte the memory of his year as a King's Cadet. The bands clanged out; the regiments marched and countermarched in gaudy new uniforms still unsullied by the field; the squadrons caracoled; and Bonaparte made a speech:

> Soldiers, here are your colours; these eagles will always serve you as rallying points; they will be wherever your Emperor judges it necessary for the defence of his throne and his people.
> You will swear to sacrifice your life to defend them, and to sustain them constantly by your courage on the road to victory. Do you swear?[1]

It was a warlike speech, but then Bonaparte was at war again, and had been since May 1803; England once more his enemy. It was never his intention tamely to settle down to a humdrum life as just another European head of state. Such a course, although so greatly to the benefit of France herself, was ruled out by his adventurer's temperament and the nature of his dictatorship alike. As he confessed to a Councillor of State, 'A First Consul cannot be likened to these kings-by-the-grace-of-God, who look upon their states as a heritage . . . His actions must be dramatic, and for this, war is indispensable.'[2] Nevertheless, he had not expected this indispensable war to start before the autumn of 1804, when the completion of twenty-three ships of the line would have enabled him to challenge England's command of the sea. That the war in fact broke out in May 1803, when he was by no means ready, resulted from his own calamitous mishandling of the English.

For rather than lull them after the Peace of Amiens by behaving like a good neighbour bent on a quiet existence, he proceeded to breach the treaty in spirit and letter. He imposed high tariffs on English goods, so striking the influential trade lobby a grievous blow in the counting house. He failed to remove his troops from Holland, thereby violating that cardinal English interest, the independence of the Low Countries. In September 1802 he took advantage of an uprising in Switzerland to send his occupation forces back there, and later degraded that once fiercely independent country into a French satellite. Between August and September 1802 he annexed Elba, Piedmont, and Parma; crude acts of aggrandizement which in English opinion outweighed his dutiful evacuation of Naples and the Papal States under the Peace Treaty. And when even the feebly appeasing Addington Cabinet was moved to protest, Bonaparte curtly informed it that the affairs of Switzerland, Italy and Holland were nothing to do with it.[3]

The English were even more disturbed by the evident rebirth of Bonaparte's ambitions to destroy their empire in the East and found one of his own on the ruins. In August 1802 he dispatched a Colonel Sebastiani on a mission of reconnaissance and goodwill to Tripoli, Egypt and Syria.[4] On 30 January 1803, the very day the English completed their evacuation of Egypt under the Peace of Amiens, the official *Moniteur* published a report by Sebastiani averring that 'six thousand men would suffice to reconquer Egypt.'[5] And on 6 March Admiral Decaen sailed for the French colony of Pondicherry in India with military cadres for training the armies of England's native enemies in the sub-continent.

The English themselves had hoped that the Peace of Amiens would usher in a period of true tranquillity and profitable trade. Doubly disappointed, they gradually came to share the view of Bonaparte so well expressed in December 1802 by Sheridan, a leading Whig (the party which once had perceived much good in the French Revolution):

> I see in the physical situation and composition of the power of Bonaparte, a physical necessity for him to go on in this barter with his subjects and to promise to make them masters of the world if they will consent to be his slaves.[6]

Bonaparte began to meet an unaccountable stubbornness in English diplomacy. The Addington Cabinet refused to evacuate Malta, the island commanding the sea route from France to Egypt and the Levant, until Bonaparte restored the *status quo* in Europe. This breach of the Peace of Amiens provoked Bonaparte, with his special regard for treaties, to a lather of righteous indignation. On 13 March 1803, after weeks of vain discussion, he lost his temper at an official *levée*, loudly upbraiding the English ambassador, Lord Whitworth, and shaking his cane at him. Whitworth, unaccustomed to such courtly manners, privately wondered whether he should draw his sword if the French dictator actually struck him. 'So you are determined to go to war!' expostulated Bonaparte in reference to Parliament's recent vote of an extra 10,000 men for the Navy. He demanded an explanation for England's rearmament. He informed the gathering that England did not keep her word. In fact his own rearmament had begun in January. 'If you wish to rearm,' he bellowed at Whitworth, 'I will rearm too; if you wish to fight, I will fight also! You may perhaps kill France, but you will never intimidate her!'[7] When Whitworth replied that England only wished to live in amity with France, Bonaparte retorted: 'Then you must respect treaties! Bad luck to those who cannot respect treaties! They must answer for their breach to Europe.'[8]

The negotiations over Malta, Holland and Switzerland dragged on through April. Bonaparte now wished either to stall the English or dupe them with a fresh formula. But the English, so gullible in 1801–2, proved deaf to his blandishments. In May the Cabinet gave him a final ultimatum: grant England ten years' possession of Malta and evacuate Holland and Switzerland, in return for which England would recognize his take-overs in Italy; or Whitworth would leave Paris. Bonaparte, huffed that anyone should issue *him* with an ultimatum, rejected these terms. The English then rejected his counter-proposals by which Malta was to pass into

Russian hands after one or two years. Whitworth took coach to Calais, pursued by last-minute French nods and winks and hints at some further compromise. On 18 May 1803 England declared war. Next day Vice-Admiral Cornwallis resumed the blockade of Brest.

Like a ship of the line in a sea fight England had laid herself alongside Bonaparte's France, implacably resolved never to draw off until Bonaparte, whom she now saw as a trickster of limitless ambition, struck his flag.

In provoking even the peace-loving and feeble Addington Cabinet into a unanimous decision for war Bonaparte had committed the most catastrophic blunder of his entire career. It sprang in the first place from a failure to understand the English character and English institutions, or comprehend England's strength. Since his youthful studies he had regarded her as the modern Carthage, a mere nation of traders doomed to destruction at the hands of a martial state like France.[9] And certainly there was little about English society that accorded with Bonaparte's own ideas as to what constituted a powerful and well-governed state. Vacillating cabinets precariously depended on the hazardous outcome of parliamentary votes. Instead of the central government directing the national life, the national life arranged itself by some mysterious organic process. The nobility and gentry governed the English shires virtually without reference to London, even controlling the militia, that important part of the English military system. The new volunteer movement had sprung up spontaneously as private and independent associations of citizens. The legal profession and the universities jealously guarded their independence. The City of London, the world's greatest financial centre, formed yet another self-governing republic. The Industrial Revolution, already well under way in England but yet to begin in Europe, owed everything to personal initiative and nothing to State direction or encouragement. All in all, English society consisted of innumerable co-existing private clubs. The apparent anarchy of the English scene found supreme expression in a free press which hounded politicians, the nobility and even the royal family with cruel lampoons. How could such a cloud of human atoms, such a nation of usurers lacking even a great army, contend against Bonaparte's own logical, efficient military state directed by a single mind of genius?

Yet although Bonaparte could not perceive it, those atoms were held together by a principle – love of liberty; the right to arrange your own affairs in association with your fellows without being told what to do by a government and its bureaucrats. He could not begin to comprehend that through such free association and debate Englishmen might arrive at a union far more resilient than the brittle artificial unanimity he had imposed on France; at a truly national purpose in contrast to the mere acquiescence of the French people in his own designs. He failed as well to note the dynamism of a country where initiative and decision flourished everywhere in the soil of liberty instead of being the monopoly of one man at the top like himself. And despite his fulminations about English gold buying allies to fight against France, he no less underestimated the strategic importance of England's resources as the world's most powerful industrial and trading nation.

By a paradox Bonaparte combined scorn for the English with a hatred such as he felt for no other enemy. Yet the paradox is only apparent, for the scorn and the hatred alike reveal the underdog's mentality. In his boyhood Bonaparte, identifying himself with Corsica, had hated France; now, identifying himself with France, he hated England, referring to her, for instance, in a signal to one of his admirals in 1805 as 'this power which for six centuries has oppressed France.'[10] On more than one occasion he described to Josephine with relish how he meant to humble England.'[11] None the less this underdog's mentality was not the only factor which warped Bonaparte's judgment in his dealings with the English in 1802–3. The English also attracted that raging impatience which had geysered up in him since childhood whenever his will was questioned, and to which Lord Whitworth had fallen personally a victim.

Yet for all the strength of Bonaparte's resentments in regard to England, it might be expected that the calculator in him, the realist, would at least have grasped the need to handle the English with prudence and tact. However, Bonaparte's intellect, for all its vaunted power and lucidity, tended to exclude unwelcome factors that might prevent his sums coming out to the answers he wanted; factors such as the strength of Mantua in 1796–7 or Acre in 1799. Experience had worsened rather than remedied this weakness, lulling him into assuming that any problem left out of his original sums could always be remedied in the event by energy, willpower and good luck. The very speed of his rise to the top helped to engender a blithe overconfidence that 'everything I undertake must succeed.' Such overconfidence, together with the heady effects of supreme power and a naturally imperious temperament, served to render Bonaparte ever more uncaring as to the reactions of others, be they individuals or nations. This was after all the period when he became First Consul for life and took the first steps towards promoting himself Emperor; and his head was already swelling to fit the future crown.

The same personal flaws which had betrayed him into provoking England's mortal enmity were now to be demonstrated afresh in his preparations to crush her by invasion.

ONCE THE ROYAL NAVY had swept French commerce from the seas and picketed the French fleets in their ports, there was little that England, lacking a large army, could do to harm Bonaparte until such time as she could build another European coalition. But in 1803 the courts of Europe proved deaf to English persuasion and blind to the glint of English guineas. Bonaparte faced an exactly opposite problem: with as yet only thirteen ships of the line fit for sea out of a total of forty-two, he could hardly seek a battle with England's fifty-two. Having occupied Hanover, George III's hereditary possession, and reoccupied Naples, Bonaparte could inflict no further hurt on England until such time as his veterans could repeat Rivoli and Marengo among the hopfields of Kent. He therefore bent himself to solving the problem of transporting 150,000 soldiers to the English coast.

The problem, as his admirals well understood, was insoluble, given the English Channel and its complicated tides and currents, its swiftly changing moods of tempest, fog and calm; given too the Royal Navy and its superlative seamanship and gunnery. Bonaparte nevertheless solved it to his own satisfaction by the simple

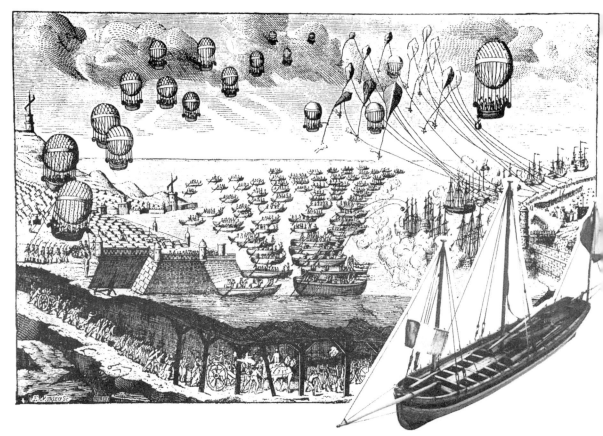

expedient of excluding the Channel and the Royal Navy from his calculations. On a day of providentially smooth weather, and when likewise providentially the English fleet had been removed from the scene by a prior gale or immobilized by a flat calm, the army would row itself across to England in a vast flotilla of special invasion craft. Possibly the hours of darkness would enable the flotilla to sneak across unscathed – without of course presenting any insurmountable problems of navigation or stationkeeping.

In March 1803, two months before the outbreak of war, Bonaparte issued orders for the construction of invasion craft, and in June orders for military camps along the coast.[12] After personally reconnoitring the invasion coastline from Dunkirk to the Somme in July, he drew up his final plans. Boulogne and Etaples were to serve as principal ports for the flotilla, with smaller bases at Wimereux and Ambleteuse. The land forces were to be concentrated in four great camps, each to hold an army corps and its artillery, at Utrecht, Bruges, St Omer and Montreuil, with a fifth at Brest as a diversionary threat to the restless English colony of Ireland.

Given only that his scheme was fundamentally impracticable, it is impossible not to admire the vigour and ingenuity with which Bonaparte pursued it. Four special types of craft were designed for the carriage of the army, its guns and horses across the Channel: the largest, the *prame*, over 100 feet long and 23 feet in the beam; the smallest the *péniche*, an undecked boat some 60 feet long by 10 feet in the beam,

The project for the invasion of England 1803–5 – fantasy and reality. The cartoon shows the invasion army rowing itself across the Channel preceded by airborne forces in balloons, while more troops pass through a Channel tunnel. The insert shows a *péniche*, one of the specially-designed but unseaworthy invasion craft. *Mansell Collection; (insert) Musée de la Marine, Paris*

An undismayed English view of Bonaparte's Army of England. *Mansell Collection*

carrying five crew and fifty-five soldiers who were to do their own rowing. None of these types of craft was fit to meet the Channel in any but its fairest moods, while the *péniche*, in which the bulk of the army was to be embarked, was suitable only for a trip round the bay on a fine afternoon. On 18 August 1803 Bonaparte laid down the armament, complement, scales of equipment and rations for these various vessels down to the number of cooking pots and pioneers' spades.[13] On the same day he sent Admiral Bruix, who commanded the invasion flotilla from a headquarters in Boulogne, a schedule of the final organization of the sea and land forces. Each division and sub-unit of the 2,000-vessel-strong flotilla was to correspond to the divisions and tactical units of the army to be carried.[14]

While the shipwrights of France and the Low Countries hammered and sawed away at constructing vessels, 50,000 labourers dug out new basins in the invasion ports to accommodate them. At Ambleteuse an entire new port had to be put in hand. Bonaparte himself minutely monitored the progress of these gigantic tasks, administering impatient long-distance kicks in the seats of his subordinates' breeches whenever the work fell behind schedule. Meanwhile, he drove his generals as hard as his admirals, urging on the completion of the great invasion camps and the concentration of the troops and guns. No matter was too small or too obvious for Bonaparte's personal attention. On 11 October he favoured Marshal Soult, commanding the camp at St Omer, with 'a drill which I have drawn up myself, having exercised the Guard on the Seine two or three times . . .'[15] The drill, for distribution to all company officers, was intended for troops operating the *péniches*, and comprised twenty-three detailed commands and evolutions beginning with 'One: Embark'. A particularly important evolution, 'Six: Row', read:

> At this command every man holding the butt of the oars stretches forward together; they lean on the butt so that the blade does not plunge into the water until they have fully extended their arms.
>
> When their arms are stretched right forward, they let the butt of the oar rise gradually, so as to plunge the blade some seven inches into the water, and at the same time they draw the oar to the rear by pulling hard on the butt.
>
> *Nota:* In order that a *péniche* be well rowed, it is essential that the two oarsmen on the rearmost bench row together and in a well-marked rhythm . . .[16]

French Volunteers, marching to the Conquest of Great Britain.

Bonaparte indeed thought of everything: on 29 November he instructed his Minister of the Interior, 'I desire, Citizen Minister, that you have a song written to the tune of the *Chant du Départ* for the descent on England . . .'[17]

Yet preparations on so vast a scale confronted Bonaparte with the old problem of cash-flow. He tried to solve it with equally old expedients: under pressure the Dutch agreed to furnish vessels at their own expense; neutral Spain was similarly coerced into a contribution of 16,000 francs a month; the Portuguese too. Despite such measures the French Treasury was bare by the beginning of 1804, ready cash only being found by borrowing from financiers at the then enormous interest rate of 15 per cent.[18] Bonaparte now proposed to resort to a measure no post-Revolution government had dared, and lay more of the cost of war on the French people themselves by imposing indirect taxes of the kind that had rendered the *ancien régime* so unpopular. 'Do I not have my gendarmes, my prefects and my priests?' boomed Bonaparte. 'If anyone should revolt, I will have five or six rebels hanged, and every one else will pay.'[19] But in the end he merely imposed a light tax on alcoholic drink.

On 2 December 1803 he resoundingly dubbed the invasion forces 'The Army of England'. All at last was ready, and the expedition would sail, Bonaparte hoped, in January. Outwardly he remained supremely confident, reporting from Boulogne to Cambacérès in Paris on 16 November: 'From the cliffs of Ambleteuse I have seen the English coast as clearly as one sees the Calvary from the Tuileries. You can make out houses and movement. It is a ditch which will be leaped whenever one has the boldness to try.'[20] But in fact the treble realities of the Channel, the Royal Navy and the unseaworthy, unwieldy and defenceless nature of his armada – realities so long urged by his admirals – were beginning to impose themselves even upon him. On 23 November he asked his flag officer in Toulon, Vice-Admiral Ganteaume: 'Give me your views on this flotilla. Do you think it will convey us to the shores of Albion? It can carry 100,000 men. Eight hours of night in favourable weather would decide the fate of the universe . . .'[21] By the turn of the year the winds of winter, filling the sails of English men-of-war and rolling steep masses of green-black water through Bonaparte's 'ditch', finally blew the illusions out of his mind. He came to accept that providence could not be depended upon to remove the Royal Navy from his path; he would have to remove it himself.

'The Plumb-pudding in danger: or State epicures taking un Petit Soupe'. Cartoon by James Gillray in 1805 on the territorial greed of Pitt and Bonaparte. *British Museum*

But hardly had he addressed himself to this fresh problem when he was distracted for several months by the royalist and republican plot involving Pichegru, Moreau and Cadoudal, followed by the kidnapping and murder of the Duc d'Enghien and then by the constitutional gerrymandering necessary to make himself emperor. Not until July did he take up the invasion project again in earnest, planning to cross in September under the protection of a French fleet which, thanks to his brilliant naval strategy, was to arrive in the Channel at just the moment when the English fleet had been tricked into vacating it. Neither aspect of this strategy came to pass, and it was then time to arrange the Coronation. Only in the winter of 1804–5 did he really get down to planning a final effort to convey his patient Army of England to its destination. Possibly he was spurred by England's disdainful response to another of his appeals for peace, this time monarchically addressed to '*mon frère*' George III.

In its reply '*mon frère's*' government, with that special English talent for snubbing upstarts, referred to the self-styled 'Emperor Napoleon' as 'the head of the French government.' Little wonder that Bonaparte vowed to Josephine that 'I will take you to London, madam. I intend the wife of the modern Caesar to be crowned at Westminster.'[22]

In pursuing his new career as amateur naval strategist, Bonaparte had to contend with the disadvantages of France's geography, with the Iberian peninsula widely separating her Mediterranean and Atlantic coasts – and fleets. Though Spain became his ally in December 1804, the Spanish fleets were themselves divided between Cadiz on the Atlantic coast and Cartagena on the Mediterranean, the English base of Gibraltar lying between. How then, in the face of English seapower and its unrelenting blockade, could these scattered fleets be united in order to force the English Channel?

Bonaparte dispatched his answer to these puzzles in instructions to his admirals on 2 March 1805,[23] laying down manoeuvres over thousands of miles of sea with a precision more appropriate to armies than fleets subject to the caprices of the winds. Vice-Admiral Ganteaume, now commanding France's principal fleet of twenty-one sail of the line in Brest, was to break out, pick up French and Spanish ships from Ferrol (capturing the English blockading squadron *en passant*) and press on to the French West Indian island of Martinique. There he would find the Rochefort squadron (which had escaped in January) and Vice-Admiral Villeneuve with the French Mediterranean fleet and the Spanish fleet. For Bonaparte simultaneously ordered Villeneuve to escape from Toulon (a base that was watched by Nelson), pick up the Spanish vessels in Cartagena and Cadiz and sail to Martinique as well. The combined fleet, some forty ships of the line, would then return to Europe 'without losing an instant' by a course as far distant as possible from the main Atlantic shipping routes, and at the same time keeping out of sight of land. If the fleet found the English western squadron on its usual station off Ushant, outside Brest, it was to attack it and then sail 'in a straight line for Boulogne, where we shall ourselves be in person . . .'[24] Bonaparte hoped that 'weather and other circumstances' would permit his combined fleet to arrive off Boulogne between 10 June and 10 July.[25]

As an exercise in throne-room strategy, pushing counters across a chart of the world, Bonaparte's cut-and-dried plan was admirable. However, like his original plan for the invasion of England, it suffered from the drawback that it did not take reality into account. In the first place Bonaparte almost entirely excluded the Royal Navy from his calculations except as a passive victim of his deceptions to be surprised and destroyed in detail by superior numbers. The Royal Navy, then at the apogee of its professional skill, was unlikely to play this convenient role. Secondly, in counting up the available ships on both sides, Bonaparte failed to take account of the immense disparity in sailing and fighting efficiency between them. The disruptive effects of the Revolution and long confinement in port had reduced the French navy to a shambles. For example, an earlier attempt by Villeneuve to escape from Toulon had lasted only three days, thanks not to Nelson but a gale. Back in harbour Villeneuve glumly reported to the Minister of Marine:

The sailors are not used to storms; they were lost among the mass of soldiers; these from seasickness lay in heaps about the decks; it was impossible to work the ships; hence yard-arms were broken and sails were carried away; our losses resulted as much from clumsiness and inexperience as from defects in the materials delivered by the arsenals.[26]

Bonaparte none the less refused to accept the evidence of this abortive cruise. 'What is to be done,' asked the old seadog in the Tuileries, 'with admirals who allow their spirits to sink, and determine to hasten home at the first damage they receive ... A few topmasts carried away, some casualties in a gale of wind, are everyday occurrences.'[27] Instead he clung to a belief that the English fleets, at sea for years at a time, must be exhausted and in poor repair, like an army after a long campaign, while the French squadrons, snug in port, must emerge in as fine a condition as an army out of winter quarters. Nothing could have been more mistaken. After the same gale that forced Villeneuve back to port, Nelson reported to the Admiralty:

The Fleet under my command is in excellent good health, and the ships, although we have experienced a great deal of bad weather, have received no damage, and not a yard or mast sprung or crippled, or scarcely a sail split.[28]

And the third aspect of reality which Bonaparte failed to take into account was that he himself was a mere landlubber pitting himself against the most formidable corps of sea officers in history; another example of an overweening conceit that no longer recognized any personal limitations. For the command of fleets in the age of sail demanded a depth of professional knowledge, amounting almost to second sight, that could only come from a lifetime at sea.

Bonaparte's grand design opened badly enough on 26–28 March 1805 when Ganteaume failed to slip away from Brest for the very kind of reasons ignored by Bonaparte in his planning. Ganteaume was beginning to make for the open sea under cover of fog when the fog suddenly lifted, revealing the distant sails of the English blockading squadron. It was plainly impossible for Ganteaume to escape without fighting – which Bonaparte's orders expressly forbade him to do. All that day the two squadrons watched each other like hostile tom-cats. Next morning the wind veered, forcing Ganteaume to retire again into Brest. A further escape attempt in April proved no more successful. Ganteaume's fleet of twenty-one sail of the line, which Bonaparte had intended to form the very keelson of his strategy, remained stuck fast in port for the remainder of the campaign.

On 30 March Villeneuve enjoyed better luck, shaking off Nelson's frigates outside Toulon in the night, and sailing through the Straits of Gibraltar to pick up the Spaniards from Cadiz. On 9 April his combined fleet set sail for Martinique.

With Villeneuve's disappearance into the Atlantic wastes there began for the Admiralty in London and the English commanders at sea four months of groping and guesswork in a sea mist of stale news, true and false sightings, and coincidences lucky and unlucky; four months accordingly of complex and continual re-deployments of England's naval strength. But when in total doubt the English admirals knew what to do: close in on the Western Squadron off Ushant. For that squadron's role was not merely, as Bonaparte believed, to blockade Brest, but to serve as the very core of the English strategic system, at once a central reserve and a

rallying-point. A century of naval struggle and victory had taught the English that
so long as they held the mouth of the Channel, no enemy combination could
succeed, and no invasion could be mounted. Bonaparte never grasped that however
ingeniously he might try to fox his enemy into dispersing his strength, he was
certain in the end to find it concentrated in that vital area off Ushant.

With Ganteaume fast in port, all Bonaparte's hopes for a successful invasion
rested on Villeneuve. On 10 April he was delighted to learn from spies that two
military expeditions were being prepared in Plymouth, apparently bound for India
and the West Indies. Gleefully he wrote to Cambacérès:

> These are neither militia nor volunteers . . . these are their best troops. If therefore our
> flotilla receives the signal and is favoured by six hours of fair wind, of fog and night, the
> English, taken by surprise, will find themselves stripped of their best troops.[29]

But in fact one of these expeditions, under General Craig, was bound for Malta,
its purpose to help cement the new European coalition which Pitt had been
patiently constructing ever since he became Prime Minister again in May 1804. On
11 April 1805 England and Russia signed an alliance, Craig's force supplying the
gage of English strategic co-operation in the Mediterranean. Bonaparte, intent
upon his own schemes, antennae calloused over by arrogance, totally refused to
accept that Europe was ganging up on him again. When his brother-in-law, Prince
Murat, reported rumours of an Anglo-Russian alliance, Bonaparte retorted on
26 May that 'what you write . . . makes no sense; it is entirely false.'[30] On the 29th

he informed Decrès, his Minister of Marine, 'England is entirely abandoned by the Continent; her situation could not be worse.'[31]

On 21 April, three days after Craig's expedition set sail, Bonaparte took up residence in the colossal baroque palace of Stupinigi outside Turin, there to prepare for a new coronation, this time as King of Italy. The conduct of the naval preliminaries to the invasion of England were to become something of a part-time activity for the next three months, what with all the ceremonial events and the putting of his new kingdom in order. Moreover, while orders and news could be exchanged between Paris and the Atlantic ports in a matter of hours by semaphore telegraph, Paris and Italy lay some four to six days apart. These impediments did not prevent Bonaparte from trying to exercise a rigid centralized direction of his fleets, laying down his admirals' movements in voluminous detail; orders out of date when sent and even more out of date when received, and based on resounding but mistaken certainties as to the positions and intentions of the English squadrons.

The real course of events at sea, however, proved less tidy. On 14 May Villeneuve dropped anchor at Martinique, only to find that the Rochefort squadron had already gone home. On 4 June, Nelson, who had been delayed by foul winds in the Mediterranean, but who on reaching Cadiz had rightly guessed that Villeneuve must have gone to the West Indies, arrived at Barbados and began to hunt for him. Only four days earlier Bonaparte had been opining to Decrès that Nelson lacked supplies for a voyage to the West Indies, that four of his ships were leaking badly, and that even if he did arrive there, he would be too weak to offer a threat to Villeneuve.[32] Villeneuve himself had now received fresh orders from Bonaparte to await Ganteaume for a further five weeks. On 8 June, however, he learned that Nelson was in the Caribbean looking for him. It was clear to the French admiral that Bonaparte's elaborate plan for concentrating his fleets in secrecy 3,000 miles away from English broadsides had fallen apart. To him the prospect of having his ramshackle fleet brought to battle by Nelson quite overruled Bonaparte's order to hang about for Ganteaume. On 10 June Villeneuve steered for Europe, followed on the 13th by Nelson. On the 14th, ironically enough, Bonaparte assured Decrès in a letter that Nelson was either in England or the Mediterranean. 'His ships', proceeded Bonaparte, 'are in no state to make long voyages, and his crews are exceedingly tired.'[33]

This was not Bonaparte's only fantasy. If indeed the Craig expedition were bound for Malta, wrote he, 'so much the better, because these movements of continental strategy based on detachments of some 1,000 men are the combinations of pygmies.'[34] On 9 June, the day after Villeneuve learned of Nelson's presence in the West Indies, and when therefore Bonaparte's grand design had already split asunder and foundered, Bonaparte loftily informed the despondent Decrès in a long and rambling letter: 'Your mistake is to calculate as if the English are in the secret; one ought to calculate in the same way as must the Admiralty . . .'[35] But the Admiralty *was* in his secret. As early as 8 April Sir John Orde, observing Villeneuve enter Cadiz, guessed that his next destination would be westward 'where by a sudden concentration of several detachments, Bonaparte may hope to gain a temporary superiority in the Channel, and availing himself of it, to strike his enemy a mortal blow.'[36] The genius Bonaparte has thus been rumbled at the outset by a run-of-the-mill English flag officer whose name few of his countrymen now remember.

Despite news that Villeneuve was on his way home without Ganteaume, Bonaparte remained as sanguine as ever. On 10 July, now back in Fontainebleau, he dispatched fresh orders to await Villeneuve at his expected landfall, the northern Spanish port of Ferrol. 'Your junction made with the Ferrol squadron, you will manoeuvre in such a way as to render us masters of the Pas-de-Calais if only for four or five days . . .'[37] Villeneuve was either to achieve this by coming straight up the Channel, collecting the Rochefort and Brest squadrons *en route*, or by sailing right round the British Isles to join the Dutch fleet in the Texel. 'Europe waits in suspense for the grand events which are in preparation. We all of us look to your courage and skill.' These orders demonstrate another of Bonaparte's landlubberly errors, for a fleet under sail could not relieve squadrons blockaded in port with the ease of an army relieving a garrison besieged in a fortress. The wind that wafted the relieving fleet on its course would very likely be foul for the blockaded fleet seeking to get out; moreover, the difficulties of communication and co-ordination between two such squadrons with an enemy fleet lying between were virtually insurmountable.[38]

Ten days later, 20 July, Bonaparte ordered Ganteaume himself to make for Boulogne should the English be good enough to remove their blockading ships from Brest and send them off to meet Villeneuve. 'When you receive this letter, we shall already be at Boulogne-sur-Mer in person, and all will be embarked, moored outside the roadstead so that, master of the sea for three days, given the weather customary at this season, we have no doubt of success.'[39] On the same day he ordered Berthier to embark all the artillery, powder and supplies so that the expedition could sail at twenty-four hours' notice.[40] So at last the preparations drawn out over two years were coming to their climax along with the naval campaign itself. On 3 August Bonaparte arrived at Boulogne and, above the port on the downs overlooking a sea studded as always with English sails, held a grand review of the Army of England – for Bonaparte, a sacrament of power, uplifting to his spirit.

Yet a secret report of this self-same date revealed the truth behind the show: out of 150,000 men intended for embarkation, only 90,000 were ready, and only 3,000 horses out of 9,000. The port of Boulogne and the specially excavated basins were stuffed with far more invasion craft than could be lifted on a single tide, and, according to this report, no one had any idea how long it would take to get the armada to sea. In fact the elaborate charts of organization, the schedules of vessels and equipment so lovingly pored over by Bonaparte since 1803 turn out to have been exercises in self-delusion. Colonel Debrière, the French soldier-historian whose research uncovered this report, and himself an admirer of Bonaparte, had to acknowledge that 'his genius indulged itself in systems simply symmetrical, bearing no relation either to the actual state of the troops and their service, or the means of embarkation accumulated in the ports . . .'[41]

The climax of the campaign thus offers, aptly enough, the climactic example of that remoteness from reality which had characterized Bonaparte's thinking throughout. In his unwillingness to accept that he had set himself an impossible task even his love of mathematics, 'where all is resolved by logic', even his appetite for facts, became transformed into just another mode of romantic fantasy.

On 13 August Bonaparte received news that Villeneuve had fought an indecisive battle on 22 July with a weaker English squadron off Ferrol commanded by Sir Robert Calder. Since the blustering language of Villeneuve's dispatch conveyed the impression of a French success, Bonaparte ordered him to 'sweep away everything in your path and enter the Channel, where we await you with anxiety.'[42] For in Bonaparte's conviction, various English squadrons, including Nelson's, still lay far distant from the area of decision.[43] But in fact only two days later Nelson's arrival off Ushant from Gibraltar finally completed the concentration of the English fleet in the mouth of the Channel; an appropriate denouement to all Bonaparte's schemings. As for Villeneuve himself, his never robust nerve had been finally shredded by his experience at the hands of Calder's inferior numbers, when he lost two ships captured and four put out of action, reporting to Decrès, 'I will not venture to describe our condition. It is frightful.'[44] On the night of 15–16 August he led his fleet out of Ferrol, not towards the Channel as Bonaparte desired, and where the English fleet awaited him, but in the opposite direction, to the shelter of Cadiz.

Bonaparte, in ignorance of this, still hung on at Boulogne in hope that he might yet see French sails to the westward. But by now he was well aware that new perils were quickly arising behind him in central Europe. On 22 August he fired off the last of his inspirational orders to Ganteaume and Villeneuve: 'I count on your talents, your steadfastness and your character', he told Ganteaume. 'Put to sea and sail here. We will avenge six centuries of insults and shame. Never have my soldiers on land and sea risked their lives for so great an object.'[45] But next day he confided to Talleyrand, his Foreign Minister, '. . . the more I reflect on the European situation, the more I see how urgent it is to come to a decision . . .'[46] Two days later he told Talleyrand that his decision was taken: 'My movements have begun; on the 30th [Fructidor – 17 September] I shall be in Germany with 200,000 men . . .'[47]

By 28 August the army was in full march. Yet this advance to the Danube constituted at the same time the retreat from Boulogne; the aftermath of the greatest strategic reverse Bonaparte had so far suffered. More, it was the consequence of the crassest blunders he had so far committed. For in addition to provoking England's renewed belligerence and then failing in his foredoomed attempt to crush her by invasion, he had needlessly stirred up Russia's enmity again – and finally Austria's as well.

VIII

THE MARCH TO AUSTERLITZ

I N 1801 ALEXANDER I had succeeded to the throne of Russia vacated by the murder of his mad father the Tsar Paul. Alexander equalled Bonaparte in self-opinion, touchiness and romantic ambition, though not in intellect. He regarded the French dictator as his personal rival for the position nearest the footlights as arbiter of European destiny. Even so there was no need for Russia and France, lying at opposite ends of Europe, to collide, providing each great man avoided trepassing on the other's manor and displayed tactful consideration for the other's vanity. But this Bonaparte failed to do, and because of the same traits of character which determined his cavalier treatment of the English. By pursuing his imperial ambitions in the eastern Mediterranean he clashed with Alexander's own designs on the Turkish Empire and Constantinople. In the summer of 1803 he upset the Tsar still further by first requesting him to mediate in his dispute with England over Malta and allied topics, then occupying Hanover and Naples without waiting for his proposals, and finally rejecting the proposals themselves. In terms of real interests, it would have cost Bonaparte nothing to accept the Tsar's proposals; he wished, however, to snub Alexander for presuming to the role of arbiter of Europe.

The kidnapping of the Duc d'Enghien from neutral German territory in March 1804 annoyed the Tsar still more, in his self-appointed role of guardian of Germany, moving him to public protest. Thereupon Bonaparte, rather than soothe Alexander down, withdrew his ambassador from St Petersburg, and vented his spite by asking the Russian *chargé d'affaires* whether Alexander would not have hastened to seize the English-paid assassins of his father, had he known that they were residing just beyond Russia's frontier. This remark concealed a poisoned blade, because Alexander was widely suspected of being implicated in his father's murder.[1]

Thus Bonaparte gratuitously opened the door for English diplomacy in St Petersburg and ushered it inside, with the result that after the customary long drawn-out negotiations the Anglo-Russian alliance was signed in May 1805 and ratified by the Tsar in July.

In Vienna English diplomacy stood in even greater need of Bonaparte's help, for the Emperor Francis shared none of Alexander's feelings of personal rivalry with Bonaparte, nor did he wish, so soon after the defeats of 1800–1, to embark on a fresh war. It was fortunate for England therefore that Bonaparte proved just as careless of Austrian susceptibilities. By proclaiming himself Emperor in May 1804 he offered a direct challenge to Francis' status as Holy Roman Emperor, heir of Charlemagne and the Caesars and hitherto the only emperor in Europe. England's patient coalition building began to make progress in Vienna too. Then, a year later, Bonaparte affronted Francis afresh by having himself crowned King of Italy and performing this act with the ancient iron crown of Lombardy, the title and the object both traditionally belonging to the Holy Roman Emperors. 'God gave it to me,' said Bonaparte at his coronation according to an equally ancient but here hardly appropriate formula, 'woe to him who touches it.'[2] By bestowing two imperial fiefs in Italy on members of his family he rubbed it in still further that he rather than Francis now occupied the high place of Charlemagne. Moreover, all these acts, together with the annexing of Genoa to France in June 1805, constituted flagrant breaches of the Treaty of Lunéville. The sleeping dog of Austria, thus repeatedly and needlessly hacked in the tender parts by Bonaparte, awoke and prepared to bite back. On 17 July 1805 the Austrian government decided to join the Anglo-Russian alliance.[3]

Only in the case of Prussia did Bonaparte fail to aid England to construct her coalition, omitting to provoke the weak Prussian king, Frederick William III, and even at the last moment offering him a bribe of another monarch's property, Hanover, to stay neutral. Despite the combined persuasion of England and Russia, Frederick William finally opted for neutrality.

Alexander I, Tsar of Russia (1777–1825). He equalled Bonaparte in self-opinion, touchiness and romantic ambition, though not in intellect. Painting (1814–18) by Sir Thomas Lawrence. *Copyright Reserved*

At the end of July 1805 it at last penetrated the carapace of Bonaparte's arrogance that a new European coalition was preparing to take the field against him; a development he had not at all intended[4] and which came at the peculiarly inconvenient moment when his own preparations to invade England were coming to their climax. On 13 August he instructed Talleyrand to send Austria an ultimatum demanding that she withdraw her troops into Bohemia and Hungary, 'leaving me to wage war against England in tranquillity', or face invasion.[5] This instruction, long, even garrulous, reveals a man surprised and stung to rage. It ends on a characteristic grace-note by referring to 'this skeleton Francis II, whom the merit of his ancestors has placed on the throne.'[6] Ten days later Bonaparte informed his foreign minister that there was no point in waiting for the Austrian reply:

> She will answer with fine phrases in order to gain time, so that I will be unable to do anything this winter . . . and in April I will find 100,000 Russians in Poland paid for by England . . . and 15 or 20,000 English at Malta, and 15,000 Russians on Corfu. I will then find myself in a critical position. My decision is taken.[7]

This time Bonaparte was not resorting to force, as on earlier occasions, to fulfil extravagant territorial ambitions, but simply to repair the calamitous consequences of mistaken and mishandled foreign policy; hardly indeed worthy of the name of policy at all. The coming campaign against Austria was therefore even more needless in terms of the real interests of the French people than those of 1796–7 or 1800.

BEHIND ITS CLANGING BANDS and under a benign autumn sun the Grande Armée (as Bonaparte had resoundingly renamed the erstwhile Army of England) tramped eastwards across the vast horizons of the Low Countries and northern France on its way to the Rhine. Rested and well fed after more than eighteen months in camp along the Channel and North Sea coasts, its gawdy uniforms for once true to the glamour of the military print and not yet befouled by war, it was the finest army Bonaparte was ever to command. The original revolutionary mixture of old royal regular soldiers and ardent citizen volunteers had now matured into veteran regiments high in intelligence and initiative, nimble in manoeuvre, devastatingly aggressive in attack. Bonaparte himself was not much of a military innovator, but content instead to make war with this hybrid army as he found it. The basic tactical manual throughout his career remained the *règlement* of 1791, which prescribed deployment into line for defence and maximum firepower, the column for attack and maximum flexibility and impetus, or the combination of both in a mixed formation. Swarms of *tirailleurs* or sharpshooters preceded the onset of the columns, their alacrity and accurate fire serving to confuse the stolid, rigid formations of the *ancien régime*.

Although Bonaparte himself was a gunner, artillery had yet to play a decisive role in his battles. In his past campaigns he had suffered a shortage of cannon for various reasons. After 1800, however, Marmont, whom he appointed Inspector-General of Artillery, had set about creating the artillery arm which was to dominate Bonaparte's later battles. For the first time civilian drivers of gun teams were replaced by military personnel. Mechanical parts such as wheels were standardized. The enormous task of recasting all France's artillery from four calibres (4-, 8-, 12- and 24-pounder) into three (6-, 12- and 24-), demanding the use of Italian as well as French arsenals, was well on the way to completion by the opening of the 1805

'. . . its gaudy uniforms for once true to the glamour of the military print and not yet befouled by war . . .'
Left: Officer of the Horse Grenadiers of the Imperial Guard; right: Trumpeter of the Chasseurs of the Imperial Guard. *Musée de l'Armée, Paris. Photos: Bulloz*

campaign. No fewer than 286 field guns were rumbling along with the columns of the Grande Armée on the roads to Bavaria.[8]

Off the battlefield, however, the Bonapartian army lacked system and discipline; it pillaged and straggled; it ignored or disobeyed its officers. On campaign its columns of route had all the regularity of migrating tribes of gypsies hung about with plunder, edible and otherwise. This was indeed the era which saw established the great French military tradition of '*le système D*', the 'D' standing for *débrouiller* – muddle through. Even by 1805 only the Imperial Guard was equipped with its own wagon-train; the rest of the army scavenged as it went.

During the Marengo campaign Bonaparte had improvised army corps, independent groups of all arms, for the sake of greater flexibility in march and manoeuvre. By 1805 the army had become, as in other European armies, a standard formation, composed of two or three infantry divisions, a light cavalry division and accompanying guns. On its march from the Channel coast the Grande Armée was divided into six such corps, a further one under Marshal Bernadotte starting from Hanover.[9] Each corps followed its own route well separated from its neighbour, so providing it with its own tract of country to feed off.

In Berthier, his chief-of-staff, Bonaparte possessed the perfect instrument for his style of command: a kind of super chief-clerk, untiring at routine work, but in no sense the equivalent of a modern chief-of-staff who proffers strategic advice or takes decisions on his own responsibility.

For Bonaparte himself, with 176,000 men under his command as against some 25,000–40,000 in Italy in 1796–7 and 60,000 in 1800, the new campaign marked a major upward change of scale. His correspondence reveals his especial pleasure in the numbers he now commanded, the sense of power they inspired; it reveals too the zest and relief with which he embarked on his new adventure, freed at last of the maddening constraints of winds and tides and of admirals, both French and English. But although he possessed so magnificent an army he could not afford to maintain it in the field for long without imposing such heavy burdens on France as to menace his imperial position. A quick war, a stunning victory, a shortcut to a glorious peace, he again must have. This time Germany was to constitute the decisive theatre, Italy the subsidiary one, where Marshal Masséna was simply to prevent the Archduke Charles marching to the aid of the Austrian armies north of the Alps. By the sheer suddenness and speed with which he 'pirouetted' (his own word) his army from the Channel to the Danube he would surprise and destroy the Austrians before their Russian allies could join them.

But while the Grande Armée was trudging eastwards some twelve to fourteen miles a day (about Marlborough's pace *en route* for the Danube 101 years before), Bonaparte returned to Paris to solve some urgent problems, such as organizing supplies for an army of nearly 180,000 men and finding the money to pay for it all. On 30 August he had written from Boulogne to his finance minister that the army had pay only for another three days, and that he found himself 'in a situation such as I never experienced at the time of the Army of Reserve.'[10] The one thing treasury officials must ensure, he wrote, was that 'at a time of penury, never to allow the pay of the army to be lacking . . .'[11] In the customary furious rush he poured out orders

Joachim Murat, later
King of Naples
(1771–1815). A hard-
driving but not always
well-judged general, he
commanded Bonaparte's
reserve cavalry. Painting
by François-Pascal
Gérard. *Musée de
Versailles. Photo: Musées
Nationaux*

for the baking of biscuit, the purchase of capes and shoes and artillery horses, the building of carts, and the stocking of depots along the Rhine. The event would reveal the slipshod nature of these hasty preparations.

Then there was also the need to explain to the French people why they had been plunged into a fresh European war:

> I march in order to repulse imminent attack, support my just rights, and punish a prince who, though twice heaped with French generosity, concealed his hatred in order to attack us with the greater perfidy . . .[12]

On 20 September he learned from Murat (sent ahead of the army to reconnoitre in the guise of 'Colonel Beaumont') that the Austrian army was taking up a position facing west behind the River Iller, with its right flank at Ulm, where the Iller runs into the Danube. Nothing could have suited Bonaparte better than that the Austrians should make this rash forward march right across Bavaria to meet him, instead of waiting well to the east for the Russians and so compelling Bonaparte to seek his battle deep inside Austrian territory, and against a united allied force. That day he issued his final directives for the army's advance from the Rhine to the Danube. While one army corps threatened the Austrians frontally from the Black Forest, the remaining six would sweep round their right at Ulm, across their communications, and finally take them in the rear. The French corps would march on a front of eighty to one hundred miles like the spread fingers of a hand, ready to clench the moment they felt the Austrians within their grasp. Ahead of them, a moving screen blinding the Austrian command, rode the 21,000 horsemen of Murat's reserve cavalry.[13] This strategy bore strong resemblances to the Schlieffen Plan of 1914: in the simple grandeur of the conception of a flank march by almost the entire army; in the reliance on the enemy's doing what was expected of him; and in the fundamental defect that instead of serving as the instrument of a wise national policy, it marked an attempt by military means to redeem a breakdown of policy:

On 25 September the marching wing of the Grande Armée crossed the Rhine at five points from Mainz to Kehl. Bernadotte's corps, coming from Hanover, was ordered to take a convenient but by no means essential shortcut through the neutral Prussian territory of Ansbach – another example, as Marshal Marmont justly observes, 'of that scorn for the rights of others of which Napoleon was often guilty when he believed himself the stronger.'[14] On 30 September Bonaparte, now in Strasbourg, wrote to Marshal Augereau: 'God will that his [the Austrian Emperor's] army continues to remain in the same position for another eight days or so, or, even better, that it advances towards the Rhine.'[15] Yet he evidently feared that the Austrians could not really be such fools as to remain motionless while he swept round on to their rear, for he told Augereau that the recent departure of the Austrian Emperor from Ulm back to Vienna meant that the Austrians had already taken alarm: 'I suppose,' he wrote, 'that the Austrians are on the point of hurrying to evacuate Bavaria.'[16]

But in fact the Austrian army remained as motionless in the Ulm position as a tethered goat in an Indian village awaiting the visit of a tiger, thus making it from Bonaparte's point of view the perfect opponent, so different from the English fleets. By 8 October the Grande Armée's questing fingers had reached or crossed the

Danube east of Ulm, ready to curl round the hapless enemy. The French were tramping now over the same rolling plains patched with forest where Marlborough and Prince Eugène had hunted Marshal Tallard in 1704 before the Battle of Blenheim; icy rain now bedraggling the army's glories of fur and feather, and veiling the finger-slim baroque church towers, pink, straw-yellow, ochre that mark the distant villages. South across the Danube swung the columns; two corps turning eastward to Munich, the rest westward to encircle Ulm. Only now did Mack, the Austrian commander, realize that his enemy was not after all going to appear along the direct route from France via the Black Forest as he had believed certain. On 20 October 1805, after frantic dartings to and fro against the encircling French like a rat caught in the corner of a barn, the Austrian army round Ulm, 33,000 men and sixty guns, capitulated, laying down its arms in a formal ceremony in Bonaparte's presence – another tableau to be painted for the legend.

Bonaparte had never won so easy or so complete a success. He exulted in it. Ulm made up – or almost – for the retreat from Boulogne. But like all his past Italian victories, it was a success that only just escaped being a disaster, and even then escaped largely because of the incompetence of his enemy. For when Bonaparte swept southwards across Mack's *derrières*, he by the same token exposed his own *derrières* to a northward counter-stroke by the Austrians. The counter-stroke never came. Yet the effect produced by the breakout of a single Austrian corps of 20,000 men (later surrounded and forced to surrender) northeastward through Heidenheim, right across Bonaparte's communications, indicates what might have been accomplished by a general less paralytic than Mack. Bonaparte is found, on 17 October, writing urgently to Murat: 'I await with impatience your news from Heidenheim in order to know what position the enemy has taken. I am eager to learn that my communications are clear and re-established, and that my park, my cavalry depots, the treasure I have at Heilbronn and my couriers are all safe.'[17]

For – as always – Bonaparte was working on the narrowest of margins. As he himself acknowledged to the Intendant-General of the army after Mack's surrender, '. . . had the army suffered some reverse, the lack of magazines would have led us into the greatest difficulties . . .'[18] Troops exhausted by ceaseless marching would arrive at their camping ground, so an eyewitness writes, 'having eaten nothing and finding no supplies waiting for them'[19] – a fate that never befell Marlborough's soldiers on *their* march to the Danube. Hunger, fatigue and the icy weather led to 'insubordination, indiscipline and marauding', according to the same officer; 'except in the Russian campaign I have never suffered so much, nor seen the army in such disorder.'[20] Even Mack's surrender did not in itself deliver the Grande Armée from its plight, for Bonaparte, in ordering his Intendant-General to rush up supplies of every kind, added: 'the least negligence, the least delay could have the most disastrous effects for the army and the Empire' – an almost word-for-word repetition of the anguished signal he had sent back to his chief commissary when trapped in the valley of Aosta in 1800 by the resistance of Fort Bard.

Nevertheless, Bonaparte's near-run gamble had again come off, and his public-relations machine made the most of it. The wordy bulletin of the Grande Armée on Mack's capitulation contains the prototype of every stock device of twentieth-

'. . . another tableau to be painted for the legend': the Austrian General Mack surrenders to Bonaparte at Ulm with 33,000 men on 20 October 1805. Sketch by Antoine–Jean Gros. *Private Collection. Photo: Bulloz*

century wartime propaganda and war reporting – the supreme commander's own comments on his triumph, given verbatim as if in a press conference; the inside story of what Bonaparte said to Mack and Mack said to Bonaparte, also allegedly verbatim; human-interest stories featuring Bonaparte and his admiring soldiery; even the device of the apt, too apt, homely comment from the ranks, in this case that 'The Emperor had found a new way of waging war; he makes use of our legs instead of our bayonets.'[21]

With his customary over-optimism Bonaparte believed that the war was now as good as over, writing to Bernadotte, for example, on 19 October that 'of the army of 80,000 which was on the Iller, nothing is left but débris', and dismissing the remaining enemy forces in the field as of no consequence. 'But what,' he asked, 'can an army of 30,000 Russians and 25,000 Austrians do against us today?'[22] Nevertheless, in a repetition of his experience in Italy in 1796–7 the search for peace dragged him further and further eastward – on into the mountains and gorges of Austria, his soldiers bending their heads before the snows of November while the Russian commander Kutusov fell back in a sometimes disconcertingly ferocious fighting retreat. Bonaparte angrily blamed his subordinates for sluggishness as Kutusov slipped away; Murat in particular drew a blazing reprimand for venturing to conclude an armistice with the local enemy commander opposite him. For each

mile of march added to Bonaparte's uneasiness about his ever-more extended flanks and communications. At least, however, he had the consolation of knowing that the Grande Armée was off French soil, its feeding no longer a charge on the French Treasury, but paid for by realizing Austrian assets; a major economy, as he pointed out to his finance minister.[23]

On 14 November Bonaparte rode into Vienna, the most resplendent capital he had so far conquered, and the first belonging to a great power. It was fortunate for him, none the less, that the Austrian government in its fright had seen the Bonaparte of legend stalking towards them instead of the vulnerable Bonaparte of reality, and therefore evacuated Vienna without a fight. He had no siege train with him with which to reduce a first-class fortress, and if Vienna had resisted like Acre or Fort Bard, his campaign might well have collapsed. Even as it was, replenishing his army from Austrian arsenals, enjoying the comforts of the Emperor Francis' huge gamboge-yellow barracks of a palace at Schönbrunn, Bonaparte faced perils enough. His army now lay as far east of Ulm as Ulm is east of Paris. To his north, round Olmütz in Moravia, was the principal Austro-Russian army; to his east, at Pressburg on the Danube, another strong force shortly to be reinforced by the Archduke Charles' army from Italy. His nine-hundred-mile-long line of communications with Paris lay under threat from Austrian troops in the Tyrol to the south – and under potential threat from the Prussian army to the north.

For Prussia, enraged by Bonaparte's casual violation of her territory during his march to Ulm, was dithering on the verge of war, and if Prussia did join in, the odds against Bonaparte would become overwhelming. Bonaparte, in fear of this from

'. . . the most resplendent capital he had so far conquered . . .': Bonaparte accepts the keys of Vienna on 14 November 1805. An interpretation in the Roman style by Bergeret. Manufacture de Sèvres. *Bulloz*

'. . . enjoying the comforts of the Emperor Francis' huge gamboge–yellow barracks of a palace at Schönbrunn.' Bonaparte was to stay at Schönbrunn again in 1809; his son was to die there in 1832. *Photo Meyer, Vienna*

Ulm onwards, reverted to his old but lately discarded tactic of the crawling appeal, writing to Frederick William from Munich on 27 October that there was 'no kind of satisfaction that I am not ready to give to Your Majesty,' and begging him not to listen to Bonaparte's enemies 'but to the feeling which I flatter myself Your Majesty still preserves in his heart for me.'[24] But on 3 November Frederick William and the Tsar signed a convention by which Prussia would offer armed mediation; in other words, if Bonaparte refused to accept Prussia's terms for a European peace, the Prussian army would march. The Prussian emissary set off to Vienna, fortunately for Bonaparte making no haste.

Yet Bonaparte faced more profound problems still, for France was going through another economic crisis, this time coupled with a financial panic in Paris; falling agricultural prices, distress among the peasantry. The crisis carried urgent military implications, for the treasury minister wrote to Bonaparte that it was impossible to send funds to pay the army.[25] In late November 1805, therefore, Bonaparte stood yet again in danger of imminent strategic bankruptcy carrying personal ruin in its wake, but this time on a scale far vaster than in similar crises in 1796, 1797 and 1800. On 17 November he reached Znaim, in Moravia, on the road to Brünn and Olmütz. That day he sent the Emperor Francis a deft promise of a 'durable and sincere friendship' if he would betray his Russian ally.[26] That day also Bonaparte received news of the epilogue to his dismal career as naval strategist: Admiral Villeneuve's fleet, which he had ordered to sail from Cadiz to the Mediterranean, had been destroyed by Nelson off Cape Trafalgar on 21 October. With more urgent anxieties on his mind, the news of Trafalgar made little immediate impact. Its significance would become clearer to him in years to come.

On 20 November Bonaparte reached Brünn, some fifty miles distant from the combined Russian and Austrian army at Olmütz, with Murat skirmishing ahead towards the village of Austerlitz. A week later Bonaparte still lay in Brünn. For he simply dared not advance that last fifty miles and attack the 80,000-strong enemy. He had now reached the limit of the distance even he would risk marching in search of a glorious peace. The impetus which had rolled with such momentum from the Channel to Ulm had finally died.

Only some 40,000 men – Soult's and Lannes' corps, the Imperial Guard and Murat's cavalry – now remained grouped under Bonaparte's own hand. The remainder lay dispersed across Austria in inevitable consequence of the concentric dangers to his flanks and communications – Bernadotte's corps in Bohemia some sixty miles to the west of Brünn, Davout's a hundred miles to the southeast near Pressburg, Mortier's sixty miles to the south at Vienna; and Ney's and Augereau's entirely out of reach at Innsbruck, Graz and Kempten (in Bavaria).[27]

Just as on the road to Turin in April 1796 or from Judenburg to Vienna a year later, only some miraculous deliverance could save Bonaparte from retreat, with all that that implied for a careerist as dependent as he was on the credit conferred by an unbroken series of successful coups. And again just as on those earlier occasions Bonaparte looked to a prompt peace to supply that deliverance. On 25 November an appeal to the Emperor Francis seemed to bear fruit when two Austrian plenipotentiaries arrived. Bonaparte sent them back to Talleyrand in Vienna. Meanwhile, the Prussian emissary was also nearing Vienna.

The precariousness of Bonaparte's situation was apparent to Francis and Alexander and their advisers at Olmütz. They had indeed only to hang on until all their forces were concentrated in the theatre, to prolong the conflict, and Bonaparte must almost certainly have succumbed to the kind of catastrophe to which he in fact fell victim at the hands of the Austrians, Russians and Prussians in the German campaign of 1813. But instead, after a fierce argument in which the cautious old Kutusov was overborne, the allied sovereigns rashly decided to venture on a battle. On 26 November their armies began to move southeast from Olmütz towards the French. On the 28th they reached a village about twelve miles short of Austerlitz. That evening Bonaparte ordered Bernadotte 'without losing a moment' to close on him; Davout as well.[28] He instructed Bernadotte to warn his troops that a battle would take place on the morrow or the day after.[29]

Some historians, basing themselves largely on Bonaparte's own later explanations,[30] have described how from 21 November onwards Bonaparte tempted his enemies into attacking him by a subtle display of military and diplomatic weakness. But although it is true that eyewitnesses remembered later how he had pointed out the terrain round Austerlitz as a future battlefield, this in itself proves nothing more than that he had chosen his ground if he had to fight. For there is in fact little evidence in Bonaparte's correspondence *before* the battle to bear out the story of an elaborate plot to induce the allied sovereigns to advance and give battle; indeed rather more evidence to the contrary. On 23 November he informed Talleyrand that 'I am not going to delay before returning to Vienna, having taken the decision to give my troops some rest, who stand in excessive need of it.'[31] On 26 November he allotted Davout some minor military errands near Pressburg, nearly a hundred miles from Austerlitz. On the same day he favoured Soult with his ideas on the best formation to adopt against the Russian masses (a mixture of line and column), but without the least overt or implied urgency.[32] Moreover, according to his orders on the 28th he was expecting the battle to take place on 29 or 30 November, by which time neither Bernadotte's nor Davout's main bodies could possibly have arrived. Nor were the medical arrangements for battle complete until 1 December.[33] Both these circumstances strongly suggest that Bonaparte was in fact taken by surprise by the enemy's advance. And finally, when informing Talleyrand on 30 November that a battle was imminent, Bonaparte averred that 'I have done much in order to avoid it . . .'[34] If this were not the case, why should he bother to tell an unnecessary lie in a private letter to his foreign secretary?

It is therefore likely that Bonaparte simply reacted to the enemy advance with the same high-speed opportunism as when attacked by Wurmser or Alvinzi in Italy, and afterwards fabricated a story by which what just happened became what he had planned all along.

By 1 December Bonaparte had encamped his army some five miles west of the village of Austerlitz which was to give its name to the coming battle. Although Bernadotte had now joined him by forced marches, there was still no news of Davout. Not for the first time Bonaparte was waiting anxiously for someone to turn up. Late that day he learned that Davout had reached Raigern – still some nine miles distant. At eight that evening, after riding along his front to observe the varying density of enemy watch fires, Bonaparte issued his final orders for deployment, any last-minute adjustments being reserved for a meeting with his marshals at seven the next morning.[35]

The army lay facing east in what seems to the casual eye just a featureless sweep of open rolling country indistinguishable from the rest of the plain of Moravia, and bleak now with winter's wet and cold. But in fact Bonaparte had chosen his patch of Moravia with care, and deployed his army to make the most of it. Defensively the position was very strong. Bonaparte's left flank rested securely on the tumbled, forest-clad hills, impassable to an army, which bounded the north of the plain. He posted his left and left-centre on a low, broad spur jutting south from this range of hills across the Olmütz–Brünn highway. Alongside the road just eastwards of this spur a lone hillock, strongly garrisoned with infantry and a battery of eighteen guns, offered further protection. To the south stretches another fine natural defensive feature, a long, low ridge, flat-topped, called the Pratzen, the steeper side of which faces east towards the Austro-Russian army's direction of approach. Nevertheless, Bonaparte did not occupy the Pratzen, but left it to fall into enemy hands in the course of their own deployment on 1 December. Instead, Bonaparte posted his right-centre and his right to the west of the Pratzen in the shallow valley of the Goldbach stream, with his extreme right flank resting on two villages, Telnitz and Sokolnitz, and the three large swampy lakes lying just to their south. For despite his inferior numbers Bonaparte was not looking to mere defence, however successful; he wanted a battle of annihilation.

In order to accomplish this, he proposed to tempt the enemy into encircling him by breaking through the south of his line and then sweeping up northwards in his rear. When the enemy had overextended themselves in this flanking move, he proposed to take them in their own flank with a smashing counter-stroke.

As the strategic bait he offered the road to Vienna, which he rightly judged would be thought by the enemy to form his line of communication, and which ran southwards very near the French positions. In fact his communications ran westward through Brünn to Linz. As the tactical bait Bonaparte offered his own deployment: strong (two corps, the Guard and the cavalry) on the northern half of his line; weak (a single corps, Soult's) on the southern half.

The enemy command swallowed these baits after much wrangling. For this time Bonaparte was facing neither an able commander like Melas or Alvinzi, nor even a stupid one like Mack, but a squabbling committee consisting of two sovereigns and their advisers. This committee finally decided that the Russian and Austrian troops already deployed on or behind the Pratzen plateau should advance southwestwards and attack the extreme right of Bonaparte's line, round the villages of Telnitz and Sokolnitz, break through, cut his supposed communications with Vienna, and swing north in order to surround him. It was an ambitious manoeuvre to undertake against so quick-thinking and quick-punching a commander and army; the more rash because it required close co-operation between corps of two different armies, one of which, the Russian, lacked war experience except against the Turks.

Late on 1 December Bonaparte issued the customary resounding pre-battle order of the day to his soldiers. Each of them, he wrote, must be inspired by the thought that 'these mercenaries of England' who hate France so much must be vanquished. This achieved, 'the peace I shall make will be worthy of my people, of you and of me' – a neat, if unintended, acknowledgment that the sovereign people were now no more than an extension of his own ego, and that he and the army formed an interest quite distinct from that of France.[36]

At two in the morning of 2 December 1805, the first anniversary of his coronation, Bonaparte learned that enemy guns, instead of being placed in battery on the Pratzen, were still on the move; indication that his bait had been taken. Had it not been taken, Bonaparte would have fallen back in retreat, an operation rendered the easier by the concentration of the main strength of the army near the Brünn road.[37] At five that morning, full darkness, hard frost, Davout with one division set off from Raigern on his nine-mile march to reinforce Soult's corps on the right of Bonaparte's line. Davout's arrival would bring Bonaparte's strength to some 65,000 against the enemy's 82,000. At seven Bonaparte met his other marshals, Soult, Bernadotte, Berthier, Lannes and Murat, at his headquarters. When the sun rose in a clear, cold sky – later to be celebrated as 'the sun of Austerlitz' – it illuminated dark masses of enemy troops sprawling across the plain directly opposite; more masses thickly smudging the crestline of the Pratzen some three miles away to the southeast. Down in the valley of the Goldbach Soult's corps lay invisible under a shroud of white mist scented and thickened by the smoke of bivouac fires. Bonaparte, upon his head the plain black bicorne hat that was to become his trademark, his now squat body clad in a grey greatcoat and the uniform of a colonel

Bonaparte's personal standard, ornamented with bees, the imperial symbol. *Bulloz*

of chasseurs of the Guard – white breeches, green jacket, red facings – surveyed the scene through his telescope. Back-lit by the rising sun, the enemy columns could be seen moving like heavy centipedes down off the Pratzen and across the low ground towards Telnitz and Sokolnitz. As the Pratzen emptied, Bonaparte knew that the enemy had swallowed his bait completely; that they lay at his mercy. After brief last-minute orders, his marshals, galloped off to rejoin their corps.

Bonaparte himself took no direct role in the often ferocious fighting of the day, remaining at his headquarters on high ground near the Olmütz–Brünn highway where he could survey the whole scene. Instead, he entrusted Soult with the conduct of the offensive against the Pratzen and the enemy centre. As he was somewhat oddly at pains to explain to his soldiers before the battle in his order of the day, if all went well 'I will hold myself far from the firing',[38] but if victory looked uncertain, 'you will see your Emperor expose himself in the front line.'

From the commencement the battle went, however, much as he had planned. While Soult's outnumbered troops round Telnitz and Sokolnitz gave ground before the onslaught of the enemy's outflanking wing, the remainder of his corps together with Bernadotte's swept up the long slope of the Pratzen and occupied it. This move, taking little more than half an hour, effectively decided the battle by separating the enemy's left wing from their right and rendering overall control of the battle by the enemy command impossible. The Austro-Russian army henceforward fought not so much in order to win as to save itself from destruction.

To the south of the battlefield the arrival of Davout, after a march of eighty miles in fifty hours, enabled the French to throw back the enemy columns which had penetrated to the west of Sokolnitz and Telnitz, trapping them between a lake to their left and the French troops on the Pratzen to their right. In the north of the field, astride the Olmütz–Brünn highway, the struggle swayed without a decision. But the centre, on the Pratzen, remained the key to the battle. All the enemy's courageous but disconnected attempts to throw French off it again and so reunite their army were repulsed. Towards midday, with mellow sunshine glowing on the slaughter of men, the French swept down southwards off the Prazten to strike the enemy's erstwhile outflanking wing in its own flank. In their panic flight the Austrian and Russian forces sought escape across the frozen lake and marshes to their south. The Austro-Russian right flank, now isolated, also gave way.

In only half a day Bonaparte had routed an army superior in number, inflicting casualties of 12,000 killed and wounded, and taking 15,000 prisoners and 133 guns, for the loss of some 8,000 men killed and wounded. Hounded by Murat's troopers, what was left of the allied army struggled away towards Olmütz in a state of dissolution. And the Third Coalition dissolved with it. Next day the Emperor Francis asked for an armistice, which Bonaparte granted on condition that the Russians withdrew to Poland. The victory equally solved Bonaparte's pressing cash problems by enabling him to fill the army's coffers with twelve million florins of Austrian gold levied from the hapless Francis; and there was more to follow.[39]

Austerlitz stands as Bonaparte's supreme professional performance; its conception brilliantly subtle, its execution as perfectly timed as a matador's sword thrust into his adversary's spinal chord. Yet Austerlitz was to become far more than merely a successful and professionally faultless military transaction; it was to become the grand set-piece of Napoleonic myth, written up again and again in lurid heroics by French historians. And Bonaparte himself launched the legend of Austerlitz on its way, himself provided the historians with all the romantic colour and detail they needed. He did so in the 30th Bulletin of the Grande Armée dated the day after the battle.[40] Not content with playing Hector, he was his own Homer as well, or perhaps rather Henty. In the 30th Bulletin we read how the Emperor visited his soldiers' bivouacs incognito the night before the battle, like Henry V, but how he was instantly recognized by his adoring soldiery; how they raised flaming faggots of straw on poles to illuminate the scene; and how 80,000 men (sic) presented themselves cheering before him, 'some to congratulate him on the anniversary of his coronation; others saying that the army would present its bouquet to him on the morrow . . .' On retiring into his bivouac, a straw shelter made for him by his grenadiers, so the Bulletin informs us, the Emperor observed: 'This is the most beautiful evening of my life, but I regret to think that I will lose a goodly number of these brave men. I feel . . . that they are truly my children . . .' The gripping yarn then carries the reader on through the events of the battle, to conclude with a thrust against England: 'May so much spilt blood, may so many miseries, be in the end visited on the perfidious islanders who are the cause of them!'

Yet a battle is not a heroic adventure, nor even a game where the prowess of the victor is to be admired for its own sake, but a piece of state business which serves – or ought to serve – national policy. The purely technical brilliance of Austerlitz has obscured the fact that but for the ineptitude of Bonaparte's conduct of foreign affairs, it need never have been fought.

On 26 December 1805 Austria signed the Treaty of Pressburg, by which she ceded the mainland territories of Venice (including the Istrian and Dalmatian coasts) to Bonaparte's kingdom of Italy, all her possessions in Germany, as well as the Tyrol and the Vorarlberg to Bonaparte's client Bavaria. She was no longer either a German or an Italian power. Had Austerlitz therefore at last brought 'the glorious peace' which the Directory and Bonaparte had first set out to win in the valley of the Po ten years before? It had not. Austria no more reconciled herself to these latest extortions than she had to earlier ones. Instead Austerlitz and Pressburg stung her into embarking on drastic reforms of her institutions and in particular her army. What she had lost by force she meant in her own good time to regain by force. And Austerlitz hardly encouraged Bonaparte himself to renounce ambition and live quietly on his winnings. Rather, so stunning a demonstration of the apparent omnipotence of force and the infallibility of his own genius loosed the last restraints. Henceforward he was driven on and on by a hunger for domination that no conquest could appease, only whet – the Casanova of power.

IX

I DESIRE ONLY YOU

BONAPARTE OPENED his new take-over programme in December 1805 with southern Italy. He announced that the Bourbon dynasty of the Two Sicilies (the territory of which comprised the boot of Italy plus Sicily) had ceased to reign, and dispatched Masséna with an army to enforce the edict. This operation entailed violating the Papal States, which straddled the waist of Italy. When Pope Pius VII protested, Bonaparte tersely informed him on 13 February 1806 that 'all Italy will submit to my rule,' and, speaking as the new Caesar and Charlemagne, demanded that 'Your Holiness will show the same respect for me in the temporal sphere as I bear towards him in the spiritual . . . Your Holiness is the Sovereign of Rome, but I am its emperor. All my enemies must be his also . . .'[1] The Pope none the less refused to bow to this ultimatum and join Bonaparte's European system. Bonaparte, incensed, withdrew his ambassador, Cardinal Fesch (his uncle; another Bonaparte family job), and all relations were broken off. Three years later Bonaparte was to resort to a more drastic solution of the problem presented by the Pope's independence of spirit: he had him kidnapped from the Vatican and imprisoned first at Savona and later at Fontainebleau.

With French troops spread throughout the Papal States and the mainland territories of the Kingdom of the Two Sicilies, armed force seemed again to have proved the effective universal tool of statecraft. Bonaparte therefore created a Kingdom of Naples and appointed his easy-going *bon viveur* of an elder brother, Joseph, as king. But affairs in southern Italy in 1806 only repeated the pattern of northern Italy ten years earlier, the initial French occupation proving the simplest part of the business. The peasants of Calabria rose in revolt, inspired by the mettlesome Bourbon Queen of the Two Sicilies, Maria Carolina, who had taken refuge in Sicily behind the guns of the Royal Navy. On 1 July 1806 a British force of 5,200 men under Major-General Sir John Stuart landed in Calabria to aid the rebels. On 4 July Stuart was attacked at Maida by General Reynier's division, 6,000-strong. The French, bawling *'Vive l'Empéreur!'*, came on in columns in their usual impetuous style. When they got within close range of the silent, scarlet English line, they were blasted to a standstill by English volleys. Reduced to a mob, the French were removed from the scene by the application of bayonets to their coat-tails. As a French officer remarked, 'Such a thing has not been seen since the Revolution.'[2] In its modest way Maida was one of the most significant military events of the era. Bonaparte entirely failed to take note of its lesson however.

News of Reynier's defeat exploded a general revolt throughout Calabria, wild mountain country much better suited to guerrilla warfare than the densely populated plains of northern Italy. Even though Stuart's force had soon to embark

in the face of overwhelming numbers, it took months of fighting by 40,000 French troops to crush the Calabrians; a fresh repetition of the lesson of 1796–7 that conquest also means entanglement. Bonaparte failed to take note of this lesson.

He had now achieved his immediate objective of submitting all Italy to his rule. This rule, an imperialism more heedless of the traditional native social and political order, and more dependent on bayonets than British rule in India ever was, has been interpreted by Bonaparte's admirers as the beneficient modernizing of a medieval, privilege-ridden society, and an idealistic attempt to forge a united and independent Italian nation.

North of the Alps Bonaparte looked to Holland and Germany for his new take-overs. In March 1806 he issued an ultimatum to the satellite Batavian Republic: accept his younger brother Louis as king, or be annexed to France. The Dutch leaders chose Louis, and what had once been one of the most fiercely independent countries in Europe was added to the Bonaparte family interests. Germany, however, presented a more ticklish problem. Before French armies first invaded the Rhineland in 1792, Germany had consisted of three hundred independent states, some of them free cities, many no larger than an English nobleman's estate; a myriad little sleepy world of tradition, privilege and fine music ruled over by electors and margraves and prince-bishops. Of all these states only Bavaria and Prussia ranked as European powers. Such political unity as Germany enjoyed lay in the allegiance of German rulers to the Holy Roman Emperor in Vienna; an allegiance often more symbolic than real. Into this remarkable civilization, a marriage of the medieval and the baroque, the armies of the French Revolution and Bonaparte had entered with the effect of a developer's bulldozer on the centre of an ancient city. Church property had been seized and sold up for cash; ecclesiastical rulers dispossessed in favour of secular neighbours; other states extinguished for the benefit of French client rulers. At each stage of the destructive process French influence had spread wider in the wake of French armies at the expense of the authority of the Holy Roman Emperor.

In 1806 Bonaparte decided that the time had come finally to rationalize Germany, as he had rationalized Italy, in order better to control it and exploit its resources. He declared the Holy Roman Empire abolished. The Holy Roman Emperor, Francis II, helpless after his disasters at Ulm and Austerlitz, could only acknowledge the deed by releasing the German princes from their allegiance and

'. . . one of the most significant military events of the era': the Battle of Maida in southern Italy, 4 July 1806, when an outnumbered English force under Sir John Stuart defeated an attack by General Reynier's division. Engraved by A. Cardon after P. J. de Loutherbourg. *National Army Museum, London*

Francis (1768–1835), elected Holy Roman Emperor in 1792 as Francis II. In 1804 he proclaimed himself Francis I, Emperor of Austria and in 1806 dropped the title of Holy Roman Emperor. Painting by Sir Thomas Lawrence. *Radio Times Hulton Picture Library*

proclaiming himself Francis I, Emperor of Austria. In place of the defunct Holy Roman Empire, which had lasted a thousand years, Bonaparte set up the Confederation of the Rhine, which was not to last so long. Petty principalities were amalgamated into larger groupings or absorbed by more important neighbours. The heads of grander German states, like Württemberg, Bavaria and, later, Saxony were promoted to the rank of king, though naturally denied the enjoyment of full sovereignty. Bonaparte appointed his brother-in-law, General Joachim Murat, as ruler of one of his new amalgamations, the Grand-Duchy of Berg. Bonaparte himself became Protector of the new Confederation, which was required to furnish him with an army of 85,000 men. For he had now moved on from realizing Europe's material assets to levying its manpower as well, so doubly lightening the cost of his ambition to France herself.

So it was that for the most immediate and personal of motives Bonaparte had carried out an act of the most far-reaching historical significance; he had disturbed a slumbering Germany and wrenched her into the nineteenth century. By rationalizing Germany's political patchwork Bonaparte opened the way towards her eventual unification into a great new nation-state – the very reverse of his own intentions. By his accompanying reforms of German institutions (and whatever the incidental benefits of the *Code Civil* and the abolition of privilege) he bequeathed to that future Germany the traditions of the Bonapartian state machine: unbridled authority at the top; an efficient bureaucracy; a passive, obedient people; the exaltation of will, force and the pursuit of power. And in the course of clamping his own domination more tightly on a subject Germany, Bonaparte bestowed one more unwitting gift, perhaps the most fateful of all – the spirit of German nationalism.

Every march of a French army across Germany since 1792 had left in its wake empty barns and byres, fields stripped bare, towns pillaged of cash and valuables, bitter memories of casual violence and insult. Bonaparte's advance to Ulm in 1805, unprecedented in numbers of troops and breadth of front, had caused the most widespread havoc of all.[3] Now in 1806, even though the war with Austria was over, the Grande Armée still lay quartered in southern Germany, partly to keep watch on Austria, partly to save the cost of feeding it at home. The sight of some 200,000 Frenchmen feeding off their country like a plague of sucking aphids deeply angered the German people. So too did the arrogant high-handedness of the occupation authorities. In July a journalist named Palm expressed German feelings in an anonymous pamphlet with the title *Germany In Her Deep Humiliation*. This pamphlet provoked Bonaparte's customary response to opposition. On 3 August he wrote to Berthier, commanding the Grande Armée in Germany:

> . . . I imagine you have had the booksellers [distributing the pamphlet] arrested . . . My intention is that they should be brought before a military court and shot within twenty-four hours . . . You will broadcast this sentence throughout Germany . . .[4]

In the event the booksellers' lives were spared at Berthier's recommendation. But Palm himself fell to a French firing squad on 25 August. Bonaparte thus handed nascent German nationalism the gift of its first martyr. He also finally if unintentionally goaded even the feeble Frederick William of Prussia into nerving himself for war.

The quarrel had been brewing throughout the year. Although Bonaparte in fact wished to have Prussia as an ally, it never seemed to occur to him that any relationship could exist between himself and a fellow ruler but that of high-handed overlord and acquiescent vassal. Even the Prussia of Frederick William did not take kindly to becoming a mere component in Bonaparte's European system. She took umbrage when without consulting her Bonaparte assumed a personal protectorate over southern Germany in the new Confederation of the Rhine. She submitted uneasily and under pressure to a treaty of alliance whereby she closed her ports to English trade in return for Hanover, which was not Bonaparte's property but George III's. She became the more uneasy and resentful when in August she discovered that Bonaparte was doublecrossing her by offering England the return of Hanover as part of a peace package (in the event abortive). False rumours that French troops were about to occupy Hanover panicked Prussia into ordering mobilization on 9 August. On 25 August the French shot the journalist Palm. On 26 September Prussia dispatched an ultimatum to Bonaparte demanding under threat of war that he withdrew the Grande Armée to the west of the Rhine by 7 October. This ultimatum marked the triumph of the Prussian war party led by the fiery and beautiful Queen Louise. But it meant that Prussia, having hung back in 1805 when her intervention alongside Austria and Russia might have proved decisive, had now chosen to fight alone except for the possible though as yet far-off aid of Russia.

Frederick William III, King of Prussia (1770–1840). By the Treaties of Tilsit in 1807 Prussia lost half her population. Painting (1814–18) by Sir Thomas Lawrence. *Copyright Reserved*

Bonaparte proved as oblivious in 1806 to evidence that Prussia was girding herself for war as to evidence of the Third Coalition the previous year. On 17 August he wrote to Berthier that they must 'think seriously about the return of the Grande Armée [to France], because it seems to me that all doubts over Germany have been dispelled . . .'[5] With something like amazement he finally accepted the fact of Prussia's 'ridiculous' preparations.[6] Whatever could have upset her? Perhaps this was a sign of another coalition, particularly since the Tsar had just refused to ratify a peace treaty with France. Were this the case, statecraft had its answer: 'I have [in Germany] 150,000 men, and with them I can subdue Vienna, Berlin and St Petersburg.'[7] Nevertheless, taking up a favourite pose as a highminded humanitarian, he sought to smooth down the Prussian King:

> If I am constrained to take up arms to defend myself, it will be with the greatest regret that I will employ them against Your Majesty's troops. I will consider such a conflict as a civil war, so closely intertwined are the interests of our states . . .[8]

Yet, however mysterious he found Prussia's hostility, there could only be one response if she failed to back down. As he put it to Berthier, 'they are asking for a lesson.'[9]

So the pattern of 1805 repeated itself – an unlooked-for war to redeem the consequences of a cavalier disregard for other countries' rights and feelings. The pattern of 1805 repeated itself militarily as well, for Bonaparte again awoke to danger so late that the logistics had to be organized and the army concentrated in a driving hurry – a breach of his own recent dictum that 'loss of time is irreparable in war; the reasons given to justify it are always bad . . .'[10] It was not until 5 September, nearly a month after Prussia began to mobilize, that he issued a warning order to Berthier; not until 15 September that he decided where to concentrate the army; not until the 19th that he evolved his final plan of campaign. Whereas in 1805 his soldiers crossed the Rhine with only one pair of shoes, in 1806 they marched without overcoats, and with the autumn and winter ahead of them.

Bonaparte's strategic plan was familiar too – another bold sweep round the enemy on to his *derrières*, with the usual object of forcing an early decisive battle and then returning in triumph to Paris. He concentrated the Grande Armée on the extreme right of the front between the Rhine and the Bohemian frontier, in the region round Bamberg, hoping thereby to tempt the Prussians into seeking to outflank his left and cut his apparently exposed communications with France. Once they had committed this false move, he would cut *their* communications instead, lunging swiftly north on a narrow front through the mountains of the Franconian Forest, past the Prussian left flank, and then wheeling westwards on Jena.

His enemy this time was formidable in reputation but little else. Half a century earlier under Frederick the Great the Prussian army, drilled to manoeuvre and fire like a machine, had been the finest in Europe. But in 1806 it still remained just as in Frederick's day, an antique weapon lovingly preserved in a glass case, worm-eaten and brittle. Like the Austro-Russian army at Austerlitz it was led by a committee, in this case of aged heroes of Frederick's campaigns. The committee now repeated Mack's mistake in the Ulm campaign by deciding on a forward strategy instead of waiting for Bonaparte behind the Elbe, where they would be in touch with their Russian ally. But the committee could not agree on the form this forward strategy ought to take: whether a direct advance on the French, or that very outflanking movement round the French left for which Bonaparte was hoping. During September the committee adopted and discarded plans like diners bewildered by an unaccustomed menu. It finally settled, in the fashion of such bodies, for a compromise offering the worst of all worlds. The main Prussian strength was deployed facing south behind the Thuringian Forest (a range of hills lying west of the Franconian Forest), with a weaker flank guard on the left, facing east behind the River Saale. No positive plan of action inspired these dispositions.

On 7 October the Prussian ultimatum expired. Next day the Grande Armée crossed the frontier of Prussia's ally, Saxony. Reconnaissance had revealed to Bonaparte the Prussian army's general dispositions; he knew that its principal weight lay to the west, on its right flank, and that therefore the way was clear for his offensive against its left flank and rear. By 14 October the Grande Armée, marching in a close, mutually supporting group of six army corps, had wheeled westward over the River Saale to a line Jena–Auerstädt. Here that day Bonaparte brought the Prussian army to battle. He had caught it while it was stumbling back along its line of communication in order to avoid encirclement, its formations in confusion, its high command in a hopeless muddle. It came into action piecemeal and fought without a plan. Even though the Prussians fought stoutly enough (one French division lost forty per cent of its strength), they proved too slow, rigid and mechanical in their tactics to withstand the turbulent onset and supple manoeuvring

of the French. In the twin battles of Jena and Auerstädt, some twelve miles apart, Bonaparte smashed the Prussian army to fragments, taking 25,000 prisoners, two hundred guns and sixty colours. The Duke of Brunswick, the Prussian commander-in-chief, was killed; the Prussian King and Queen themselves only just managed to escape in the press of fugitives.

Yet Bonaparte's own performance was nothing like so immaculate as at Austerlitz, marred this time by carelessness and misjudgment reminiscent of his Italian battles. Whereas he believed that he himself, at Jena, had defeated the bulk of the Prussian army, in fact his 75,000 men were attacking only 47,000 Prussians. Meanwhile, Davout with only 26,000 beat 45,000 at Auerstädt. Moreover, Bernadotte's corps took no part in either battle, lying instead all day midway between. For Bonaparte had omitted to amend Bernadotte's previous orders, and Bernadotte refused to depart from these even though Davout showed him his own new instructions from Bonaparte, which contained the following highly ambiguous reference to Bernadotte's role: 'If Marshal Bernadotte is with you, you can both march together; but the Emperor hopes that he will have reached the position [previously] assigned to him . . .'[11] For failing to act on his own initiative and march with Davout, Bernadotte later incurred Bonaparte's violent displeasure. Yet on other occasions subordinates who did depart from the strict letter of their orders could earn just as stinging a rebuke. The truth is that from the very outset of his career as a general-in-chief Bonaparte practised tightly centralized control of all operations, however distant, and demanded blind obedience to the orders which defined his subordinates' roles in his master plan.[12] Nor was Jena-Auerstädt the first occasion in his career when Bonaparte allowed a formation to lie idle for want of orders. During the Castiglione campaign in 1796 he left Serrurier's division, a sixth of his strength, without orders for four days at Marcaria, some twenty-five miles

Bonaparte at the Battle of Jena, 14 October 1806, as romantically visualized by the painter Horace Vernet. *Musée de Versailles. Photo: Musées Nationaux*

Marshal Bernadotte (1764–1844). Adopted as son and heir by the King of Sweden in 1810, he fought against Bonaparte, his old chief, in the 1813 campaign. *Radio Times Hulton Picture Library*

away. It only reached the battlefield after fighting began; another of Bonaparte's anxiously awaited and needlessly last-minute arrivals.[13]

Yet in Jena-Auerstädt Bonaparte had outwardly achieved an even more brilliant success than Austerlitz, bringing about the collapse of the leading military monarchy of the *ancien régime* in a single-day's fighting. The rest of the campaign was a tale of surrender with hardly a shot fired as the Grande Armée swept through Prussia in remorseless pursuit. By the end of the first week of November 1806 all that remained to King Frederick William III except for a few isolated fortresses were East Prussia and one army corps. So the gates swung open to yet another kingdom, and Bonaparte rode in to take possession, a conqueror to whom no feat now seemed impossible. On 24 October he slept in Frederick the Great's palace of Sans Souci at Potsdam, adding the Prussian hero's sword and decorations to the plunder he had sent back to Paris since 1796. On 27 October he made his entry into Berlin, passing beneath the Brandenburger Tor, monument to Prussia's vanished glory, in the midst of marshals and horse grenadiers of the Guard. On the steps of Frederick William's palace Bonaparte was welcomed by his own Grand Master of the Palace – the most illustrious squatter in Europe about to occupy another desirable but vacated residence.

It only remained to wrap up the war in routine fashion. On 28 October Bonaparte instructed his Intendant-General: 'You will forbid the paymasters to pay with money from France; they will pay with money from Berlin . . .'[14] Prussia was eventually to be mulcted of 160 million francs.[15] On 30 October the Prussian King signed a peace treaty ceding all his territories west of the Elbe and closing his remaining ports to English trade. All now seemed clear for Bonaparte to return to Paris and enjoy another triumph.

He chose not to do so. For the victory over Prussia heated his imagination, swelling it with a buoyant sense of limitless power and lofting it heavenwards. He repudiated the peace treaty with Prussia and on 21 November in a message to the Senate proclaimed vast new war aims which transformed the nature of the European conflict. He would conclude no more separate peace treaties with individual powers, but only a general settlement. As the *sine qua non* of such a settlement England must return all the colonies she had captured from France, Spain and Holland. Until such a peace was concluded he, Bonaparte, would evacuate no part of Prussia that he at present occupied. In other words he meant to dictate peace to Europe and England, using Prussia as a hostage.

> . . . we are certain that our peoples will appreciate the wisdom of our political motives, that they will decide with us that a partial peace would be nothing but a truce which would make us lose all the advantages we have won and only lead to another war, and that in the end it is only in a general peace settlement that France can find happiness. We are at one of those turning-points in the destinies of nations . . .[16]

Bonaparte's new policy brought immediate and far-reaching strategic consequences. A Russian army was advancing through Poland (a country then partitioned between Prussia, Austria and Russia) to support Frederick William III. By ratifying his peace treaty with Frederick William Bonaparte would have aborted this army's mission without firing a shot. Instead, remaining still at war with both Frederick William and the Tsar Alexander, Bonaparte now resolved to march on into Poland, smash the Russian army and so bring the Tsar to heel as well. Thus for the first time in his career Bonaparte undertook of his own volition a further long-distance march of the kind hitherto forced on him by circumstance; for the first time embarked on a fresh strategic gamble without a pause to rest his army and return to Paris.

But this new march would lead him into that desolate region of the North European Plain where Europe fades into Asia, a countryside of unimagined squalor and poverty, of few roads and those mostly unpaved. Here the Guibertian or Bonapartian system of warfare whereby an army fed itself by scavenging could not work, least of all with winter coming on. In November and December 1806 Bonaparte seriously addressed himself to the task of quartermaster for the first time in his life; sought to emulate his eighteenth-century predecessors by establishing a system of supply trains and magazines. The task was all the heavier because after the Jena campaign the Grande Armée stood in urgent need of re-fitting. A Wellington or a Marlborough would therefore have regarded the campaign in Poland as requiring a whole season's careful preparation. Bonaparte drove his army on into Poland without a pause, counting on captured stores to nourish the advance while he mobilized Prussian money and Prussian economic resources.

On 14 November he issued his Intendant-General, Daru, with an exhaustive instruction about clothing the army for a winter campaign – 85,000 overcoats and 250,000 pairs of shoes to be made and stocked in forward magazines, a fifth of the quantity by 1 December and at least two-fifths by 20 January 1807.[17] These were enormous burdens to lay on a pre-industrial economy. Painfully Bonaparte learned that to create an adequate supply system demanded more than the dictation of a series of comprehensive orders. On 12 December, for instance, he was complaining bitterly from Posen about the failure to fulfil his month-old orders about clothing; the administration, he groaned, could not be making worse progress.[18] But at the same time he dispatched another of his shopping lists, in this case for the equipping of field hospitals in Poland. Twelve thousand tents were to be turned into 9,000 pairs of sheets; 12,000 others into 40,000 shirts and pairs of trousers – an indication of the expected scale of sick and wounded.[19]

But in any case Prussia could not supply him with new recruits. Even after making levies on his German satellites he was forced to call up 80,000 French conscripts of the 1807 class, boys still under eighteen, to serve at home in order to release older men for field service. As he explained to his Director-General of Conscription on 23 November:

> I have by no means lost a lot of men; but the project which I have embraced is more vast than any I ever have [in the past], and as a result of this, it is essential that I am in a position to respond to all eventualities.[20]

So the cycle of Bonaparte's career revolved yet again, as success inspired further ambition, and further ambition beckoned him into yet more colossal undertakings. On 19 December Bonaparte arrived in Warsaw to direct in person the operations against the Russian army in Poland under General Bennigsen, who had now retired to Pultusk. Four days later the French advance began, a flounder along unpaved roads now reduced to swamps by the ceaseless rains. On 26 December the Grande Armée attacked two Russian corps at Pultusk and Golymin; clumsy and indecisive frontal assaults in the teeth of Russian cannon-fire. Bennigsen thereupon drew off again. The French, starving, exhausted, mud-bound, with more than 3,000 killed and wounded, could do no more. The course of events had fully borne out Bonaparte's prediction that 'the greatest difficulty will be in the means of subsistence'[21] – a difficulty he had nevertheless quite failed to overcome. For the first time since 1796 Bonaparte's gamble had failed to come off; he had failed to achieve his objectives in a single campaign; for the first time he would have to winter in the field and fight again the following year.

Yet to maintain the Grande Armée in its chosen winter quarters along the Vistula and the River Passarge (in East Prussia), a region where the peasants could barely feed themselves, demanded that virtually all food and fodder would have to be brought up from the rear. This task dwarfed even the unprecedented efforts Bonaparte had already had to make over supply since embarking on his Polish venture: six great magazines to be established and stocked – and kept stocked; the supplies then to be distributed from the magazines to the troops themselves. From then until the coming of spring brought relief he struggled ceaselessly with these unaccustomed problems. His correspondence teemed with complaints about the poor quality, late arrival or non-arrival of the stores he had ordered; overcoats and shoes from Berlin, for example, were 'worth nothing', coats from Leipzig 'ridiculously short'.[22] But even when supplies had been collected in the rear, want of wagons and the state of the roads prevented them reaching the troops. So the troops too soon came to realize that this was a different kind of war from those past promenades through the lush fields and rich cities of Italy and South Germany. On 6 March for instance Bonaparte was writing to Ney in reply to the marshal's complaints, 'I am truly distressed by the sufferings endured by your troops . . . but means of transport are lacking . . .'[23] The traditional system relying on private contractors to supply the transport having broken down, Bonaparte drew up a wonderful scheme for an army transport corps.[24] Nothing came of it because a transport corps on the scale required by the huge French conscript armies lay well beyond the resources of the French exchequer. The scheme was just another of Bonaparte's fantasies, as were – at least in part – the grandiose shopping lists for stores he kept issuing and impatiently following up. By July 1807, for instance, only 26,000 overcoats had been delivered out of the 85,000 he had ordered the previous November.[25] Confronted once again with a reality beyond his power to dominate he had sought refuge in makebelieve, just as in regard to the flotilla for the invasion of England.

And all through this gruesome winter of 1806–7 Bonaparte was attempting at the same time to run in person the internal affairs of western Europe, the foreign policy of his empire and a trade war with England. It is perhaps hardly surprising therefore that although his army escaped actual destruction through starvation and sickness on this particular occasion, Bonaparte showed himself no more than mediocre as a quartermaster – less able than Raglan, nowhere near as able as Wellington or Marlborough.

At the end of January 1807 the Russian army, whose patient ranks of peasants were inured to misery, proceeded to add to French distresses by launching a winter offensive in East Prussia against the left flank of Bonaparte's overextended line of winter quarters. Bonaparte reacted like a reposing lion whose tail has been trodden on, swiftly gathering his army together and pouncing at the Russian communications with Königsberg, their main base and Frederick William III's temporary capital. Yet of the French army's total strength of more than 400,000 men, only a quarter were available to take the field under Bonaparte in East Prussia; a sign of the extent to which French military power had now become dissipated in garrisoning Bonaparte's conquests and protecting his communications from partisans.[26] The pounce at the Russian communications failed, for the Russians realized their danger in time and fell back swiftly in retreat. Instead, Bonaparte had to content himself with merely pursuing the enemy; a slow march of horror through frost and blizzard in which the supply system completely broke down, and the French cavalry stripped the thatch off the peasants' hovels to feed their horses.[27]

At Preussisch-Eylau the Russians, 80,000 strong, halted to offer battle in defence of Königsberg. On 8 February 1807, a day of smothering snowfall, Bonaparte attacked them, even though his total strength had now shrunk to some 50,000–60,000 men. The Battle of Eylau displayed Bonaparte at his worst as a commander. At the beginning of the battle only two of his five corps were present under his own hand; another failure to concentrate in time. Although Davout was marching to support his right flank, Ney, off to the left pursuing a Prussian corps, did not receive an order from Bonaparte to close in on the main body until 2 p.m. on the day of the battle;[28] Bernadotte again received no order at all, and took no part in the battle. Meanwhile, the assaulting French columns, struggling forward blinded by snow over unreconnoitred ground, ran into murderous Russian cannon-fire; they fell back, shredded. The Russian commander, Bennigsen, launched his ponderous masses in a counter-stroke against the French centre. Only repeated charges by the French cavalry saved the army from collapse until Davout at last came into action on the right, threatening the Russian flank. Ney's corps, however, did not reach the battlefield until the very end of the day, just in time to counterbalance the arrival of the Prussian corps it had been pursuing. The battle died away in stalemate. Next day, when the Russians fell back towards Königsberg, Bonaparte did not, could not, follow them.

For Eylau was a battlefield such as neither he nor his army had ever yet seen. Over 15,000 Frenchmen, nearly a third of the army's deployed strength, lay dead or wounded in the snow. As Marshal Ney remarked when he surveyed the scene aghast on the day after the battle: 'What a massacre, and without result!'[29] To this then Bonaparte's pursuit of his personal adventure had now brought the men of France. In his papers there is a curious note in his own handwriting, which reads almost as if intended for insertion in some public-relations handout, and needs no comment:

On that occasion the Emperor said: 'A father who loses his children tastes none of the glamour of victory. When the heart speaks, glory itself holds no more illusions.'[30]

'... a battlefield such as neither he nor his army had ever yet seen': Eylau, in East Prussia, 8 February 1807, where nearly a third of the French army's deployed strength was killed or wounded. A propaganda version by the painter Adolphe Eugène Gabriel Roehn. *Château de Grosbois, Boissy-Saint-Léger. Photo: Librairie Hachette*

On 17 February he began his retreat to his winter quarters; the temperature twenty-two degrees of frost; the snow falling and falling, a silent terror enfolding the army's vehicles in its gentle but inescapable grasp; the wounded in the vehicles pleading in vain not to be abandoned; men and beasts struggling on, bellies empty. In the canon of Bonapartian disasters the retreat from Eylau stands midway in scale and suffering between the retreat from Acre and the retreat from Moscow. When the news seeped through to France, a nation used to being feasted on victories and forward marches became uneasy. Why had not the Emperor taken Königsberg after the 'victory' (for so Bonaparte's propaganda said it was) of Eylau? When Cambacérès voiced this disquiet to him, Bonaparte denied that Königsberg had ever been his objective – a flat lie.[31]

The campaigns against the Russians between November 1806 and February 1807 mark Bonaparte's second great strategic reverse in three years. Like the first, the failure to defeat the Royal Navy and invade England, it stemmed from overweening self-opinion and a consequent failure to acknowledge the magnitude of the task he was setting himself. The dynamic of French expansion – and of Bonaparte's own adventure – had faltered to a halt.

YET DURING THIS WINTER of care and setback Bonaparte did not lack consolation. The office of his *femme de campagne*, filled in Egypt by Bellilote Fourès, was taken up by Marie Walewska, the young wife of an elderly Polish nobleman. In November and December 1806, on his way to Warsaw, Bonaparte had hoped soon to be reunited with Josephine, who had reached Mainz on her way to join him. Josephine was tearful and unhappy, jealous and lonely. The freedom and frolic of her days at Louis XVI's court, the uncorseted opportunities of life under the Directory, had yielded to a kind of crowned imprisonment. For the Bonapartian court combined a Byzantine stiffness and hierarchy with the oppressively restrictive attitude to females of the Victorian bourgeoisie; and no female at that court dwelt under closer restriction than Josephine, whose entire day was spent under the wardership of ladies-in-waiting and other functionaries. Since she had failed to provide Bonaparte with a son to carry on his dynasty she lived in fear of being discarded in favour of a fertile second wife. All in all she was more eager now to receive her far-off husband's letters than she had been ten years ago when he was in Italy:

'. . . his essential power-base, the instrument by which he had finally reached the top . . .': the Army. Above left: Infantry of the line – Sergeant-Major eagle bearer, 1809; above right: Infantry of the line – sapper, 1809; below left: Infantry of the line – drummer, 1809; below right: Light infantry – *cornet de voltigeurs*, 1811. Details from the painting *Types militaries du 1ᵉʳ Empire* by Pierre and Hippolyte Lecomte. *Musée de l'Armée, Paris*

> Today is the anniversary of Austerlitz [he wrote from Posen on 2 December]. I have been to a ball in the city. It is raining. I am well. I love and desire you. My troops are in Warsaw. It has not yet turned cold . . . There is only one woman for me. Do you know her? I might paint her picture excellently for you; but I would have to make it too flattering if you were to recognize yourself; however, to tell the truth, my heart would only have agreeable things to say to you.
> These nights here are long, all alone . . .[32]

On 20 December he was writing to her from Warsaw that he hoped to be able to send for her in five or six days.[33] But on 2 January, after his return to Warsaw from Pultusk, he told her that though her misery touched him, she must submit to events; Warsaw was too far for her to journey; he recommended her to return to Paris. In the face of repeated entreaties from Josephine in the coming weeks, he stuck adamantly to this decision and for good reason. On 1 January 1807, at Broni, on the way back from Pultusk to Warsaw, he had met Marie Walewska and fallen in love with her at first sight, like a hero in one of his own youthful stories.

Certainly the circumstances of their meeting might have come straight from a romantic novel: the hero's coach stopping in a little town for a change of horses, a girl's voice calling in French from out of a crowd of peasants to plead for an interview; the encounter in his coach, when she was almost dumb with awe, and he gazed in wonder at a face like a child's, all beauty and innocence; with huge blue eyes lustrous with emotion, and an aureole of blonde hair. She pleaded for Poland's freedom and independence; Bonaparte handed her a bouquet of flowers he happened to have in the coach; and she vanished again into the crowd, a fair unknown.

After his return to Warsaw, Polish leaders divined who this fair unknown of Bonaparte's might be. She was therefore presented to him at a ball, inspiring him to send her a note afterwards: 'I saw only you, I admired only you, I desire only you . . .'[34] This missive struck the keynote of his courtship: the pudgy, jowly dictator had taken up afresh the part of Clisson, the lovelorn young warrior-hero. But Marie was the virtuous, devoutly religious wife of Count Walewice-Walewski. Bonaparte's breathy missive did not therefore strike a sympathetic note. But fortunately for him the success of his wooing did not only depend on his own love letters, for eminent Poles, led by Prince Poniatowski, saw Marie's body as a means towards the restoration of Poland's independence. They sent her a letter signed by all of them arguing that it was her patriotic duty, akin to a soldier's sacrifice in battle, to close her eyes and think of Poland. Meanwhile, Bonaparte was showing in his own letters to Marie that he had lost none of his romantic novelist's talent. 'You deprive me of rest!' ran one letter. 'Oh! Give a little joy, happiness, to a poor heart all ready to admire you . . .'[35] And again: 'Oh! Come! Come! All your desires will be fulfilled. Your country will be the dearer to me when you have taken pity on my poor heart.'[36] Marie, doubly besieged, finally surrendered. The amorous appointment was arranged. The lady, profoundly veiled, entered the gentleman's residence by a side entrance. The gentleman's unthinking reference in the course of a preliminary chat to 'your old husband' reminded the lady too vividly of her position, and she burst into tears. But Bonaparte, with a rare restraint which did him credit, forbore to enter into possession of his new conquest that night. Later the lady, back in the matrimonial home, received from her wooer a bouquet and garland of flowers all in diamonds. This she threw across the room in her emotional turmoil. A letter accompanied the gift:

> Marie, my gentle Marie, my first thought is for you, my first desire is to see you again. You will return, won't you? You promised me. If not, the eagle will fly to you . . .'[37]

In the event there was no need for the eagle to flap its wings; she repaired again at a later date to Bonaparte's apartments and discharged her patriotic duty. Thereafter, for the remainder of the campaign, she lived with him wherever his headquarters were stationed; perhaps in his estimation the perfect woman, being docile, soft, and

'... in his estimation the perfect woman, being soft, docile and lacking the disadvantages of a mind and will of her own': Marie Walewska, Bonaparte's Polish mistress. Painting by Robert Lefevre. *Radio Times Hulton Picture Library*

lacking the disadvantages of a mind and will of her own. Yet her sacrifice for Poland was to prove all in vain, so it was as well that she came to be genuinely attached to Bonaparte. For although he set up a puppet Polish administration (he had done so before he met Marie) and created a Polish army to serve him, he had no intention whatsoever of restoring an independent Polish state. This could only lead to the risk of unwanted embroilments with Russia and Austria in the future. One Pole at least, the national hero Kosciuszko, got Bonaparte's true measure: 'He thinks of nothing but himself. He detests every great nation, and he detests even more the spirit of independence. He is a tyrant.'[38]

FOR JOSEPHINE who, tormented with suspicion, jealousy and rumour, wrote to accuse him of consorting with unnamed ladies, Bonaparte had reassurance and comfort. In a letter of 10 May 1807 from the castle of Finkenstein, where he and Marie lived together, he told her:

> I love only my little Josephine, good, sulky and capricious, who knows how to pick a quarrel with grace, as she does everything, because she is ever lovable, apart however from the times when she is jealous; then she becomes all devilment. But let us return to these ladies. If I needed to busy myself with one of them, I assure you that I would wish her to have pretty pink nipples. Is this the case with those you speak of to me?[39]

X

AMBITION IS NEVER CONTENT

EVEN BY THE COMING OF SPRING Bonaparte had still not surmounted the problems caused by his failure to keep strategic ends and logistic means in due proportion. On 6 March 1807 he wrote to his Intendant-General that 'It is the penury of victuals which shackles all our operations.'[1] On the 12th he dispatched an urgent, even desperate, plea to Talleyrand in Warsaw, beseeching him, 'Perform miracles, but have sent to me 50,000 rations of biscuit per day . . .',[2] and adding later in the same letter, 'Today the destiny of Europe and the grandest calculations hang on supply' – a flourish of rhetoric already employed on more than one occasion in his career when he had similarly gambled himself into a quartermaster's nightmare. Yet beyond this crisis lay the larger question of the enormous effort required to mount a second campaign against the Russians.

All through the winter reinforcements of the 1807 conscript class had been trudging piecemeal through Germany. But now Bonaparte ordered the 1808 class to be called up as well: another 110,000 men to be pulled from the villages, clad, shod, and equipped; more unpopular work for the prefects; a heavy extra strain on the administrative machine. Early in April Bonaparte was enraged to learn that the 1808 class would not be ready to depart for three months. 'This is not the time to indulge in childsplay,' he fulminated to Cambacérès on 15 April, abjuring him: 'but, for God's sake, do not lose a moment; cut through all red-tape . . . It is soldiers we need in France and Germany, and not empty formalities. The speed of this call-up could make the [enemy] powers decide on peace . . .'[3] The satellite states too were forced to yield up their tribute of manpower – 112,000 men, or not far from double the number for 1806. The Grande Armée in Germany swelled to 400,000 men, twice its size in the previous campaign, although only a quarter of this total was actually available for operations against the Russians.

On 24 May the fortress of Danzig, stubbornly defended by a Prussian garrison since the autumn, fell at last; a treasure trove of stores which eased Bonaparte's immediate supply problems at a stroke. Nevertheless, it was not Bonaparte who opened the campaign of 1807, but the Russian commander Bennigsen, who on 4 June attacked Ney's exposed corps near Allenstein, amid the lakes and pine forests of East Prussia. While Ney fell back, Bonaparte launched a counter-stroke and brought Bennigsen to a halt. With typical opportunism Bonaparte decided to transform this successful counter-stroke into a great summer offensive. Manoeuvring constantly round Bennigsen's left flank in order to menace his communications with Königsberg, he forced him back in a series of hard-fought actions to Friedland, on the River Alle, twenty-seven miles southeast of Königsberg. Here, in a bridgehead west of the Alle, Bennigsen offered battle. It proved a major miscalculation which played into Bonaparte's hands. For the bridgehead was too narrow to offer room for manoeuvre under attack; it was split into separate sectors by an unbridged stream; and there was only one bridge leading back over the Alle in the rear of the Russian army, should it need to retreat. Bonaparte fully exploited these weaknesses. The Battle of Friedland, 14 June 1807 (the anniversary of Marengo; a happy omen to a superstitious Corsican), displayed him at near the top of his form as a man of battle. Pivoting his army on its left wing, he sent his right and centre smashing into the Russian left flank, lying to the south of the stream which bisected the field. The Russians, who fought with their customary stoicism, bloodily repulsed the initial French onslaught. But after the enemy masses had been torn open by the fire of a battery of thirty-six guns – the first time that artillery really decided a Bonapartian battle – the French fought their way into the heart of the Russian bridgehead. The enemy struggled back across the Alle by a ford and retreated towards Königsberg, leaving behind them nearly 20,000 dead, wounded and prisoners and eighty guns. Bonaparte had at last gained that decisive victory which had eluded him for eight months. The worry and the waiting were over; he was on the move again; the adventure had recommenced. Gleefully he wrote that night to Josephine:

> My love, I can only write you a word, because I am really tired . . . My children have worthily celebrated the battle of Marengo; the battle of Friedland will be just as famous and just as glorious to my people . . . it is a worthy sister of Marengo, Austerlitz, Jena . . .[4]

Next day Königsberg fell, yielding more booty in food and fodder. On 19 June Bonaparte entered Tilsit on the Niemen, and Bennigsen asked for an armistice. On 25 June Bonaparte met the Tsar Alexander, at the Tsar's suggestion, to open discussions about a peace settlement. A raft moored on the Niemen midway between the banks held by each army supplied the venue for their private meetings. No scene could have been more worthy of romantic drama than this encounter between two emperors for the purpose of carving up eastern Europe from the Baltic to the Bosphorus, more satisfying to Bonaparte after the anxieties of the winter, or more gratifying to the underdog of Brienne who would always dwell within him.

Accompanied by suites of grandees whose garb would have dimmed the plumage of coveys of Lady Amherst Pheasants, the two leaders were rowed over at noon on the 25th to their waterborne pavilion of striped and bepennoned canvas. They met; they embraced; they passed into the privacy of their conference chamber. It seemed that a lovely friendship had begun to burgeon, each of them seeing the other's greatness as a reflection of his own, and Bonaparte in any case being apt to treat a victory over a fellow ruler as a sound basis for inaugurating cordial relations. That night he reported to Josephine that he was really pleased with Alexander: 'He is a truly handsome, good and youthful emperor; he has a better mind than is commonly supposed . . .'[5] Day after day the two men met, the most exclusive club in the world. The courtesies continued: on one occasion when the Tsar was to dine with Bonaparte in the French camp, Bonaparte would not let him return to his own camp to change, but sent for all the articles of his evening

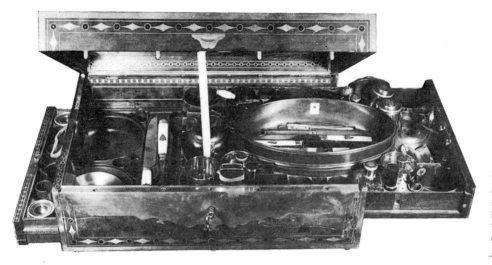

'. . . his own gold toilet-
case . . .': the *nécessaire*
used by Bonaparte during
his campaigns and lent at
Tilsit to the Tsar. *Musée
Carnavalet, Paris. Photo:
J. Hyde*

costume, offered him the services of his, Bonaparte's, own valet, his own gold
toilet-case, cravats, handkerchiefs.[6]

On 7 July their communion bore fruit in the Treaties of Tilsit. Prussia (which had
been barred from the negotiations) lost all her territories west of the Elbe, partly to
Murat's Grand-Duchy of Berg, partly to a new Kingdom of Westphalia bestowed
by Bonaparte on his youngest brother Jerome; she also lost all her Polish lands apart
from a narrow strip linking Pomerania to East Prussia; a total of half her population.
By a separate treaty Bonaparte imposed on her a heavy war indemnity, French
evacuation of her territory being conditional on its payment. The Prussian army
was limited to 42,000 men. In an empty gesture towards Polish aspirations to
independence, Bonaparte created the puppet Grand-Duchy of Warsaw out of
Prussia's lost Polish territory. As for Russia herself, she ceded no lands on her
western borders, only certain possessions in the eastern Mediterranean; she agreed,
however, to join Bonaparte's blockade of English commerce, the so-called
Continental System.

So Bonaparte seemed to have pulled it off again, emerging from perhaps the
grimmest episode of his career to his most spectacular triumph. Yet Tilsit was not
quite so brilliant a coup as it appeared. By making a separate peace with Russia and
Prussia Bonaparte had retreated from the resolution he had proclaimed in the
previous November of being satisfied with nothing less than a general peace
settlement (that is, including England and based on the return of all the colonies
captured by her). Moreover, the mildness of the peace terms with Russia reflected
the fact that Russia had no more suffered a national defeat than Austria at the time of
the Peace of Leoben ten years earlier, but only lost a single battle and that outside her
own territory. The terms also reflected, again like Leoben, the underlying
precariousness of Bonaparte's own situation. His army now lay nearly 1,000 miles
from Paris as the crow flies, its communications through Germany exposed to
attack by partisans. Despite the victory at Friedland and the stores captured in
Danzig and Königsberg Bonaparte was neither militarily nor logistically strong
enough to march on into Russia in order to cow Alexander into a proper

'. . . the most exclusive
club in the world . . .':
the raft in the middle of
the River Nieman where
Bonaparte and the Tsar
Alexander negotiated the
Treaties of Tilsit in 1807.
Mansell Collection.

Bonapartian peace. Politically moreover he stood in urgent need of an early return to Paris, where, as his Minister of Police kept reminding him, the mice were beginning to stir after the long absence of the imperial tom-cat.

Tilsit therefore represents, as had Leoben, Bonaparte's determination to capitalize on a transient and superficial military success before time could dissipate its effect. And true to the tradition of Bonaparte's peace treaties, it rendered a future conflict more rather than less likely. For each emperor went home believing that the other had fallen under his own sway; illusions that could only lead to future mischief, especially since they nourished clashing ambitions, unresolved at Tilsit, with regard to the Turkish Empire and the eastern Mediterranean.

O N 27 JULY 1807 the boom of cannon from the Invalides announced to the citizens of Paris that their master had returned after ten months in the field. Heralds in mock-medieval costume proclaimed the Treaties of Tilsit in the smoking glare of torches, and Bonaparte had the title of 'the Great' awarded to himself, like Louis XIV after the Peace of Nijmegen in 1678.[7] The French people, haplessly chained to his destiny as they were, hoped that true peace had come at last; for them, for Bonaparte also, the winter of Eylau was now like a mere uneasy dream forgotten in the warmth of a bright morning. It was a time for celebration: military parades, balls, fêtes. Bonaparte's own fête on 15 August – 'the Emperor's Birthday' and 'the Feast of St Napoléon' – was remembered afterwards as the most glittering, the most evocative of popular joy, in the whole brief history of his Empire. Upon entering the Cathedral of Notre-Dame for his birthday devotions, Bonaparte assured the Archbishop of Paris in a brief speech that:

> . . . everything comes from God. He has granted me great victories. I come in the premier capital of my Empire to render thanks to Providence for its gifts, and to recommend myself to your prayers and those of the clergy.[8]

Next day, in a speech from the throne on the opening of the *Corps Législatif*, he reported on his triumphs and the glossy condition of his Empire; 'all nations,' he said, 'rejoice with one accord to see England's malign influence on the Continent destroyed for ever.'[9] Only a week afterwards came the wedding between brother Jerome, now King of Westphalia, and Princess Catherine, daughter of the King of Württemberg. It gave occasion for further lavish entertainments, of which the discerning judged the ball given by Murat ('the Grand-Duke of Berg') at the Elysée Palace on 29 August to have been by far the smartest. And still military parade succeeded military parade in celebration of peace. Bonaparte seemed now to stand safely on a sunbathed summit of achievement, far above the swirling clouds of struggle and danger; ruling an empire that extended from the Pyrenees to the Vistula, from the North Sea and the Baltic to the Ionian Sea; commanding an army – Frenchmen, Dutchmen, Germans, Italians, Poles – that numbered 800,000, a total without precedent in European history.[10] Only England still continued to oppose him, and she would soon succumb to economic collapse, now that virtually every port in Europe had been shut to her exports. In his study at St Cloud, engorged with power, Bonaparte bent himself afresh to the task of making Europe fit for his ego to live in.

'. . . military parade succeeded military parade in celebration of peace . . .': the city of Paris celebrating the return of the Imperial Guard in November 1807. *Bibliothèque Nationale, Paris. Photo: Collection Viollet*

Much of this task had already been accomplished. Beyond the frontiers of Greater France the new 'Grand Empire' created by the aggrandizements of 1805–7 was ruled by Bonaparte either through obedient native potentates like the kings of Bavaria or Saxony, or through members of his own family by blood or marriage – King Louis of Holland, King Jerome of Westphalia, King Joseph of Naples, Murat, Grand-Duke of Berg, Eugène de Beauharnais, Viceroy of Italy – whose sovereignty was limited to carrying out Bonaparte's detailed instructions like super-prefects. After appointing Eugène in 1805, for example, he wrote to him: '. . . you must not under any pretext whatever, even if the moon threatened to fall on Milan, do anything that falls outside your authority . . .'[11] This system of satellite hereditary monarchies within the family curiously blended traditional methods of extending and ruling an empire, and a Mediterranean clan connection, a *cosa nostra*.

Yet although Bonaparte has been credited with a strong family sense, the family none the less remained for him simply the closest of all extensions of his own self. Each of his kin was expected to yield his or her own desires to Bonaparte's will. When Jerome returned from a visit to America with an American wife, Elizabeth (Betsy) Patterson, Bonaparte and his mother forced an annulment of the marriage in 1804, even though Betsy was pregnant, on the score that Jerome, at twenty-five, was under age by French law and could not marry without his parents' permission. When Lucien married his mistress, Madame Joubertheau, a notorious *horizontale* who had born him a son, Bonaparte sought to bully Lucien into giving her up and marrying a Spanish princess. Despite Lucien's resolute refusal, Bonaparte continued

to pester him over the matter year after year. In April 1804 Lucien even quit public life and retired into exile in Italy because of this quarrel. In December 1807 the two brothers met in Mantua while Bonaparte was making a royal progress through his Italian kingdom. Again Lucien refused to trade his wife for a throne and a place in Bonaparte's grand dynastic design. He did, however, promise to send his daughter Charlotte to Bonaparte's court. Bonaparte's report of the interview to brother Joseph well conveys his view of family relations:

> His [Lucien's] thoughts and language are so far from mine that I had difficulty in grasping what he wanted . . . I have exhausted all the means in my power to recall Lucien, who is still in his first childhood, to the employment of his talents for me and for the country. If he wishes to send his daughter, she must leave without delay, and he must send me a declaration whereby he places her entirely at my disposition, because there is not a minute to lose, events are pressing, and it is necessary that my destinies be accomplished . . .[12]

But on this occasion Charlotte stayed at home, after all, instead of providing another usefully marriageable Bonaparte.

Even Letizia incurred her son's impatient displeasure. The habits of a harsh early life and an instinctive distrust of the future made her frugal; simplicity of character made her prefer a quiet domestic existence. So Bonaparte nagged away at her without success to squander money on ostentation worthy of 'Madame Mère'. And since his relatives kept on regarding themselves as individuals pursuing their own lives instead of components neatly fitting into Bonaparte's schemes, more family trouble lay in store for him in the future.

As personal ruler of Greater France – which now included Belgium, the Rhineland, Piedmont, Genoa and the French-speaking parts of Switzerland – Bonaparte provides the prototype of the ruthless corporation boss of the modern age. Yet as a corporation boss he suffered from the serious defect of being temperamentally unable to delegate responsibility or trust his subordinates:

> Within a State, nothing goes by itself [he explained to the Viceroy of Italy on 11 February 1808]; every month I make a review of the orders I have given, and I check on their execution. This is the only way business makes progress; otherwise ministers go to sleep and willingly let everything slip into oblivion . . .[13]

In the dank shadow of such a domination neither talent nor initiative could flourish; only the fungus growth of bureaucratic mediocrity. One of his first acts on returning from Tilsit was to sack his Foreign Minister, Talleyrand, a man too independent in ideas and behaviour, and replace him with a dutiful chief clerk, Champagny; the diplomatic equivalent of Berthier. One by one the able ministers who had adorned the Consulate were to give place to ciphers and sycophants. The magistracy and the prefects were subjected to periodic purges aimed at replacing old revolutionaries or independent spirits of any kind with subservient creatures, often local members of the old noblesse. Year by year Bonaparte whittled down or ignored the elective principle still written into French institutions. He busied himself personally with the censorship, the printed word being specially given to the sin that, in his own words, 'it appeals to public opinion instead of to authority'.[14] The prefects, *gendarmerie*, informers and the postal censorship kept watch over opinion, particularly those persons suspected of potential opposition, like old Chouan rebels. The awkward were imprisoned without trial or forced to reside, like Madame de Staël, in a designated place under supervision; even consigned to lunatic asylums like the poet who in 1804 clearly demonstrated his madness by uttering the epigram: 'Yes – Napoléon is great – a great chameleon.'[15] The life of ideas in France, so rich before 1789, sputtered out.

Yet Bonaparte was much concerned with encouraging culture, so desirable an embellishment of a grand empire like his. Among his varied wardrobe of personalities, the role of man of letters and *savant* still remained a favourite, especially since it could now be combined with that of imperial patron. In April 1807, for example, he took time off from the East Prussian campaign to dictate a homily to the Minister of the Interior in his *Discours de Lyon* style on the nature of history, the purpose of poetry and other such simply decided questions, and directing the Minister as to how historians, poets and their fellow intellectuals might be most efficiently deployed.[16] All then that bursaries, prizes, honorific titles and bureaucratic organization could do for culture was therefore done in the Bonapartian empire. A new class of official literary lackeys prospered; precursors of the Writers' Union hacks of Communist states in the twentieth century. Composers wrote stirring hymns to victory. Architects, politically harmless fellows, greatly flourished, for triumphal arches were much in demand, new quays along the Seine were under construction, a new opera house was projected, a new bourse. The modern Caesar meant to have his own Rome. 'What is grand is always beautiful,' he pronounced; and official architecture, as the world now knows it, was born.[17] Engineers too thrived, for true to the Roman example Bonaparte inaugurated canals, aqueducts and roads. In the case of such roads as the new Mont Cenis Pass, the purpose was strategic. Otherwise, as he himself explained in a letter to the Minister of the Interior on 14 November 1807, he was prompted by a mixture of motives:

> I mean the glory of my reign to consist in changing the face of the territory of my empire. The execution of these great works is just as necessary to the interests of my peoples as to my own satisfaction . . . One must not pass by on this earth without leaving behind remains which recommend our memory to posterity . . .[18]

Yet even though he had now harnessed so much of European life to the service of his own satisfaction, the parvenu's hopeless wish to be the genuine article still haunted him. Josephine recorded how the court life of Louis XVI (whom Bonaparte actually referred to as 'my uncle') was rummaged for precedents as to exactly the correct etiquette to be followed; how surviving ornaments of that court came to occupy the key ceremonial posts in the entourage of the self-made emperor.[19] His admiring personal secretary, Méneval, wrote: 'I will not deny that the Emperor had a penchant for the remaining representatives of the elite of the old noblesse at court . . . Those polite manners . . . the tradition of taste and urbanity which they brought to his court had an effect on his mind which he strove to conceal. He thought that in his relations with European courts, their membership of the freemasonry of aristocracy would prove highly useful to him.'[20] In March 1806 Bonaparte began to create his own hereditary noblesse by awarding dukedoms to his marshals. Where possible, each took his title from the scene of some distinguished service, so that, for example, Davout became Duke of Auerstädt. All were granted hereditary fiefs in order to support their new style in appropriately splendid fashion. In March 1808 Bonaparte's noblesse became fully fledged. Ministers, prefects, mayors of large towns could aspire to baronies; members of the Legion of Honour to knighthoods[21] – more work for the costumiers. Here was yet another abandonment of a fiercely held conviction of Bonaparte's youth, in this case that aristocracy was a social evil, a prop of royal tyranny. The abandonment was prompted by a characteristic blend of romantic glorying of self and political engineering. In his own words when inaugurating dukedoms in 1806, he wanted to reward 'great civil and military services which have been or which will be rendered to us, and in order to give new support to our throne and surround our crown with fresh lustre.'[22]

With regard to the mass of the nation Bonaparte's principal exercise in political engineering in 1806–8 lay in evolving a state education system, the *Université de France*, divided into primary, secondary and higher grades. Bonaparte or his agent, the Grand Master of the University, prescribed in detail the syllabuses and regulations which governed the life of every school and college, and appointed all the staff, even down to the primary schools. From one end of France to the other every child of an age was to take the same lesson at the same time, and change class to the beat of drum. A corps of teachers, properly indoctrinated, subject to an oath of obedience, would ensure that Bonaparte possessed, as he put it, 'the means of directing the political and moral opinions of the country.'[23] For he had long believed that such direction was vital:

> So long as the people are not taught from their earliest years whether they ought to be republicans or royalists, Christians or infidels, the State cannot properly be called a nation, for it must rest on vague and uncertain foundations . . . In a properly organized State there is always a body destined to regulate the principles of morality and politics.[24]

Meantime, he relied on the priests and the Imperial Catechism for French children:

> Q. What are, in particular, our duties towards the Emperor, Napoleon?
> A. We owe him love, respect, obedience, fidelity, military service, all the contributions ordered for the defence of the Empire and Throne, and fervent prayers for his welfare and the prosperity of the State.
> Q. Why are we bound to show these duties towards the Emperor?
> A. Because God has established him as our Sovereign, and has rendered him His image here on earth, overwhelming him with gifts in peace and war. To honour and serve our Emperor is, therefore, to honour and serve God himself . . .

QUEEN LOUISE OF PRUSSIA, who pleaded in vain with Bonaparte at Tilsit in her country's cause, said of his appearance that he had the head of a Caesar. She did not say which – Julius, or one of the later emperors whose busts were rendered by their sculptors as images of crude power, meaty and massive. Queen Caroline's lady-in-waiting, the Countess von Voss, a violently hostile witness, saw a Bonaparte 'with a fat, swollen face, very corpulent, besides being short and entirely without grace. His great eyes roll gloomily around; the expression of his features is severe; he looks like the incarnation of fate; only his mouth is well shaped, and his teeth are good . . .'[25] Even the official painters, however, could not conceal that Bonaparte now verged on the stout; that the Byronic features of 1800 had coarsened into a thick-cheeked mask of self-will. The savageness in the little boy at Brienne, the force of personality cracked like a whip by the new commander of the Army of Italy, had matured into a presence so formidable that Bonaparte had only to enter a room for its occupants, be they even marshals, to fall into apprehensive silence. He employed rage – always unleashed on the victim in front of an audience – as a weapon of ascendancy. On such occasions, according to his secretary, Méneval, 'his face took on a severe and even terrible expression. He worked his forehead and in between his eyebrows . . . the eyes flashed lightning. The flanks of his nose swelled, blown up by the storm within . . .'[26] This tumescence of the features served as the prelude to torrents of barrack-square abuse. As Lord Malmesbury fastidiously put it in 1803, 'when Bonaparte is out of his ceremonious habits his language is often coarse and vulgar.'[27]

'. . . a thick-cheeked mask of self-will . . .': Bonaparte, about 1808, in a painting by Jacques-Louis David. *Musée Bonnat, Bayonne. Photo: Musées Nationaux*

Yet such rage served him as a cane in the cupboard rather than one in constant use. Towards his loyal entourage he usually displayed another face: 'In its normal state', wrote Méneval, 'his visage was calm, gently serious. It lit up with the most gracious smile whenever he was warmed by good humour or by a wish to be agreeable . . .'[28] He loved to tease, gilding his own pleasantries with 'a noisy and bantering laugh',[29] and the ladies of the court had to accustom themselves to imperial critiques of their costume. It was the highest compliment for a subordinate to have his ears pulled, or undergo some similar physical familiarity. Méneval records that on days when Bonaparte found himself bored and restless, he would 'come and sit on the corner of my desk, or on the arm of my armchair, sometimes on my knees. He would pass his arm round my neck, and amuse himself by gently pulling my ear, or tapping me on the shoulder or on the cheek . . .'[30] Such condescension won for Bonaparte the love and devotion so often accorded to famous men by those about them. And Bonaparte himself, who could be so ruthless towards those who crossed him, displayed profound attachment to any person who had ever served him or played some role in his life. He awarded pensions to the former head of the *Ecole Militaire* at Brienne and to the former royal inspector-general of *écoles militaires* for example; gave preferment to old fellow pupils at Brienne. A drunken and useless coachman was kept on simply because he had driven a wagon at Marengo. No old household servant could be sacked without Bonaparte's personal permission.[31] Nevertheless, even the admiring Méneval had to acknowledge that as the price of his kindness Bonaparte demanded not merely loyal service but total self-abnegation, subjecting even his servants' friendships to his approval.[32] Marshal Lannes, shrewder than Méneval, wrote of his own personal relationship with Bonaparte: 'I have always been the victim of my attachment to him. He only loves you by fits and starts, that is, when he has need of you.[33]

B Y ONE OF THOSE curious discords in his makeup, Bonaparte, despite his hardiness amid the fatigues and discomforts of a campaign, liked his physical luxuries when in a palace. He soaked himself in baths so hot that his physician warned that they could enfeeble him. Each morning he brushed the skin of his shoulders and torso himself, whereupon his valet completed the delicious process by roughly rubbing down his back. A sponge of eau de Cologne over his fine hair and the rest of the flask over his white body completed his toilet. His working day began before breakfast, when he conferred with his closest officials and studied papers which had been prepared for him overnight. He breakfasted alone; usually a ten-minute affair, although sometimes prolonged by interviews with scientists, artists or men of letters. Then, in a sombre study – it might be at St Cloud or the Tuileries or Fontainebleau – rich with the olive-greens, the mahogany, the gilt and the bronze, the sphinxes and the griffons of that decorative style to which his empire gave its name, he set about transacting the affairs of his dominions. His powerful mind ground up one topic after another, from diplomacy and war to the internal arrangements of the opera. Of all the state papers stacked before him, it was the monthly orders-of-battle of the army and navy, complete to each unit's numbers and colonel's name, and bound in red moroccan leather, that he found most rewarding:

> He ran over them with delight, and said that no work of science or literature gave him so much pleasure. His astonishing memory took in all the details . . . he was less at home with the spelling and pronunciation of names; he never remembered them correctly . . .[34]

Partly because he wrote so illegibly and spelled so badly, partly because his thoughts outran his power to put them on paper, he relied on dictation:

> Napoleon dictated only while walking about. He sometimes began when seated, but at the first sentence he would get up. As he got into his subject he would yield to a kind of twitching movement of the right arm, which he twisted while pulling at the cuff of his uniform . . . He found the words he wanted without effort. If they were sometimes inaccurate, even this inaccuracy added to their energy and still painted marvellously on one's mind what he wanted to express . . .[35]

In the absence of shorthand, however, which was yet to be invented, the scribbling of his secretaries tended to lag behind Bonaparte's voluble dictation, and they therefore learned to draft when necessary their own versions of his instructions for him to sign.

Bonaparte usually lunched alone; simple fare accompanied by watered Burgundy and a single cup of coffee, which he gobbled down like a dog. He dined at six *à deux* with Josephine, sometimes later if business was pressing, and afterwards they would pass an hour together before she returned to her own apartments; for all their jealousies, infidelities and tantrums he still loved her after his fashion. Then his librarian would call with a selection of the latest books. Bonaparte would rummage through them with the itchy-fingered impatience he displayed in all he did, chucking on the floor or even on the fire any that failed to take his fancy or, worse, annoyed him. At ten o'clock he issued orders for the morrow's business and retired, whereupon Josephine would often come and sit on the end of his bed and read to him; a cosy domestic close to the imperial day. But insomnia or urgent affairs would frequently fetch him out of bed again in the small hours, and set him striding up and down in turban and white nightgown, hands behind back, fingers in his snuff box, and dictating away to a sleepy secretary freshly dragged from the pillow.

Here then was another Bonaparte, domestic, living a life of virtuous routine enlivened only by official meetings or functions, imperial progresses and weekly forays into the forests of Rambouillet or Fontainebleau to hunt or shoot. Yet this was still the same person who on the day after his coronation had regretted that:

> I have come too late; men are too enlightened; there is nothing great left to do . . . Look at Alexander; after he had conquered Asia and been proclaimed to the peoples as the son of Jupiter, the whole of the East believed it . . . with the exception of Aristotle and some Athenian pedants. Well, as for me, if I declared myself today the son of the eternal Father . . . there is no fishwife who would not hiss at me as I passed by . . .[36]

Tilsit, for all its éclat, could hardly satisfy the aspirations of a man who entertained regrets that he was unable to make himself into a god. As Bonaparte himself had written with the sageness of youth in *Le Discours de Lyon*, 'Ambition is never content, even on the summit of greatness.'[37]

So it was that within barely three weeks of signing the Treaty of Tilsit he had set in motion preparations for his next adventure.[38] This time he looked southwards beyond the Pyrenees; to the Iberian Peninsula; to Lisbon, on the River Tagus, where English ships, barred from the rest of Europe's ports, still flaunted in his face the union flag.

XI

HIS CURIOSITY TO SEE THE DEAD

Although in 1807 the balance sheet of Empire, with its assets of peoples and territories and military manpower, looked so impressive, the true situation was otherwise – one of strain and overstretch. For Bonaparte's power rested on no stable foundation of consent either on the part of the peoples he ruled or of the remaining independent states of Europe. No natural equilibrium prevailed on the Continent therefore; only one maintained artificially by the constant exertion of force, like a hand holding down one pan of a pair of scales to counterpoise a heavy weight in the other. This did not disquiet Bonaparte, for a decade of experience had only served to confirm his belief that an army offered the solution to all political questions. For this reason he felt no hesitation in embarking on yet another ambitious take-over bid.

On 12 October 1807 he ordered General Junot, commanding the 'Corps of Observation of the Gironde', 20,000 strong, to march forthwith on Lisbon across the territory of Spain, his subservient ally. Very soon Junot's men became the first of hundreds of thousands of French soldiers to discover that Spain was a country of immense and empty distances, a gaunt land of barren plateau and brown rock where an army without its own supply train must go famished. Junot's army went famished; a circumstance which evoked the stern reproach from Bonaparte on 5 November that 'I will not hear of a march being slowed for a single day on the pretext of lack of victuals: such a reason is only good enough for men who wish to do nothing; 20,000 men may live anywhere, even in a desert.'[1] With this pronouncement Bonaparte sounded another major theme of the Peninsular War, that of his own unwillingness to confront its realities.

On 12 November 1807 he dispatched further instructions to Junot. He was to seize the Portuguese fleet and fortresses, disband the army, send the Portuguese Prince Regent back to France under guard; seize all English goods and ships, all jewelry and objects of value and sequester the Portuguese revenues.[2] Junot's troops, soon to be renamed 'the Army of Portugal', were of course to live and be paid entirely at Portuguese expense.[3] On the last day of the month Junot brought 2,000 men into Lisbon, his other 18,000 straggling behind him along the 560-mile line of march – only to find that two days earlier English men-of-war had rescued the Portuguese royal family and its treasures, and all the contents of English warehouses. Bonaparte had to content himself with levying 100,000 francs from the Portuguese. 'The great number of troops which I am obliged to maintain,' he wrote to Junot on 23 December, 'renders my expenses enormous.'[4]

It was now the turn of Spain to bend the neck. Bonaparte reckoned that although she made an inefficient ally she would prove a valuable enough asset once reconstructed under his control. Throughout the winter of 1807–8 he pursued a tortuous game of doublecrossing with regard to rival members of the Spanish royal family and the Spanish chief minister, Godoy, the self-styled 'Prince of the Peace'.[5] Meanwhile, he fed French troops into northern Spain under colour of supporting Junot's operations and guarding against an English invasion.

Yet the Iberian Peninsula did not by any means constitute the sum total of Bonaparte's new ambition; in his imagination a far, far vaster design had wreathed into shape. England – as always his central obsession – was to be brought to surrender by a gigantic pincer-movement on the Mediterranean and Middle East via Gibraltar and Constantinople, followed by a second and even more gigantic pincer-movement on India via the Middle East and the Cape of Good Hope. In this design Bonaparte was deterred neither by his utter failure as a maritime strategist in 1803–5 (it was all the fault of his admirals), nor by his equal failure in 1796–8 in an earlier attempt to vanquish England via the Middle East and India. He was not a man much given to learning from experience, least of all when it was disagreeable.

On 2 February 1808 he invited the Tsar Alexander to participate in the eastern arm of his pincer-movement:

An army of 50,000 men, Russian, French, perhaps even to some extent Austrian, marching on Asia via Constantinople, would only have to arrive on the Euphrates in order to shake England and make her go down on her knees. I am prepared in Dalmatia; Your Majesty is on the Danube. A month after we agreed to it, the army could be on the Bosphorus. The blow would resound throughout India, and England would be subdued . . .[6]

The Tsar's price for his co-operation, Constantinople, proving too high, Bonaparte had to limit himself to the western arm of his strategy. In March he took his steady occupation of Spain a step further by ordering Murat to march on Madrid, the capital, with 50,000 men.[7] In April and May 1808 his intrigues to gain control of Spain came to their climax with a particularly fine example of his statecraft. He arranged for King Charles IV of Spain, who had abdicated under popular pressure in favour of his son Ferdinand, to be brought under escort to Bayonne with his Queen. He then persuaded Ferdinand as well to repair to Bayonne, dangling as bait the suggestion that he and Bonaparte might discuss the possibility of Bonaparte recognizing him as king, perhaps even furnishing him with a French princess in marriage.[8] In fact nearly three weeks previously Bonaparte had offered the Spanish crown to his own brother Louis.[9]

When Ferdinand reached Bayonne he found himself clapped under close guard and threatened by Bonaparte that unless he recognized his father Charles as rightful king, he would be treated as a rebel.[10] Ferdinand, a relentlessly bullied prisoner without hope of aid, gave way. His father, in little better case, also surrendered, signing away his kingdom to Bonaparte and going into exile at Valençay. Since brother Louis had by now declined to leave his present kingdom of Holland, Bonaparte bestowed Spain on brother Joseph, who passed on his own realm of Naples to Murat ('King Joachim').

Even Bonaparte felt some twinge of shame at this raw work, writing that 'My

'Then, in a sombre study . . . rich with the olive-greens, the mahogany, the gilt and the bronze, the sphinxes and the griffons of the decorative style to which his empire gave its name, he set about transacting the affairs of his dominions': Bonaparte's study at Malmaison. *Photo: Studio Laverton*

action is not good from a certain point of view, I know. But my policy demands that I shall not leave in my rear, so close to Paris, a dynasty hostile to mine.'[11] Years later on St Helena he was to admit: 'I embarked very badly on the Spanish affair, I confess; the immorality of it was too patent, the injustice too cynical . . .'[12]

Nevertheless, at the time he congratulated himself that his knavery had delivered Spain into his hands. 'I regard then,' he wrote to Talleyrand on 6 May, 'the biggest part of the business as being done . . .'[13] True the people of Madrid had risen four days earlier against French occupation troops, but Murat, Bonaparte's 'Lieutenant of the Realm' in Spain, had crushed the revolt in standard fashion with case-shot and summary executions. Even if some further agitation took place, wrote Bonaparte, 'the good lesson just meted out to the city of Madrid must without question promptly decide matters . . .'[14]

But never in his insensitivity to the feelings of others had he committed more crashing misjudgments. The Spanish business, far from being done and decided, was only just beginning. On 20 May the pro-French governor of Badajoz was killed by a mob; two days later the governor of Cartagena too. On the 23rd the province of Valencia rose; next day the Asturias, at the opposite end of the country; Seville on the 27th. One by one the provincial governments or juntas declared war on France in the name of the captive Ferdinand VII, raised armies and sent them against the French. In this spontaneous national uprising the nobility supplied the leadership, the Church the inspiration and the people loyalty to these traditional authorities and a proud abomination of foreigners in their land. Suddenly the French found themselves in the middle of a roaring scrub fire of hatred. Suddenly the 117,000 troops Bonaparte had in Spain seemed all too scant a number. Suddenly the whole fabric of French control began to totter in the flames.

Yet there was nothing novel about the Spanish uprising in itself. On previous occasions, after all, Bonaparte had barged into deeply traditional societies and set about reconstructing them on the model of Bonapartian France, so insulting their customs, loyalties and religions. And on those occasions too outraged peoples had taken up arms against him, with the result that the deceptively easy shortcut of conquest had proved only to lead him into a morass of political and social complication. The novelty about the Spanish revolt, that which made it a decisive historical event, consisted in its order of magnitude, both human and geographical.

For this time an entire nation, and a nation of an unequalled ferocity and national pride, had risen against French occupation. And this time the arena of people's war amounted to nearly 200,000 square miles, as against the some 16,000 square miles of northern Italy or barely 8,000 square miles of Calabria. Moreover, the Spanish arena was even wilder, emptier and poorer country than Calabria. In following his star into Spain Bonaparte the romantic had saddled Bonaparte the mathematician with an unprecedented, and indeed insoluble, problem of space, time, numbers and logistics. The problem was further complicated by that imponderable moral factor (here in the shape of the Spanish character) which he himself reckoned as outweighing other factors in war by four to one.

Bonaparte reacted to the uprising like a beehive vigorously prodded with a stick, orders swarming out of him in all directions. Not until into the new year did his

A tapestry once in Bonaparte's study at the Tuileries and now at Malmaison, rich in Napoleonic and Roman imperial symbolism: eagles, imperial crowns, laurel wreaths, his monogram, and bees.
Photo: Studio Laverton

hectic buzzing on the topic of Spain subside. At first, with his usual contempt for an opponent, he ordered his commanders to sweep on through the country, smash the Spanish armies and extinguish the revolt by expedients he had employed in Egypt and again and again in Italy, such as shooting, burning of villages and taking of hostages. Thereby, however, he scattered his strength across a front of some four hundred miles. On 14 July Bessières routed the Spanish army of Galicia at Medina del Campo; cheering news. But in Aragon the French failed to take Saragossa;[15] in Catalonia General Duhesme was forced to seek refuge in Barcelona; down in the southeast, Moncey had to fall back from Valencia on Ocaña, a retreat which Bonaparte, conducting the campaign at long distance from Bayonne, characterized as 'inconceivable'.[16] An even more inconceivable event was pending. The most exposed French formation of all was Dupont's corps of 19,000 men in Andalusia, which Bonaparte had ordered to advance from Toledo on Cadiz. After pillaging Cordoba on his way, Dupont learned that he was now facing 30,000 Spanish troops and 10,000 irregulars under General Castaños. He therefore fell back to Bailén in order to await reinforcements. There, on 22 July 1808, his communications with Madrid through the passes of the Sierra Morena having been cut by Castaños, his men without water under a broiling southern sun, without food or ammunition, Dupont surrendered.

The news of Bailén reverberated on the ears of Europe with the lasting resonance of a great bell. For the first time since the Revolution a French army had been forced to capitulate in the open field. For the first time the run of Bonapartian victory had been unmistakenly broken. Bonaparte naturally blamed Dupont for what he called

The signing of the Treaty of Bayonne, April 1808. Bonaparte himself later said that 'the immorality was too patent, the injustice too cynical.' *Bibliothèque Nationale, Paris. Photo: Collection Viollet*

this 'horrible catastrophe',[17] rather than himself, who had ordered Dupont to undertake so rash and unsupported an advance in the first place. 'Dupont has disgraced our colours', he wrote to brother Joseph. 'What ineptitude! What baseness!'[18] His rage was the more intense because he recognized full well the immense damage Bailén could inflict on an empire so dependent on the prestige of victory as his. 'Events of such a nature,' he told his brother, 'demand my presence in Paris. Germany, Poland, Italy etc. are all bound up with it . . .'[19] Indeed Bailén could not have come at a worse moment, for Bonaparte already had intelligence that Austria appeared to be preparing for another war.[20] Quite suddenly Bonaparte was confronted with the task of holding together a European power structure that threatened to crack apart. To General Clarke, his Minister of War, and others he dispatched copious instructions for preparing a fresh campaign in Spain: huge supply depots to be formed at Bayonne and Perpignan as the army's main bases; two corps of the Grande Armée to be ordered from Germany to Spain.[21] Nevertheless, he had words of comfort for brother Joseph, now a fugitive from his new capital: '. . . Spain will be conquered in the autumn . . . Tell me that you are cheerful, in good spirits and accustoming yourself to the trade of soldier; here is a fine opportunity to study it . . .'[22]

Still Bonaparte's troubles increased. For the courage of the Portuguese and Spanish peoples gave England her opportunity to intervene effectively on land at last. The Spanish juntas invited the aid of England, Spain's erstwhile enemy, against France, her erstwhile ally. On 1 August 1808 Lieutenant-General Sir Arthur Wellesley and an expeditionary force of 10,000 men landed at Mondego Bay, on the coast of Portugal. With the wisdom of one who had learned his soldiering in India, Sir Arthur immediately began to hire bullock carts so that his army might be properly supplied; a grasp on essentials never to be relaxed. Sir Arthur had remarked at a farewell dinner party in London that while the French might overwhelm him, he did not think they would outmanoeuvre him:

> First, because I am not afraid of them, as everybody else seems to be; secondly, because, if what I hear of their system of manoeuvres be true, I think it a false one against steady troops. I suspect that all the Continental armies were more than half beaten before the battle was begun. I, at least, will not be frightened beforehand.[23]

At the Battle of Vimiero, on 21 August 1808, he vindicated these judgments by crushingly defeating Junot's Army of Portugal. Just as at Maida in Calabria in 1806, the tumultous French rush was stopped and broken up by the blasting musketry of the English line. Only the arrival of officers more senior than the thirty-nine-year-old Wellesley saved Junot from Dupont's fate, for instead of insisting on his capitulation these ageing bumblers signed a convention whereby he and his army were to be transported back to France in English ships. Nevertheless, Bonaparte had lost Portugal, another disastrous setback; and the English had acquired a firm base easily supplied by sea. The redcoats had taken the field again, and this time they were there to stay.

Bonaparte returned to Paris that August wearing a personality few at Court had seen before, although possibly it would have been familiar to anyone who had known him at Brienne or Auxonne: 'unquiet, sombre, dreamy' was how Josephine expressed it, adding, 'The courtiers trembled with affright.'[24] But it never occurred to him to cut his losses and restore Ferdinand VII or Charles IV. Instead he flung his supreme qualities of will and energy into the task of repairing his Iberian bungle by a fresh application of force, this time massive enough to sweep away any opposition. But on top of the news of Junot's surrender and of a withdrawal of the Army of Spain behind the Ebro came further confirmation that Austria was arming.[25]

For the first time in his career Bonaparte had to contend with the possibility of a war on two fronts. The crushing of the Spanish nation would, he now recognized, demand the major part of the veteran troops of the Grande Armée. How then could Austria be kept in check and Germany safeguarded? Bonaparte decided to ask his new friend the Tsar to lean on the Austrians on his behalf, and for that purpose invited him to a conference at Erfurt. Here the two emperors met on 27 September 1808. Bonaparte spared no effort to render the occasion even grander than Tilsit: the courtesies to Alexander even more overwhelming. Kings and queens abounded. Ornaments of German intellectual life like Goethe and Wieland were there, to be personally enlightened by Bonaparte on such topics as philosophy and religion. The friendship of Tilsit was formally renewed in a fresh alliance. But the Tsar refused to commit himself to go to war on Bonaparte's side in the event of a conflict between France and Austria; refused to put pressure on Vienna to remain at peace. Erfurt, for all the military show with which Bonaparte dressed it, was an act of wheedling; and one which failed of its main purpose.

On 12 October 1808 Bonaparte ordered the Grande Armée to be broken up.

While 40,000 men remained in Germany to watch Austria, the remainder took the road to Spain. By January 1809, so Bonaparte had promised brother Joseph, 100,000 veterans would ensure that in the whole country 'there will not be a single village in revolt.'[26] On 5 November Bonaparte himself reached Vittoria in northern Spain in order to conduct this unlooked-for and hastily improvised campaign. His troops found themselves as ill-supplied as ever despite Bonaparte's dispatch of a fresh salvo of imperious shopping lists to his supply department. 'I have nothing, I am naked,' he complained to his commissariat in Bayonne on 14 November, 'my army is in need and your bureaux are making fun of me . . .'[27] and on 21 December, with the weather now searingly cold, 'My hospitals are filling up with sick because I have neither overcoats nor shoes. I have been cruelly let down in all this . . .'[28]

But these were transient problems, for the campaign would soon be over. Providing the Spanish armies remained within reach, as at present, he believed that the war 'could be ended with a single blow by an ably combined manoeuvre . . .'[29] In November and December 1808 Bonaparte carried out this manoeuvre with the 191,000 men now under his command. While he protected his right flank and communications by driving the Spanish army of Galicia back on León, the rest of the Army of Spain swung southwards in another of those majestic Bonapartian wheeling movements and smashed through the Spanish defence of the Sierra de Guadarrama. On 4 December Bonaparte entered Madrid. Wherever the scarecrow Spanish armies had stood and fought, as at Tudela on the Ebro on 23 November, the veterans of the erstwhile Grande Armée effortlessly scattered them. While himself pausing in Madrid in order to reorganize Spanish society and administration, Bonaparte pushed his troops on down the Tagus valley southwestwards towards Portugal and his next intended victim, the English expeditionary force.

General Sir John Moore, its new commander, more senior than Wellesley and possibly as able, was not, however, waiting tamely in Portugal to be engulfed by overwhelming numbers. By 10 December 1808 he had transferred his base to Corunna, on the northwest coast of Spain, and concentrated his army, now in a strength of 28,000 men and sixty-six guns, at Salamanca. He had come to the conclusion that his best hope of aiding the Spanish patriots lay in striking at Bonaparte's isolated right-flank guard, under Soult, at Carrion de los Condes, some two hundred miles north of Madrid. Only fifty miles to the east of Carrion, at Burgos, lay Bonaparte's only line of communication with France. In the second week of December Moore began his manoeuvre against Bonaparte's flank and derrières. On the 21st his cavalry brushed with Soult's cavalry at Sahagun, some fifty miles west of Carrion.

Thus far Bonaparte had remained oblivious to the threat beginning to curl towards his back, intent instead on preparing his own further advance southwestward down the Tagus valley. On the 22nd, however, came sure intelligence that the English, instead of being as he thought in southern Portugal, were within striking distance of Soult. Thus unpleasantly taken by surprise, Bonaparte reacted with the same kind of animal leap as on those occasions when Wurmser or Alvinzi had caught him at a disadvantage in Italy, conducting a forced march over the high pass of the Puerto de Guadarrama in a blizzard in an attempt to sever Moore's own communications. But though he drove his frozen troops some one hundred miles in four days, he was too late. On 23 December Moore had learned that Bonaparte was after him, and that therefore his own gamble against Soult had miscarried; and next day he began the retreat to Corunna. Nevertheless, Bonaparte still remained hopeful of success, instructing brother Joseph on 27 December: 'Have it put in the newspapers and broadcast everywhere that 36,000 English are surrounded . . .'[30] By the first week of January 1809, however, he had come to realize that Moore had escaped, and that it was now a question of tediously following him back to Corunna. This unrewarding task he handed over to Soult.

Yet even in failing, Moore's thrust towards Bonaparte's rear had fulfilled a great strategic purpose. It had wrecked Bonaparte's chances of clearing up the Spanish entanglement at one blow according to plan. For by postponing his intended sweep through southern Spain it accorded the Spanish patriots the breathing space they needed to save them from extinction. From Bonaparte's point of view this postponement could not have been more ill-timed, because while he was resting his army after his leap at Moore, confirmation came that Austria was now actively preparing for war. On 15 January 1809 Bonaparte informed brother Joseph: 'The state of Europe obliges me to go and spend twenty days in Paris. If nothing prevents me, I shall be back here towards the end of February.'[31] But he was never to see Spain again. The Bonapartian killing stroke against the Portuguese and the Spaniards and their English allies had been postponed for good. So too had the grand design for pincer-movements by land and sea against the Middle East and India.

IN PARIS BONAPARTE flung himself into hectic preparations for war on two fronts; a novel problem peculiarly of his own making since it was the Spanish insurrection which finally spurred Austria into opting for a fresh struggle. He called up in all another 140,000 conscripts. But two-front wars demanded more than merely men. As Bonaparte confided to Davout, commanding the Army of the Rhine, 'Spain costs me much and returns me nothing. My armies have just been augmented, which demands heavy expenditure on my part.'[32] Once again he bent himself to the problem of cash-flow, mulcting the hapless Prussians and selling up some of his own imperial and royal domains in France and Italy. So fragile was France's true financial condition that Bonaparte took care to conceal it by cooking the public national accounts like a smart company accountant.[33]

The army Bonaparte cobbled together in the early months of 1809 for service against Austria while the majority of his veterans were in Spain far from equalled the Grande Armée he had led to Austerlitz four years before. The newly-raised troops approximated in quality to a militia, because under the Bonapartian military system recruits received little formal training. Since conscripted citizens were now allowed to supply substitutes at their own expense, the ranks saw fewer of the intelligent middle classes, more of society's poorest and dimmest, like an army of the ancien régime. The officer corps too had deteriorated, both because of the ravages of war and because Bonaparte, out of consideration for morale and his own

popularity, promoted officers for feats of bravery or their comrades' liking for them
rather than for their professional qualities. The makeshift 'Army of the Rhine'
could as a whole only manage crude tactics in clumsy mass formations; it depended
on massed cannon to blast a path for it. By a paradox the very decline of Bonaparte's
army was to breed another Napoleonic legend; that of the master of artillery.

And in any case, of all the forces mobilized against Austria in Italy and Germany
only half were native Frenchmen; the rest more or less unenthusiastic
satellite troops.

The Austrian army on the other hand had never been more formidable, its
organization and tactics reformed under the sting of defeat, its rank and file – indeed
the peoples of the Austrian Empire as a whole – inspired by a new spirit of loyalty
towards the Habsburg dynasty. And this time command of the army in the main
theatre north of the Alps fell to Austria's ablest soldier, the Archduke Charles.

On 9 April the Archduke took Bonaparte by surprise by invading Bavaria,
France's ally, six days earlier than Bonaparte expected,[34] so catching the Army of
Germany still far from concentrated, the Guard still *en route* from Spain and the
cavalry corps still being assembled. It did not help that Bonaparte had left Berthier,
a man unfitted for command, in temporary charge.

On 14 April Bonaparte left Paris to wage war against Austria for the fourth time.
Arriving in Donauwörth in Bavaria early on the 17th, he found his army in peril of
being destroyed in detail by the advancing Archduke. But rather than retreat
behind the River Lech and regroup, Bonaparte chose to gamble on an immediate
counter-stroke. While Davout fell back fighting from Regensburg to Ingolstadt,
drawing the Austrians after him, Masséna and Oudinot were to strike to the east
round the Archduke's left flank and sever his communications with Vienna along
the Danube. Bonaparte appended to his order to Masséna the heartfelt postscript:
'Action, action, speed! I implore you.'[35]

Davout, however, was brought to battle by the Austrians on a front between
Regensburg and the village of Eckmühl (as the French called Eggmühl). Bonaparte
thereupon swung Masséna away from his eastward march against the Austrian
communications, and directed him and Lannes north from Landshut to take the
Austrians in their left flank at Eckmühl. On 22 April Bonaparte himself led the race
to reach Eckmühl before Davout was overwhelmed by numbers. At about 2 p.m.
they wound down the slope into Eckmühl, a hamlet and a huge baroque watermill
in the valley of the Raaber stream. While Davout attacked the Austrian front,
Bonaparte launched his own columns across the water-meadows beyond the
Raaber into the Austrian flank. 'Then was seen,' said Bonaparte's bulletin after
the battle, 'one of the most beautiful sights war has offered' – in other words, the
retiring backs of the Archduke's army. Next day Lannes capped this brilliant
reversal of fortune by storming Regensburg; an event nevertheless slightly marred
because Bonaparte was bruised in the right foot by a spent musket-ball, his first
wound since Toulon.

To have thrown the Austrians back out of Bavaria did not suffice for Bonaparte;
Vienna it again must be, and another dictated peace. On 12 May 1809 he took up
abode at Schönbrunn once more, issuing a standard greeting to the Viennese: 'I take

the good inhabitants under my special protection. As for trouble-makers, I will inflict condign punishment upon them.'[36]

But where was the Archduke Charles and his army? After Eckmühl the main body had retired northeastward into Bohemia while a single corps retreated down the Danube through Vienna. But owing to a complete breakdown in reconnaissance and a no less complete absence of maps,[37] Bonaparte had no idea of the Archduke's present whereabouts. Yet if he lacked maps and information he had his star. He therefore decided to cross to the east bank of the Danube opposite Vienna and hunt about for the Archduke somewhere between Vienna and Moravia; a gamble in a void. Since the Austrians had destroyed all the Danube bridges, this operation would first require the building of a pontoon bridge, and at a season of year when the river was subject to sudden devastating surges of floodwater. In committing his army to this operation beyond the Danube Bonaparte had embarked on perhaps his rashest military undertaking thus far; an act of recklessly bad generalship.

As a bridging point Bonaparte chose the hamlet of Albern, some six miles south of Vienna, where islands split the Danube into three streams, the largest about as wide as the River Thames at Richmond, the narrowest perhaps 150 yards across, so easing the task of the engineers. The shining grass, bright with buttercups, of the Albern water-meadows vanished beneath piles of timber, cordage, anchors and outdoor workshops. On 20 May, a week later than Bonaparte had optimistically ordered, the army began to cross the new bridge and march on through the largest of the Danube islands, Lobau, a lush wilderness shaded by poplars enormous in height and spread. On the far side of Lobau the troops traversed the narrow third channel of the river and emerged on an immense naked plain, the Marchfeld.

On 21 May, when only some 20,000 of Bonaparte's army had so far deployed in the Marchfeld, the Archduke Charles, who had been patiently waiting with his whole army a mile back from the Danube, sprang his trap. Under cover of a bombardment by 250 guns, 100,000 Austrians smashed into the French and drove them out of the villages of Aspern and Essling back towards their bridge. As the French struggled to hold a narrow bridgehead beyond Lobau, a four-foot wave of floodwater carried away part of Bonaparte's pontoon bridge. Repaired in the night, it was destroyed again in the morning, this time by barges sent down by the Austrians. Bonaparte's stubborn hope of renewing his offensive with fresh reinforcements from Vienna was destroyed along with the bridge. In the afternoon he withdrew his exhausted troops from the bridgehead in the Marchfeld into the sanctuary of Lobau.

In the two-day battle of Aspern Bonaparte had suffered the first outright personal defeat of his career. Aspern tolled in the ears of Europe with even greater resonance than Bailén. And neither Bonaparte nor his soldiers had ever experienced so bloody a struggle. Each side lost over 20,000 men killed, wounded and missing. One casualty touched Bonaparte into genuine grief. Marshal Lannes, Duke of Montebello, one of his oldest comrades, had both legs smashed by a cannon-ball, and was to die after lingering on for eight days of agony and fever. Yet Bonaparte even made propaganda capital out of personal grief by publishing in the official bulletin on the battle a highly-coloured account of his visit to the side of Lannes' stretcher, not omitting mention of the shedding of imperial tears.

> The Duke of Montebello had lost consciousness; the presence of the Emperor revived him; he threw himself on his [Bonaparte's] neck, saying to him: 'Within the hour you will have lost the man who dies with glory and the conviction of having been, and of being, your best friend.'[38]

With his defeat at Aspern Bonaparte had got himself into the most gruesome plight of his career, with half his army marooned on Lobau and the Danube repeatedly in flood. But he still would not abandon his main purpose. In contrast to the casual, even slapdash, way in which he had originally dispatched his army across the Danube, he now set about organizing a second attempt with meticulous care, a task which took him six weeks. While the engineers constructed a triple bridge on piles driven into the river bed, he rustled up reinforcements from France and Italy. By the beginning of July the island of Lobau, perfect cover for the assembly of a great army, swarmed with men like an ants' nest concealed in tall grass. In the meantime Bonaparte's hopes that the Austrian court would make peace overtures met with bitter disappointment.[39]

On 2–4 July he issued minutely detailed orders for the most elaborate set-piece operation he had ever mounted: the breakout from Lobau into the Marchfeld and the deployment of 187,000 men, three times his numbers at Austerlitz. At 9.30 p.m. on the 4th, an evening of thunder and bucketing rain, the army began to cross the third

arm of the Danube on the eastern side of Lobau by pontoon bridge and ferry, brushing aside Austrian covering troops. By mid-morning the army began to wheel its front from east to north in obedience to Bonaparte's master-plan of enveloping the left flank of the Archduke Charles' army and sweeping it away. This majestic evolution encountered nothing but skirmishing parties. Bonaparte had failed to carry out reconnaissance sufficiently thorough to discover the enemy's actual dispositions.

The Archduke once more intended to entice Bonaparte into a trap and this time finally destroy him. With his right flank resting on the Danube near Aspern, he had posted the Austrian army facing south along a fifteen-mile arc running through the villages of Aderklaa, Wagram (which gave its name to the coming battle) and Markgrafneusiedl. The final segment of the arc, between Markgrafneusiedl and the Danube, was to be filled by his brother, the Archduke John, now on his way with his corps from Pressburg.

By early evening Bonaparte had marched his army deep inside the Austrian half-circle, discovered its existence, and deployed facing outwards to it. He established his own command post on an earthy bank some eight feet high next to the road leading north from the village of Raasdorf to Wagram; a position nearly at the hub of the vast semi-circle of the armies. Here he could observe the entire Austrian perimeter from north of Aspern round to Markgrafneusiedl. The scene before him in the torrid sunshine following the rain dwarfed in its vastness of scale any of his previous battlefields, perhaps any previous battlefield of history. Along the level and almost treeless horizons of the Marchfeld lay ranged more than 300,000 men and nearly nine hundred cannon; all brought together by Bonaparte's pursuit of his destiny for the purpose of slaughtering each other: 136,000 Austrians and nearly four hundred guns, and 187,000 men and five hundred guns under Bonaparte's own command.

The monotony of the Marchfeld is broken by only two natural defensive features, the marshy Russbach stream, thick with trees, which protected the Austrian left between Wagram and Markgrafneusiedl, and a slope running behind it some thirty feet above the plain. Inexplicably Bonaparte selected this strong sector as the object of his opening attack, by Davout's and Oudinot's corps. They were thrown back with bloody loss. Bonaparte tried again, this time with Bernadotte's Saxon corps in the centre of the Austrian ring at Wagram. They too were repulsed, breaking to the rear on the verge of panic. When night fell the Austrians still stood firmly in their original positions.

Next morning Bonaparte launched further disconnected attacks in the centre, and again without success. So far he had wholly failed to produce a commanding plan of battle. It was the Archduke Charles who now launched the one grand manoeuvre of the engagement, a long meditated stroke near Aspern against Bonaparte's left flank. Accompanied by furious cannon-fire two Austrian corps lumbered forward against a single French corps under Masséna with the object of driving right across Bonaparte's rear and cutting his whole army off from the Danube bridges. For a time, as Masséna's line sagged, the Archduke came close to one of the great victories of history. But Bonaparte was always at his best in the

'. . . his fourth Austrian war was ended by the Treaty of Schönbrunn': an order of the day proclaiming peace. *Bulloz*

confusions and emergencies of a battlefield. He shifted Masséna's corps to its left in order to block the most dangerous enemy thrust towards the Danube bridges, and closed the gap opened by Masséna's sidestep with the fire from a battery of one hundred guns. By this swift regrouping Bonaparte saved his left wing from immediate collapse and his army from total catastrophe. The battle resumed its pattern of bloody attrition; punch and counter-punch. But on the opposite side of the sixteen-mile arc of smoke from Aspern, Davout turned the left of the Austrian position at Markgrafneusiedl and began to fight his way behind the Russbach towards Wagram. Around midday Bonaparte launched his last available reserves of cavalry and infantry against the Austrian centre at Wagram in the wake of a bombardment by sixty guns of the Guard artillery. The Austrian army, still fighting stoutly, began slowly to give ground, a movement which gradually merged into a fighting retreat. The Archduke left behind no unwounded prisoners and only seven guns, those being damaged. Bonaparte did not pursue; the French army was too shattered for that.

So yet again he had narrowly won through. Nevertheless, Wagram shed no lustre on his generalship, for it was a victory won by sheer bludgeoning. The French artillery fired a record total of 71,000 rounds. At least 32,000 of Bonaparte's own troops and a roughly similar number of Austrians lay dead or wounded on the field. Wagram proclaimed a new order of warfare; it looked ahead to such combinations of massed manpower and firepower as the battles of the American Civil War; as Verdun and the Somme; as Stalingrad.

Next day Bonaparte rode over the Marchfeld to view its ghastly litter. Marshal Marmont, who accompanied him, remarks in his memoirs:

> I have never understood his curiosity to see the dead and dying so covering the ground. He stopped in front of one officer grievously wounded in the knee, and had the strange idea of having the amputation performed before him by his surgeon Yvan. The latter had difficulty in making him understand that this was neither the place nor the time.[40]

On 12 July 1809 Bonaparte and the Archduke Charles signed an armistice, for, lacking allies, the Austrian government was not prepared to emulate the Spaniards and fight on come what may. This was well for Bonaparte, for 40,000 peasants had risen against him in the Tyrol, menacing his communications, while from Spain he received only tidings of gloom. Marshal Soult, whom he had ordered to reconquer Portugal, had instead been routed by Sir Arthur Wellesley, now at the head of the new English army in the Peninsula which had replaced the one evacuated after Moore's successful stand (and death in action) at the Battle of Corunna. In August 1809, to Bonaparte's fury, another of his marshals, Victor, was beaten by Wellesley at Talavera. Since running the Spanish war from Schönbrunn 1,400 miles away did not seem to be working very well, Bonaparte's closer presence seemed desirable.

On 14 October his fourth Austrian war was ended by the Treaty of Schönbrunn, whereby Francis I ceded further lands, this time in Poland and along the Adriatic. On this occasion, however, to appease Bonaparte was going to cost the Austrian Emperor more than territory; it was going to cost him a daughter too.

XII

BUT HOW WILL ALL THIS END?

ALTHOUGH JOSEPHINE bore a son and a daughter to the Vicomte de Beauharnais, she failed to bear either to Bonaparte despite all the remedies prescribed by Bonaparte's physician and such expedients as taking the waters at Plombières, renowned for their stimulating effect on the reproductive system. After Bonaparte became Consul for Life in 1802 and began to assume the trappings of monarchy, his want of progeny became a source of dynastic anxiety to him. Josephine, now in her forties, began to be tormented lest he should discard her and try his luck with someone else in the prime of child-bearing age. When in 1804 the Pope arrived in Paris to conduct the Coronation, Josephine therefore cunningly let him know that she and Bonaparte had never been married by the Church, only in a civil ceremony. The Pope insisted that this must be put right before the Coronation, otherwise he would lay down his crozier and officiate no more. Bonaparte, thus outmanoeuvred, gave way; and his uncle Cardinal Fesch married them two days before his crowning.

But if it now appeared to be harder for Bonaparte to get rid of Josephine, it proved no easier for her to conceive. Bonaparte's patience became more and more tried by thwarted paternal and dynastic ambition. On one occasion at Malmaison when he suggested going hunting and Josephine protested in tears that all the deer were in kid, Bonaparte kindly remarked to the company: 'Come, we shall have to give up the idea; every creature here is pregnant except madame.'[1] Nevertheless, a rumour thrived that the trouble lay with the sire rather than the consort, a question not so much of sterility as impotence.[2] Another – and contradictory – rumour credited Bonaparte with being the true father of Napoléon-Charles, the son of his brother Louis and Hortense, Josephine's daughter by her first marriage. This rumour by no means put Bonaparte out, because for a time he contemplated adopting him as his heir; a project scotched by the child's death in 1807.

At the end of December 1806, however, Bonaparte at last received what seemed like sure proof that given a suitable female he could father children. A passing mistress, Eléonore Revel, wife of a captain of dragoons and formerly Murat's mistress too, gave birth to a son to be christened, significantly enough, 'Léon'. It was said that Bonaparte's chance encounter with Eléonore had been carefully arranged by Murat for the very purpose of enabling Bonaparte to prove himself as a sire. As it happened, the news of Léon's birth reached Bonaparte just as he was falling for Marie Walewska, so doubly dooming Josephine. He returned from Tilsit in July 1807 resolved at last on a divorce.

Yet it took him who was usually so brutally decisive more than two years to make up his mind to carry out the deed. Long habit, that friend of fading wives, lay on Josephine's side; that and the attachment Bonaparte always evinced towards the companions of his early years, the memory he cherished, like a lock of hair in a drawer, of his first tumultous experience with her. Indeed, his real difficulty was that he loved her after his fashion. Indecision tormented him. Remorse rekindled passion, as when he drew Josephine – in full fig for a court assembly – on to his bed and wept all over them both, protesting that he could not leave her.

Nevertheless, dynastic egotism proved the stronger pull in the end. He wanted a son in order to found a new line of Caesars. He wished to marry into one of the great royal houses of Europe. Such an alliance would confer legitimacy on his own self-made royalty. It would satisfy that upstart's snobbery which had griped him since childhood, and which although once naïve enough to be appeased by marrying a mere viscountess now aspired to a princess.

When Bonaparte travelled to meet the Tsar at Erfurt in September 1808, he was in hopes of the Tsar's sister, the Grand-Duchess Catherine. But the Tsar, forewarned by Talleyrand, put the matter off on the grounds that she was not yet pubescent. Thereafter, Bonaparte's search for 'a womb', as he exquisitely put it, was delayed for a year by the Spanish embroglio and the fourth Austrian war. It was while at Schönbrunn after Wagram – where he enjoyed the society of Marie Walewska, who had journeyed to see him and who as the result of her visit bore a son, Alexander, in May 1810 – that Bonaparte finally made up his mind to divorce Josephine.

But so painful did he find it to break the news that, rather than tell her directly, he subjected her to a kind of cold war. His letters ceased. He ordered the doors and passages linking their suites at Fontainebleau to be blocked up by builders. Back at Fontainebleau early in October 1809 he took care never to see her alone but always in company. He dropped hints to intermediaries about his intentions. Only when he learned that his stepson Eugène was on his way from Italy at Josephine's entreaty to intercede for her did he nerve himself to convey his decision in person. Fifteen days later, on 15 December 1809, the divorce took place in a lamp-lit room in the Tuileries in the presence of his family and the Arch-Chancellor, Cambacérès. Bonaparte, tearful, holding Josephine's hand, read out the imperial declaration dissolving the marriage (later confirmed by a Senatus-Consultum and compliant clergy). After the brief ceremony, Josephine returned to her own apartments, Bonaparte to his study, 'sad and silent; he let himself flop back on to his favourite couch in a state of utter prostration; he remained there several moments, head resting on his hand, and, when he got up, his face was in turmoil.'[3] Although a carriage was waiting to take him to the Trianon, he first went down the private spiral staircase to Josephine's apartments with his secretary, Méneval.

> At the sound we made on going in, she quickly got up and threw herself sobbing on the Emperor's neck, who pressed her against his chest while kissing her over and over again; but such was her emotion that she had fainted.[4]

Having provided for Josephine by a generous financial settlement, Bonaparte resumed his search for a fertile 'womb'. The Tsar again, however, politely evaded his proposal with regard to his sister. The excuses were plausible – the girl, at sixteen, was still too young; there was the problem of different religions. None the less the negotiations marked the widening of a hairline crack in the friendship between Bonaparte and Alexander. But by now Bonaparte had turned his thoughts towards the Archduchess Marie-Louise, the eighteen-year-old eldest daughter of the Austrian Emperor. Politically this match would finally remove Austria from the ranks of his enemies. Gynaecologically as well it appeared a sound investment, for painstaking reconnaissance had assured him that in Marie-Louise he had found

'. . . soft, good, innocent and as fresh as roses . . .': the Archduchess Marie-Louise, daughter of Francis I of Austria, whom Bonaparte married in 1810. From a painting by Jean-Baptiste Isabey. *British Museum*

the belly he needed. She was a strapping girl herself, while her mother had borne thirteen children, her grandmother seventeen and her great-grandmother twenty-six.[5] She had been subjected to exactly the kind of upbringing Bonaparte thought suitable for women and indeed prescribed for them in his own educational reforms – nun-like seclusion; inculcation of the duty of complete submission to father and husband; genteel accomplishments like music, drawing and needlework; avoidance of all ideas and higher knowledge as might disturb the weak female mind. Such, however, was the prudery of the Habsburg court that all the books to which Marie-Louise had access were emasculated of sexual content with the scissors, and only female pets were allowed within her sight.

On 9 and 11 March 1810 the civil and religious marriages were concluded in Vienna by proxy, as was the custom. In Paris Bonaparte found himself in an unaccustomed twitter at the prospect of a Habsburg bride of eighteen. He

personally supervised the decoration of her apartments. Much concerned with producing an elegant personal effect on this young woman of ancient lineage, he got Murat's tailor to make him a wedding costume so encrusted with embroidery that it was painful to wear, and changed his shoemaker in order to have yet finer footwear. Never a good dancer, he learned the latest dance, the waltz. As Queen Catherine of Westphalia reported to her father, '. . . these are things such as neither you nor I would have imagined.'[6]

The bride progressed across Europe, greeted at every stage with messages or flowers, even wild boars shot by the imperial hand. It had been arranged for the couple to meet on 28 March in a magnificent pavilion erected in the park at Compiègne. The troops, the nobility and the great and small flunkeys of the Court deployed themselves. But on the 27th Bonaparte, strung to concert pitch, rode off from Compiègne through drenching rain with only Murat as escort, ambushed

Marie-Louise in the little village of Courcelles, drove with her to Compiègne without sparing the horses past waiting mayors and their speeches, past the Court and the pavilion, and conducted her straight into the bedroom. By this characteristically brusque violation of the accepted rules of conduct the portly forty-year-old dictator took premature possession of his young princess, 'soft, good, innocent and fresh as roses', as he enthusiastically described the qualities of Teutonic women to one of his generals next day.[7] As so often in his life Bonaparte's bad behaviour was provoked by a sense of social inferiority and personal unease; a sense which Marie-Louise herself was not slow in divining, for three months after the solemnizing of the marriage in the Grand Gallery of the Louvre on 22 April 1810 she was writing to Metternich, the Austrian Chancellor, that 'I am not afraid of Napoleon, but I begin to believe that he is afraid of me.'[8]

O N 20 MARCH 1811 Marie-Louise gave birth to a son (named François-Charles-Joseph) so vindicating Bonaparte's faith in choosing as early as the February of the previous year the title of 'King of Rome' for his future son. The *accouchement* nevertheless had its moment of drama when the *accoucheur*, alarmed at a long hold-up in the proceedings, offered Bonaparte the choice of saving the life of the mother or the child. Without hesitation Bonaparte answered, 'Save the mother! Save the mother!' – evidence of how much he had now come to dote on his young wife.

The King of Rome's cradle, designed by Prud'hon, now at Schönbrunn. *Bulloz*

So at last he had his heir; his Empire a future beyond his own lifetime. Was this the fulfilment for which he had been searching so restlessly and so long? Or had he, in the phrase coined by Lieutenant Buonaparte twenty years before to describe the fate of those who achieve worldly success, 'sought happiness and found only glory'?[9]

For the sake of ambition he had abandoned his wife; one of the most selfish and dishonourable actions of his life; moreover, a deep self-inflicted emotional wound. He had cut himself off from the closest relationship he was ever to form with a woman, perhaps with anyone; the fruit of fifteen years of shared experience, good times and bad. Dote as he might on Marie-Louise, she could hardly fill Josephine's place in his life, she a newcomer only present because her father and the interest of Austria required it. No wonder Bonaparte would steal away from time to time to Malmaison, there to recover for a moment what he had cast aside.

And even within his own family too, Bonaparte by his egotism was exiling himself on a lonely island of the spirit. As his elder brother Joseph had wistfully remarked in 1806, 'Ah! The glorious emperor will never compensate me for that Napoleon whom I so much loved and whom I wish I could find once more just as I knew him in 1786.'[10] By August 1810 Bonaparte's quarrel with his brother Lucien had become so bitter that Lucien decided to exchange exile in Italy for the more distant sanctuary of America. Captured in the Mediterranean by the Royal Navy, he ended up in England instead, there with his family to live the life of a country gentleman until the coming of peace. In 1810 brother Louis abdicated from the throne of Holland rather than submit to Bonaparte's ultimatum to enforce the Continental System even at the cost of ruining his subjects. He did more than abdicate; he disappeared for a time and finally turned up in Bohemia, beyond the

bounds of Bonaparte's Empire, so inflicting a grevious blow on Bonaparte's *amour-propre*. The news of Louis' flight provoked in Bonaparte that astonishment he always felt when people or states manifested hostility towards him. What ingratitude! His secretary Méneval records:

> ... anguish and vexation wrung tears from him. 'Should I have expected,' he cried, 'such an outrage on the part of someone to whom I have been a father? I brought him up on the scant resources of my pay as a lieutenant of artillery; I have shared my bread and the mattress on my bed with him ...'[11]

And Joseph in Spain, Jerome in Westphalia and sister Caroline in Naples (wife of 'King Joachim' Murat) found it no less hard than Louis to reconcile the kingship that had been thrust upon them (the perks and pretensions of which they much enjoyed) with Bonaparte's treatment of them as mere agents whose task it was to exploit their subjects for his benefit. Their interests and his therefore diverged more and more; their affection for him yielded increasingly to resentment. Like their mother Letizia, they wondered if, and how long, Bonaparte's Empire would endure, and they governed their actions accordingly.

IN 1810–11, with all the great powers of the Continent not only at peace but also allied to Bonaparte, the struggle with England – his central obsession, the ulterior object of all his marches – came to the forefront. The struggle remained primarily economic; the basic issue simple. Bonaparte continued to seek to bring England to financial ruin and a peace of surrender by shutting her out of her richest export market, the Continent of Europe. Each new conquest enabled him to further this purpose by bringing fresh coastlines and ports within his Continental System from which English ships and goods were barred. By the Berlin Decrees of 1806 he declared England to be in a state of blockade and forbade all trade with her on pain of draconic penalties; in 1807 he tightened his boycott still further with the Milan Decrees, and again in 1810 by the Trianon and Fontainebleau Decrees. In theory every port in Europe should now have been shut to England either by himself or by his allies. But in practice English goods kept leaking in. Smuggling thrived; the local authorities connived; the products reached the customer, even if not in the desired quantities. For Europe wanted – needed – English goods: cottons from the new steam mills of Lancashire; Yorkshire woollens; coffee and sugar from the tropics. There were even units of the Grande Armée wearing English greatcoats and shoes.

And as fast as Bonaparte tried to stop up one leak, another would begin to gape. In the case of Spain and Portugal, he himself by his blundering had ended by opening them to English trade instead of closing them as he intended – and the markets of their empires as well. Fuss and fume as he might, Bonaparte could inflict no more than partial damage on the English economy, most severe in 1808 and 1811, but never enough to bring down so powerful, buoyant and resilient an industrial and trading power.

At the same time the Continental System, with its harsh regulations and penalties and its prying legions of narks, came to seem to Europeans the very embodiment of

Bonaparte's despotism. Nor was the System in any sense an idealistic precursor of the Common Market, as some partisans of Bonaparte contend, for France herself enjoyed a privileged role within it, safe behind high tariffs from competition from the rest of Bonaparte's dominions. In Bonaparte's admission in 1810, 'France comes before everything else.'[12] For European consumers the System spelled denial of necessities and luxuries from abroad; for merchants ruin when their stocks of English goods were burned by Bonaparte's customs officers; for the great maritime traders of Europe like the Dutch and the Hanseatic ports, the drying-up of their commerce with the rest of the world.[13]

While Bonaparte was playing the customs officer in hot pursuit of the English smuggler, the war in the Iberian Peninsula sucked in more and more French troops – the total rose from 190,000 in 1809 to more than 360,000 in 1811 – and still the Spaniards fought on; still Wellesley (now raised to the peerage as Viscount Wellington) and his redcoats kept the field.

AFTER WAGRAM BONAPARTE had fully intended to return to Spain in January 1810 and clear the whole messy business up once and for all by marching to Lisbon. 'When I show myself beyond the Pyrenees,' he modestly promised the *Corps Législatif* on 3 December 1809 'the terrified Leopard [England] will seek the Ocean in order to avoid shame, defeat and death. The triumph of my arms will be the triumph of the spirit of good over that of evil . . .'[14]

But instead he stayed in France for the next two years, although kept there for so long a period by no overriding political or strategic considerations. At first he stayed in order to prepare for Marie-Louise's arrival; then in order to enjoy his young bride and take her on imperial progresses; then because Marie-Louise, now pregnant, wished him to remain near her; and then because he had a new baby son. Measured against the scale and urgency of the Spanish entanglement, these were frivolous motives. However dynastically important it was for him to provide himself with an heir, it did not take two years to marry and beget a child. Were there perhaps deeper reasons for failing to return to Spain? Bonaparte genuinely believed in his 'star'; perhaps it no longer gleamed at him beyond the Pyrenees. Perhaps instead he felt instinctively that now Spain meant trouble and drudgery rather than glory, like the post he had declined in 1795 with the army fighting the Vedéean rebels, or Egypt when he deserted his command in 1799.

It was Wellington who accurately analysed the basic French problem:

> Bonaparte cannot carry out his operations in Spain, excepting by means of large armies; and I doubt much whether the country will afford subsistence for a large army, or if he will be able to supply his magazines from France, the roads being so bad and the communications so difficult.[15]

By the end of 1809 Wellington had come to a further conclusion that so long as the English army could remain in the field the Peninsular War would go on, and that as much as the French might wish to drive the English army out:

> . . . they must employ a very large force indeed in the operations which will render it necessary for us to go away; and I doubt whether they can bring that force to bear upon

'. . . the Continental System, with its harsh regulations and penalties . . .': Bonaparte's customs officers destroying illicitly imported English goods. *Historisches Museum, Frankfurt*

Portugal without abandoning other objects and exposing their whole fabric in Spain to great risk.[16]

The course of the struggle in the winter of 1810–11, when Bonaparte launched his most formidable proxy attempt to drive 'the Leopard' into the sea, demonstrated the accuracy of Wellington's analysis. In September 1810 Marshal Masséna's Army of Portugal, numbering only 70,000 out of more than 300,000 French soldiers in the Peninsula, advanced on Lisbon. After a painful march through the countryside stripped by the Portuguese of all supplies and a sharp repulse at Bussaco by Lord Wellington, Masséna neared his destination only to find his path barred by three powerful lines of field fortifications stretching from the Atlantic to the Tagus across the neck of land on which Lisbon stood. From October 1810 to March 1811 he resolutely starved in front of these impregnable Lines of Torres Vedras, then retreated back into Spain with a loss of 25,000 men. Henceforward the strategic initiative lay with Wellington.

Bonaparte, conducting the campaign at long distance from Parisian palaces, never grasped the fundamental strategic truths so plainly perceived by Wellington. In the first place he would not see or admit how utterly inadequate was the French supply system in a barren country where the Bonapartian or Guibertian system of subsistence by scavenging could not suffice. Marshal Marmont, appointed to command the 'Army of Portugal' in 1812, wrote:

> The English army had its pay on time; the French army received not a penny. The English army had magazines in abundance, and the English soldier never needed to forage for himself; the French army lived only by the efforts of those who composed it . . . The English army had six thousand mules for its food supplies alone; the French army had no other means of transport but the backs of our soldiers . . .[17]

Secondly, in directing strategy Bonaparte fell into the same kind of error – or fantasy – as in his maritime war against England in 1803–5, by playing a war game off the map without regard to operational realities. He counted manpower as he had once counted ships, unable or unwilling to grasp that guerrilla warfare in such a country as Spain meant that his armies' strength must be continually dispersed in defence of their own communications or bases, or in sweeps after guerrilla bands. With that curious scorn of his for the enemy who obsessed him beyond any other, he underestimated the fighting quality of the English army and its general, as he had once that of the English fleets and admirals. Until 1812 he sought to co-ordinate all operations himself, dispatching inflexible directives based on out-of-date information or wishful thinking, and even more out of date when received; again an echo of the naval struggle of 1803–5. When he did appoint a supreme commander in Spain with authority over the squabbling marshals, his choice fell on his brother 'King Joseph', whom he had judged as long ago as 1785 to be totally unsuited for a military career, and whose directives in 1812–13 were largely ignored by the marshals.

All in all, therefore, the Spanish war offers an outstanding example of Bonaparte's habit of retreating from reality once it ceased to be congruous with his wishes. In Marmont's measured but justified indictment:

The extreme division of command, which he never wanted to renounce, the rivalry of every kind which he never succeeded in repressing, his absence from a theatre where he alone could do good, his habitual refusal to provide the most essential help and resources, his constant obstinacy in shutting his eyes to the light and his ears to the truth; finally, the mania which he would not give up for directing from Paris operations in a country which he neither wished to study nor understand, completed the mass of evils to which the best armies of Europe must in the end have fallen victim.[18]

When in February 1812 Marmont sent one of his officers to explain the truths of warfare in Spain to Bonaparte in person, Bonaparte, according to this officer, replied: 'Here is Marmont complaining about the lack of many things, victuals, money, resources etc. Ah well, as for myself, I am going to throw myself with vast armies into the middle of a country which produces nothing.' According to Marmont's emissary, Bonaparte thereupon fell into deep meditation, emerging from it to observe: 'But how will all this end?'[19]

THE FRIENDSHIP between Bonaparte and the Tsar Alexander created at Tilsit in 1807, a beautiful makebelieve, had become year by year harder to sustain. Their ambitions clashed over the Near East, over the future of Turkey and its capital Constantinople, and again over the future of Poland. At Erfurt in 1808 the smiles were pinned back on the imperial visages, but the Tsar none the less declined to promise to fight on Bonaparte's side in the event of another Franco-Austrian war. The shifty mutual dealing over Bonaparte's search for a bride at the turn of the year 1809–10 deepened the mistrust. Yet underlying the specific issues of dissent was the fundamental problem that each man regarded himself as the greatest emperor in the world and providence's chosen instrument. Such convictions could hardly be reconciled. After Tilsit Bonaparte wrongly assumed that Alexander had accepted second place to him, and in particular would loyally enforce the Continental System on Russia. But by 1810 Russia's Baltic ports provided one of the largest leaks in the Continental System. Thanks to the defaulting of his imperial friend, therefore, Bonaparte saw his squeeze on England's throat relaxing. He nagged Alexander that if he let English goods in, 'the war will go on; if he seized and confiscated them . . . the counter-blow that will strike England will be terrible . . .'[20]

Alexander, however, chose to consult the crying economic needs of his own country rather than Bonaparte's wishes. To meet these needs meant reopening overseas trade in place of stifled exports and enforced reliance on dear French goods. At the end of 1810 Alexander laid heavy duties on French products; light ones on imports from America and colonial countries. Although he still formally barred English goods and ships, the ingenious English slipped in, as Bonaparte complained, under cover of the flags, documents and labels of all nations, even France. In any case, within a year the Tsar was positively conniving at two-way trade between England and Russia. These developments doubly enraged Bonaparte by opening a fresh hole in the Continental System and by demonstrating an insufferable spirit of independence on the part of the Tsar. Bonaparte on his side had nevertheless not neglected to anger Alexander in his turn, for in October 1810 he annexed the north German coastal state of Oldenburg and deposed its duke; an outright breach of the

Tilsit Treaty, and the more tactless because the duke's heir was married to the Tsar's sister – the very grand-duchess who had not been available to Bonaparte.

There could of course in the end be only one answer to the Tsar's pretensions to an independent role; pretensions which, despite Bonaparte's pressure, he refused to give up. In the first week of December 1811 Bonaparte began preparations for his grandest, riskiest military adventure ever, its objects to plug the holes in the Continental System and teach Alexander to return to his proper orbit as a planet revolving round the Bonapartian sun. Sober, let alone sagacious, statecraft had nothing to do with the project; nor the true interests of France, long since lost to sight. For Bonaparte's will to domination was in the saddle again and riding hard. He brushed aside the warnings of his diplomats and soldiers, who recalled how Charles XII of Sweden's army in 1709 had been swallowed up in the vastness of Russia and destroyed at the Battle of Poltava. The spirit of adventure which drives the mountain climber or the explorer to tackle ever more formidable challenges held Bonaparte in thrall. And as with every adventurer the thrill lay in the doing rather than the accomplishment. But in Bonaparte's case there was more to it than that. Action disguised the essential emptiness of his existence, the void in the heart.

> As for me [he once confided to one of his ministers] I care nothing for St Cloud, nor for the Tuileries. It would matter little to me if they were burned down. I count my houses as nothing, women as nothing, my son as a little. I quit one place, I go to another, I quit St Cloud, I go to Moscow, not out of inclination or to gratify myself, but out of dry calculation.[21]

Then again, action provided an answer to the most haunting of questions, that of identity: 'I act, therefore I am.' For power and glory had not served to remedy but only to conceal Bonaparte's lack of a true identity, in the sense of that homogenous core of character, that pure metal of integrity, to be found in such men as Wellington or Lincoln. Success had failed to weld into a consistent whole his various jarring personalities: cold manipulator and emotional romantic, mathematician and dreamer, boss and underdog. Rather it had brought about new discords – between, for instance, the self-appointed know-all of Europe and the victim of neurosis and superstition he had always been. Because of his horror of open doors, anyone briefly entering his room had to open the door just wide enough to squeeze through, then hold it by the handle tight shut behind his back until the moment came for going out again.[22] When during a row with one of his brothers some years earlier he knocked Josephine's picture off a table and smashed the glass, he had paled with superstitious fear. 'I have often seen him,' Josephine recorded, 'fall into a terrible rage if one of his *valets de chambre* happened to place on the left what belonged on the right; for instance, his box of razors . . . In taking off an article of clothing he would often throw it over the left shoulder, saying "lands"; another, adding "castles"; and so on to the end repeating "provinces", "kingdoms" etc. . . .'[23]

And superstition, in the shape of belief in his 'star' or destiny, influenced his decision to invade Russia not less than the will to domination or the spirit of adventure. Once when criticized by his uncle Cardinal Fesch over his treatment of the Pope, Bonaparte took him by the hand and led him out on to a balcony:

'Look up there,' he told him, 'Do you see anything?' 'No', answered Fesch, 'I see
nothing.' 'Very well, in that case, know when to shut up,' replied the Emperor, 'Myself,
I see my star; it is that which guides me. Don't pit your feeble and incomplete faculties
against my superior organism.'[24]

It was in such a state of mind, halfway between faith and fatalism, that Bonaparte
set about organizing the most gigantic military operation in history to that time.
Month by month troops flowed across Europe and into Prussia and the Grand-
Duchy of Warsaw, the assembly areas for the invasion of Russia. They came from
Greater France, from Switzerland, from Italy, from the Illyrian provinces, from the
satellite states of the Confederation of the Rhine, even handfuls of them from Spain
and Portugal. Prussia, an unwilling ally and even more unwilling host to this vast
concourse, was called upon to provide an army corps; Austria too. In all Bonaparte
mobilized 700,000 men, of which some 600,000 were to see service in the Russian
campaign. The main striking force, the Grande Armée, itself numbered 450,000
men and 1,146 guns.[25] To concentrate an armed force of this size posed an
unprecedented problem of planning and organization. It was tackled not by the
collective brain of a general staff, like the Prussian mobilizations of 1866 and 1870,
but by Bonaparte's own brain alone, for as usual he employed his subordinates
merely as errand boys. An even more daunting problem lay in the logistical
preparations needed in order to supply such an army on such a campaign; this again
Bonaparte reserved for his initiative alone. He fully recognized that he could not
apply the Guibertian system of warfare in the coming campaign. As he wrote to
Davout in May:

> The result of my movements will be to unite 400,000 men in a single place; there will be
> nothing then to hope for from the countryside, and we will have to carry everything
> with us.[26]

He therefore devoted himself to organizing the collection of enormous stocks of
supplies and dumping them at Danzig, the army's main base. On 13 January 1812 he
informed his Director of War Administration, Lacuée, that as a result of the
instructions which he, Bonaparte, had issued:

> I will have 20 million rations of bread, or enough for an army of 400,000 men for fifty
> days; I will have 20 million rations of rice at one ounce per day, or enough for 400,000
> men for fifty days. I will have 2 million bushels of oats, or enough for 50,000 horses for
> fifty days . . .[27]

No less elaborate were the measures Bonaparte took to create a transport service
on the scale he calculated necessary to move such quantities of stores to Danzig, and
thereafter carry them up to the army during its advance. He ordered military
transport battalions to be formed with a total of nearly 6,000 wagons, either horse-
drawn or ox-drawn – sufficient to carry enough flour for 200,000 men for two
months.[28] He ordered new designs to be produced for lighter-weight wagons that
could still carry the same quantity of stores. He requisitioned 15,000 horses in
Prussia alone for draft purposes. Great herds of cattle were to accompany the army
as meat on the hoof.

On paper then Bonaparte thought of everything, calculated everything, just as he had on paper while preparing to invade England. But once again Bonaparte's instructions conflated fantasy and reality. It was one thing to draft these compendious documents without reference to actual resources or manufacturing capacity, and quite another to implement them. By the beginning of March Bonaparte was having to write to Lacuée that:

> ... my intention is that the manufacture of wagons should not retard the departure of [transport] battalions; once again, I am pressed for time . . . I find myself in a situation of fearing not to have enough ambulances for the first encounters, which are always very sanguinary . . .[29]

By the middle of June, the eve of the campaign, Bonaparte's original grandiose target of enough supplies for 400,000 men for fifty days had shrunk to twenty to twenty-five days.[30] Even during the approach march through Germany to the assembly areas contingents of the Grande Armée resorted to pillage in order to eat. With regard to medical services too a wide gap existed between the Bonapartian instructions – and expectations – and the reality on the ground. Skilled surgeons, bandages, medicaments, hosptial beds and bedding, all were lacking in the quantities required for an army of 450,000 men (or 600,000, counting all those deployed in eastern Europe). So poor was the care of the army's health that even before the campaign opened there were more than 60,000 sick; perhaps double that number.[31]

While therefore Bonaparte had succeeded in assembling the largest army of history in Prussia and Poland by mid-June 1812 (and numbers acted on him as a powerful stimulant drug), he had also produced at the same time the largest military muddle in history; a mass of men, beasts and vehicles like a thousand Derby Days in one.

On 16 May Bonaparte reached Dresden with Marie-Louise, there to hold a fortnight's round of festivities ornamented by most of the royalty of Europe; a classic case, as it turned out, of the last ostentatious party thrown by a self-made tycoon before the receivers are put in. On 13 June he arrived in Königsberg, the army's forward base, to take command in person and launch the most ambitious of all his gambles. He was nearly forty-three now; no longer simply plump, but stout, thanks partly no doubt to two years of daily four-course lunches with Marie-Louise instead of his old midday snacks. The uniform he wore during the Russian campaign (now on exhibition in the Musée de l'Armée in Paris) shows him to have had a paunch protruding as if in pregnancy and upper arms like small legs of lamb. Even the court painters of the time portray a great head sitting almost neckless on massive shoulders. As his secretary Méneval remarks:

> The stoutness which he acquired during the last years of his reign had given his torso greater development than the lower part of his body, which since his fall has made it said that he gave the impression of a majestic and imposing bust which lacked a base in due proportion to its size.[32]

Thus in curious fashion Bonaparte's physique continued to express those inward flaws and disproportions of his nature, those coarsening sensibilities and that gluttony of power which had brought him and 600,000 men to the borders of

Russia. Yet over the native-born French contingent of the army, barely a third of
the total, Bonaparte still cast all his old spell of leadership. The German poet Heine
had watched him review the Guard during its passage through Germany:

> For ever I see him high on horseback, the eternal eyes set in the marble of that imperial
> visage, looking on with the calm of destiny at his Guards as they march past. He was
> sending them to Russia, and the old grenadiers glanced up at him with so awesome a
> devotion, so sympathetic an earnestness, with the pride of death: '*Te, Caesar, morituri
> salutant*'.[33]

Presented with the problem of war against so vast a country as Russia, orthodox
eighteenth-century grand strategy would have thought in terms of a step-by-step
advance, establishing magazines as it went, with the object of conquering a province
or two for use as bargaining counters at a peace conference. A solution so dim, so
cautious and so slow never occurred to Bonaparte, even in this special case. A rapid
swoop, a great battle, a resounding victory, a peace dictated to an abject foe – that as
ever was the way to do it. Indeed, since Bonaparte had only succeeded in organizing
supplies for three weeks' marching, it was the *only* way he could hope to do it. The
maps were spread; he plotted the majestically advancing arrows.

While he feinted south of Warsaw with Schwarzenberg's Austrian corps, the
Grande Armée, divided into three armies (the main body under himself in person, a
left-flank army under his stepson Eugène and a right-flank army under brother
Jerome) would cross the Niemen east of Kovno and advance, left shoulder forward,
on Vilna.[34] By this means Bonaparte hoped to thrust through the enemy centre,
splitting the Russian army under Prince Bagration which lay in the area west of
Minsk from other Russian forces north and northeast of Vilna; and at the same time
getting between Bagration and St Petersburg, the Russian capital. Thereafter much
would depend on Russian reactions, for opportunism formed as strong an element
in Bonaparte's strategy in 1812 as it had in 1796. In particular Bonaparte fervently
hoped that Bagration would respond to his advance on Vilna by launching a major
counter-stroke either on Warsaw or against the right of the Grande Armée. This
would enable him to carry out a favourite manoeuvre, bringing the Grande Armée
swinging down behind Bagration's own right flank and across his *derrières*, so
cutting him off and destroying him.[35]

On 24 June 1812 – sunshine and humid heat, a day for sweating wet inside serge
and braid, fur and steel and brass – the Grande Armée crossed the Niemen by
pontoon bridge and set foot on the soil of Russia. This happening had already of
course called forth an imperial order of the day:

> Soldiers! . . . At Tilsit Russia vowed eternal friendship to France and war on England.
> Today she breaks her oath! . . . Russia is drawn on by fate; her destinies must be fulfilled.
> Does she think we are degenerate? Are we no longer the soldiers of Austerlitz? She gives
> us a choice between dishonour and war: the choice cannot be in doubt. Let us then march
> forward . . .[36]

In marching forward, however, there were to be certain practical difficulties, one
of the earliest being, in Bonaparte's words on the second day of the invasion, that
'. . . our maps are so defective that we can find nothing further on them.'[37]

XIII

HIS MAJESTY'S HEALTH HAS NEVER BEEN BETTER

THE GRANDE ARMÉE'S DISSOLUTION began from the moment it took the road to Vilna, less than seventy-five miles distant from the Niemen. Although the soldiers carried four days' rations in their knapsacks, many guzzled them on the first day and thereafter left the ranks marauding for food. The weather hardly favoured the march: sunshine tropical in strength and humidity; torrential downpours; chilly nights. Bonaparte's hopes that the nearest Russian army under Barclay de Tolly (a Russian of Scots ancestry) would fight for Vilna met with disappointment, for hardly an enemy soldier was seen. Vilna itself, its supply dumps fired by the retreating Russians, proved an empty prize; so far, then, so bad.

Although the essence of Bonaparte's strategy lay in speed, he remained in Vilna. himself for over a fortnight, leaving his subordinates to conduct forward operations. Political problems, such as the need to settle the role of Polish leaders in the government of occupied Russian territory, hereabouts once belonging to the Polish kingdom, partly dictated this lengthy sojourn. But the main reason lay in a supply crisis which threatened Bonaparte's campaign with collapse and his army with starvation at the very outset of his march; a repetition on a vast scale of the crises he had faced on the road from Ceva to Turin in spring 1796, on the road to Gaza in 1799; on the Great St Bernard in 1800, and on the march to Ulm in 1805.

For the vast concourse of supply wagons and carts collected together by Bonaparte lay far to the rear, hopelessly jammed on rain-softened dirt roads sliced into impassable mince by iron-shod wheels; roads anyway inadequate to carry the volume of traffic. Slapdash staff-work completed the chaos. Despite all his unprecedented efforts to ensure his army's supply in Russia, Bonaparte had proved as a quartermaster no more equal to operational needs and difficulties than in earlier campaigns. The effect on the army was immediate and ruinous. The troops marched on empty stomachs in best Napoleonic style while Bonaparte sought to eke out scant available supplies;[1] units losing their cohesion in the hunt for food in a miserable countryside; stragglers and deserters clogging the rear, apt victims for marauding Cossacks.[2] The horses, now reduced to eating green corn from the fields in place of oats, sickened and died in vast numbers, so weakening the cavalry and artillery and redoubling the transport problem.[3]

During his fortnight's stay in Vilna Bonaparte, true to his dictum that character must dominate circumstance, therefore set about improvising new arrangements for supply and transport. He ordered roads to be repaired, fresh routes to be opened, bridges constructed, bread ovens to be built (a task delayed for want of horses to bring up the loads of bricks).[4] Yet as early as 7 July he had come to accept that the Grande Armée after all must depend largely on living off the country –

the very thing he had pronounced impossible in his preliminary planning.[5]

So within two weeks of the campaign's commencement the Grande Armée found itself reduced to living a few mouthfuls away from starvation according to standard Bonapartian precedent. And as a consequence of this Bonaparte himself, again true to precedent, hungered ever more anxiously for the deliverance of a decisive battle.

UNFORTUNATELY for Bonaparte the commander of the Russian army in eastern Poland, Prince Bagration, failed to launch that westward stroke on Warsaw which would have exposed his own *derrières*. Instead, he retreated eastwards. Though Bonaparte in Vilna hopefully ordered Davout to cut off Bagration's retreat while brother Jerome hemmed him in from the west, Bagration slipped away safely towards Smolensk. He escaped partly owing to Jerome's inexperience (it was one thing to appoint a brother to a mere king's job, quite another to place him in command of an army); partly because of the sheer difficulty of locating the enemy in these vast spaces of plain and forest where Poland merged into Russia. From Bonaparte downwards the French command could only grope and guess.

In the second week of July Bonaparte issued fresh directives for the French advance. On his extreme left flank Macdonald (a French general of Scots ancestry) and the Prussian corps were to besiege Riga; a sideshow. On his right Davout (Jerome, huffed at being placed by his brother under Davout, had returned to his Kingdom of Westphalia) was to pursue Bagration southeastwards in the direction of Moghilev. In the centre Bonaparte himself with the main body would thrust eastwards to Vitebsk, so, he hoped, shouldering his way between Bagration and Barclay, whom he correctly believed now to lie in a fortified camp at Drissa on the Dwina northwest of Vitebsk. With luck Bagration might be thrown southwards into the River Dnieper while Barclay was forced to retreat northwards to cover St Petersburg, the Russian capital.[6]

On 28 July Bonaparte rode into Vitebsk, disappointed in his hope that Barclay would give him a battle, his plan to split the Russian centre already a failure. For thanks to a timely order from the Tsar, Barclay abandoned the camp at Drissa and marched southeast to cover the road to Moscow. On 3 August Barclay and Bagration (who had evaded Davout) united their armies at Smolensk. So Bonaparte's second great lurch into the Russian void came to nothing. He found himself confronting a strategic problem as novel as it was baffling. For in most of his other campaigns his enemies had been kind enough to come forward to meet him, often in offensives of their own, thus offering the chance of that early decisive encounter upon which his gambler's strategic system so much depended. Yet the Russians were not pursuing a deliberate policy of evading action and drawing Bonaparte ever deeper into the country. It was simply that rivalry and indecision within the Russian command had thus far prevented them from giving battle. Nevertheless, the effect on the Grande Armée was just as destructive, for every extra mile of advance sharpened the French supply crisis. The Grande Armée struggled into Vitebsk like a dynosaur slowly expiring of sickness and hunger, while behind it along the roads to the Niemen lay its bloodstained dung in the form of the carcasses of uncounted horses and men; abandoned wagons, ambulances and guns.

For Bonaparte's efforts to solve his logistic problems during his stay in Vilna had completely failed; the combination of roads like swamps, want of fodder, the sheer number of vehicles to be moved and staff incompetence proved beyond the power of orders, however imperious, to surmount. The magazines of Vilna remained empty; the sick lacking even straw to lie on.[7] In Vitebsk itself only a hospital of 1,400 beds could be set up for an army which still numbered 230,000 men with the colours, such being the dearth of supplies. Even Bonaparte, devotee of 'sword in the kidneys' (a favourite phrase) pursuits though he was, had to call a halt:

> . . . the condition of the cavalry, infantry and artillery [he wrote on 29 July] is such that I have resolved, unless the enemy forces me to the contrary, to remain [here] seven or eight days in order to rest the army.[8]

It was not the weather, trying as it had been, which had brought the Grande Armée to this lamentable condition after only five weeks in the field, but Bonaparte's own professional shortcomings. To cite an expert opinion, that of the Duke of Wellington (expressed many years later after he had studied French accounts of the campaign):

> . . . those who know what an army is well know that a storm of rain, whatever its violence and character, does not destroy the horses of an army. That which does destroy them, that which renders those who survive nearly unfit for service throughout the campaign . . . is hard work, forced marches, no corn or dry fodder at the period of which green corn is on the ground, and is invariably eaten by the horses of the army. It is the period of the year at which of all others a commander who cares for his army will avoid enterprises the execution of which requires forced marches or the hard work of the horses.[9]

Nor, in the Duke's judgment, did rain and heat destroy infantry:

> . . . but forced marches on roads destroyed by storms of rain, through a country unprovided with shelter, and without provisions, do destroy soldiers, as every one left behind is without resources, is exposed, unsheltered and starving, to the effects of the storm; he cannot follow and overtake his corps and must perish.[10]

Now Bonaparte in Vitebsk sought to repair the damage by rapping out another series of comprehensive instructions. But as General de Fezensac, who was present, observes:

> . . . it is not enough to give orders, it is necessary that the orders are capable of execution; and given the speed of movement, the concentration of troops in the same place, the poor state of the roads, the difficulty in feeding the horses, how was it possible to make regular issues of rations and organize the hospital services?[11]

Bonaparte himself blamed his subordinates for the failure of his orders to result in well-stocked magazines and a smooth flow of supplies. The Duke of Wellington notes however that:

> . . . these orders were not given as other Generals at the head of armies have given similar orders, pointing out the places where, and the means by which, these provisions were to be collected and stored in magazine; and by supplying the money necessary to pay for their cost . . .[12]

But ready cash – that is, *French* ready cash – was the very thing revolutionary and Imperial France had always lacked; the very thing therefore that Bonapartian or Guibertian warfare was designed to dispense with as far as possible.

The truth is that in undertaking to invade Russia at all Bonaparte had again deceived himself, as in the case of the project to invade England, that 'genius' could find an answer to an inherently insoluble strategic equation. For an army large enough to crush Russian resistance simply could not be adequately supplied, given the capacity and condition of available roads and the poverty of the countryside; Spain all over again.

Now, in Vitebsk, he had to take possibly the most momentous decision of his career. Should he close down the 1812 campaign, restore his army, reorganize his supply system and try for victory in 1813? Or should he march on still further in hopes that he might yet force the Russians to a decisive battle? On arrival in Vitebsk he had talked grandly of establishing a vast base in western Russia, and taking Moscow in 1813 and St Petersburg in 1814. 'The war with Russia,' he proclaimed, 'is a three-year business!'[13] He failed, however, to issue orders for this base area to be organized; proof of inner doubt. He prowled and paced his room, touchy and abstracted, restless and bored. His secretary sent urgently to the imperial librarian in Paris for 'some amusing books' to soothe his spirit.[14]

By the first week of August Bonaparte seemed to make up his mind. He would go on, as he had gone on across northern Italy; as he had twice gone on to Vienna and beyond. Volubly he justified this decision to his entourage. In Moscow, in his words, Russia's 'holy city', he would find peace with or without a battle. In any case he could not remain in Vitebsk with the campaign still undecided 'without weakening the spell of his infallibility . . . and without arousing dangerous hopes in Europe . . .'[15] But his subordinates argued the dangers of going on, given the already grim state of the army. The arguments were long and loud.[16] For once Bonaparte listened; dithered for several days, hoping that the Russians would kindly oblige by attacking him. On 8 August enemy cavalry drove in his outposts. Surely this meant that a battle lay within reach at last? So on 10 August the Grande Armée set off eastwards again. Wishful thinking, that traitor within Bonaparte's powerful mind, held him in thrall once more. 'Everything leads one to believe,' he wrote to Ney on the 12th, 'that there will be a great battle at Smolensk.'[17]

There was not. Late in the afternoon of the 16th he saw the city before him in the westering sun, a vision of gilded onion domes. Next morning he ordered an immediate assault on its eighteen-feet-thick walls; the assault failed with heavy loss; Fort Bard or Acre all over again. That night the Russians completed their evacuation of Smolensk, their departure concealed by the flaming destruction of its wooden buildings, ignited either by French shells or the Russians themselves or both. The city went up like one vast roaring bonfire of dry sticks, a strong breeze whirling showers of sparks high into the darkness. While Caulaincourt, the Master of the Horse, was watching this appalling scene, Bonaparte joined him with Berthier and Marshal Bessières.

> 'An eruption of Vesuvius!' cried the Emperor, clapping me on the shoulder . . . 'Is not that a fine sight, my Master of Horse?'

'Horrible, Sire!'

'Bah!' rejoined the Emperor. 'Remember, gentlemen, what one of the Roman emperors said, "The corpse of a dead enemy always smells good!"'[18]

This, however, was the limit of the pleasure which Smolensk, yet another empty prize, another unfought battle, was to afford Bonaparte.

Now he had to decide afresh whether to call a halt or march all the way to Moscow, still 240 miles distant. After a brief hesitation he opted for Moscow, not least because, as he confided to one of his generals, 'this army can no longer halt . . . movement alone keeps it together. One can advance at the head of it, but neither stop nor retreat.'[19] On 24 August the Grande Armée, now reduced to only 156,000 men, set off into the east again, hungry, tormented by the heat, riddled with dysentery, shedding sick men and beasts as it went. Behind it, along the ever-lengthening French communications, Cossacks and local partisans pursued the same kind of war as the Spanish *guerrilleros* 1,500 miles away: a war of the ambushed convoy or courier, the sudden assault on the lonely post or depot, the knife across the throat.[20] In this violence that knew neither rules nor mercy was consummated the process begun by Bonaparte himself sixteen years earlier when he first 'brilliantly' broke eighteenth-century warfare's code of conduct and threw aside the wisdom of its self-imposed limitations.

On 2 September, at Gzhatsk, more than halfway from Smolensk to Moscow, Bonaparte at last received the tidings for which he had been waiting so eagerly for nearly six weeks, and which promised the deliverance of which he stood in such dire need. The Russian army was digging in across the Moscow road near the village of Borodino in evident preparation for a battle.

'. . . cunning and dangerous as an old bear . . .': General Kutusov (1745–1813). Contemporary woodcut. *Society for Cultural Relations with the U.S.S.R., London. Photo: John Freeman*

THE TSAR ALEXANDER, perturbed by his armies' continued retreat and by bickering between Barclay and Bagration, had appointed General Kutusov to supreme command. Kutusov was sixty-seven years old, bloated, dissolute, lethargic, drunken, but as cunning and dangerous as an old bear. In 1805 he alone had argued against the rash forward move that led to the catastrophe at Austerlitz. Throughout the present campaign he had urged a strategy of withdrawal and evasion which would ruin Bonaparte's army without a fight; a strategy that Russia had in fact carried out without intending to. Now by a paradox Kutusov found himself under orders from the Tsar to fight a battle. None the less Kutusov's cunning found scope enough in the planning of this battle. Instead of ambitiously either attacking Bonaparte or seeking to outmanoeuvre him like so many of Bonaparte's enemies in the past, he proposed to fight a completely defensive and static battle in positions as strong as nature and spades could contrive; such a battle being, moreover, exactly suited to the stubborn valour of the Russian soldier. Kutusov's right flank was protected by the River Moskva, his left by a thick woodland. His centre lay on rising ground behind ravines cut into the surface of the plain by winter torrents; and he further buttressed it by powerful redoubts packed with artillery. Along this four-mile front he deployed 120,000 men and 640 guns; a very much greater density than the Austrians had enjoyed at Wagram.

Bonaparte himself was slightly stronger in infantry, with about 130,000 men,

and weaker in artillery, with 587 guns. For the first time in his career he had to attack a static enemy strongly and densely posted in a fortified position, whereas almost all his victories so far had been won in encounter battles in which his own and his army's qualities of quick thinking, adroit footwork and hard punching told to best effect. In evolving a plan of attack he was, moreover, hampered by want of detailed information about the Russian position and by inadequate maps, his perpetual bane in Russia. Davout, impressed by the strength of Kutusov's line, proposed that the Grande Armée should turn it by advancing round its left, or southern flank. But Bonaparte feared lest the Russians should slip away again while this manoeuvre was in progress. He opted instead for a frontal offensive, meaning to smash the Russian army to pieces where it stood. According to his general instruction for the battle, massed French batteries were to crush the artillery in the enemy redoubts, after which infantry would take the redoubts by storm. 'The combat having thus begun,' continued Bonaparte a trifle feebly, 'orders will be given according to the enemy's dispositions.'[21]

The 6th of September was spent by both armies in preparing for action. Bonaparte, a victim of a feverish cold and of difficulty in passing urine, was much cheered by the arrival of a painting of his son, the King of Rome, playing with a toy. He quickly put it to propaganda use by having it propped on a chair outside his tent for his soldiers to see, an inspirational purpose served in the Russian camp by ikons and incense. Bonaparte had been rather less cheered by the arrival of an account by Marshal Marmont of his resounding defeat at Wellington's hands at the Battle of Salamanca. This event Bonaparte blamed on Marmont's disobedience to his, Bonaparte's, orders, a charge as factually baseless as the similar one levelled by Bonaparte against Admiral Brueys, defeated and killed at Aboukir in 1798.[22]

At two in the morning of the 7th, Bonaparte, his cold liberally dosed with punch, finished writing the customary pre-battle order of the day; a tired exercise in the style of Henry v's speech before Agincourt:

> Soldiers, here is the battle you have so much wanted! Henceforward victory depends on you: we need it. It will give us abundance, good winter quarters and an early return to the homeland! Conduct yourselves as at Austerlitz, at Friedland, at Vitebsk, at Smolensk, so that the remotest posterity will cite with pride your conduct on this day. *Let them say of you: He was present at this great battle under the walls of Moscow!*[23]

Though it was of no moment to the imperial copywriter, the walls of Moscow in fact still lay some seventy miles distant.

At six in the morning of 7 September 1812, with sun dispersing the night mists ('The sun of Austerlitz!' exclaimed Bonaparte hopefully), the French guns opened the Battle of Borodino.

The course of the day proved Bonaparte to be no better at achieving a breakthrough than the derided allied generals on the Western Front during the Great War. His preliminary bombardment failed either to demolish the enemy's redoubts or silence his artillery. The French assaults that followed were inspired by no simple but effective plan such as Marlborough carried out at Blenheim and Ramillies, of attacking one wing of the enemy to compel him to draw troops from his centre, which could then be breached in a final offensive blow. Instead, successive French piecemeal attacks gained ground only slowly and at horrifying human cost in the face of Russian cannon-fire and savage counter-strokes. As was Bonaparte's custom, he made no attempt to conduct the French attack in person, but observed the proceedings from a knoll in the rear. What with his bladder trouble and feverish cold he was not in any case feeling at his most dynamic.

In the late afternoon the Grande Armée forced the Russians out of their redoubts, only to see them forming up again in the rear, their resolution and cohesion still unbroken. Rather than risk the Guard, his personal reserve and last undamaged formation, Bonaparte now renounced any further attempt to bring about the enemy's collapse. The exhausted, eviscerated armies bivouacked where they had come to rest, the French facing the grim possibility of having to attack again on the morrow. The Grand Armée had lost between 30,000 and 40,000 (no exact figures exist) in killed and wounded – a quarter to a third of its total engaged strength.

Next day Kutusov drew his army off towards Moscow, so enabling Bonaparte to claim the victory.

AROUND MIDDAY on 14 September, the Grande Armée – now only some 100,000 strong – crested a range of low hills and saw the onion domes and towers of Moscow before it, 'the sun making the city sparkle with a thousand colours', as General Ségur remembered:

> . . . the entire army clapped its hands and repeated with rapture: 'Moscow! Moscow!' as sailors cry out 'Land! Land!' at the end of a long and hazardous voyage . . . Napoleon himself hurried forward. He stopped in excitement; a cry of happiness escaped him . . . 'There at last is this famous city! . . . And about time!'[24]

Eighty-two days had elapsed since the Grande Armée crossed the Niemen; five hundred miles of Russian road. All that now remained was for Moscow's civic dignitaries ceremonially to hand him the keys of the city, like their confrères over

'. . . the stubborn valo of the Russian soldier': soldier swinging a sab Pencil and watercolou drawing by C. Alexan Ivanovich Sauerweid. *Wellington Collection, Stratfield Saye*

the years in Turin, Milan, Cairo, Vienna and Berlin, and he could make his triumphant entry amid the expected watching crowds; the military grand-tourist rendering a visit to yet another ancient capital. But like so much else in the Russian campaign, the event did not run according to pattern. No civil leaders turned out to surrender the keys; no crowds watched him ride in. For the French discovered that with the exception of its humblest citizenry Moscow was a deserted city; a literally empty prize apart from stocks of guns and ammunition for Bonaparte and loot for his soldiers. And in the course of the four days following Bonaparte's depressingly unceremonial entry, Moscow's value to the Grande Armée was further impaired by a spectacular fire kindled in obedience to orders issued by Count Rostopchin, the city's governor, before his departure. Only a small area round the Kremlin remained as shelter for the French amid acres of charred and stinking débris, the blind façades of burned-out buildings. Moscow, the distant sight of which had so lifted the army's sinking morale only a few days earlier, presented, in General de Fezensac's words, 'a spectacle at once horrible and weird'.[25]

Bonaparte now found himself in a familiar enough situation: outwardly one of successful conquest, actually one of weakness and peril. In all his previous Continental campaigns his enemy had got him off the hook either by rashly attacking him or by concluding a peace. However, Kutusov, now lying at Kaluga to the southwest of Moscow where he equally protected Russia's rich southern provinces and threatened Bonaparte's communications, showed no sign of attacking. Nor did the Tsar manifest a desire to make peace, even though Bonaparte sent him repeated peace feelers and assured him that his invasion of the Tsar's domains had been inspired by no personal ill-will.[26] The days, the weeks, passed. Still Kutusov made no move; still the Tsar made no reply. This time therefore the grand-strategic magician kept waving his wand in vain; no doves of peace fluttered from the cocked hat. The trick, though so often successful since 1796, seemed to have gone wrong. How baffling! How embarrassing! Pacing his study in the

'Moscow's value to the Grande Armée was further impaired by a spectacular fire . . .': the burning of Moscow, September 1812, as visualized by the English cartoonist, George Cruikshank. *British Museum*

Kremlin, preoccupied, less garrulous than usual, Bonaparte none the less typically clung to a belief that with Moscow in his hands the Tsar must and would make peace in the end; a belief from which his entourage could not wean him.[27]

And while he hung on, the Russian winter loomed nearer and his army decayed day by day. The ambulance service had virtually collapsed;[28] the cavalry alone needed 14,000 horses;[29] the five hundred miles of road back to the Nieman lay under constant partisan attack. With mounting alarm his subordinates urged him to retreat while there was yet time. But he had withdrawn again into that halfway world of his between reality and fantasy. The unusually warm autumn weather encouraged him to sneer at his Master of Horse's warning of snows and frosts to come: 'So this is the terrible Russian winter that M. de Caulaincourt frightens the children with.'[30] He refused to hear the truth about the state of his army, instead resorting as in the Eylau campaign to fantasy orders. As one of his generals wrote:

> . . . At one time we were . . . to protect the peasants who would bring in supplies to market, although all the surrounding districts had been stripped bare and the peasants had taken up arms against us; another time it was a question of buying 10,000 horses in a countryside which had neither horses nor inhabitants; then the project was announced of passing the winter in a ravaged city where we were dying of hunger in October.[31]

And still not a word came from the Tsar. Still the Russian campaign, and with it Bonaparte's career, lay poised between advance and recoil.

BY MID-OCTOBER, however, reality had pierced coldly through Bonaparte's wrappings of self-delusion. The Tsar was *not* going to make peace; the Russian winter *was* going to happen; and he, Bonaparte, had no alternative but to retreat. On 14 October he began to issue preparatory orders.[32].

So at last it had finally come to pass – that total collapse of his strategy which had very nearly occurred in every single campaign he had fought from 1796 onwards.[33] The Russians had proved the first to discover, if largely by accident, the weapons inevitably fatal to a gambler such as Bonaparte – time, space, evasion and sheer tenacity. And other nations too would now learn the Russian lesson. Bonaparte had been rumbled. Never again was he to enjoy that essential prerequisite of his earlier success, opponents who conveniently played into his hands.

ON 18 OCTOBER Kutusov launched a surprise attack on Murat at Winkovo which was beaten off only with difficulty; the final prod to Bonaparte's reluctant purpose. During the night of the 18th–19th what was left of the Grande Armée began to steal away from Moscow, furtive like a thief, loaded with valuables like a thief. 'There was something lugubrious about this march', wrote General de Fezensac. 'The darkness of night, the still smoking débris we trod underfoot, all seemed to combine to strike gloom into the imagination.'[34]

This was more than the turning-point of the Russian campaign; it was the turning-point of Bonaparte's life adventure. For what he had said of the Grande Armée back in Smolensk was equally true of his Empire: 'movement alone keeps it together. One can advance at the head of it, but neither stop nor retreat.'

THE GRANDE ARMÉE took the road to Kaluga rather than the direct westerly route to Smolensk, partly in order to support Murat, partly in order to find unravaged country to live off during its retreat. On 24 October Bonaparte found Kutusov blocking his path at Malo-Yaroslavetz, and attacked him: a smaller Borodino. For a moment a vision enticed Bonaparte of saving the campaign after all by attacking Kutusov again and crushing him. The lateness of the season, the state of his army and the arguments of his marshals dissuaded him. He turned back; back to the devastated Smolensk road. Now the retreat began in earnest; the confusions and sufferings of the advance all over again. According to Caulaincourt, Bonaparte's Master of the Horse:

> Never was a retreat worse planned, or carried out with less discipline; never did convoys march so badly. Precautionary calculations and dispositions had no place in the arrangements that were made and it was owing to this lack of forethought that we owed a great part of our disaster . . . Shaped and drilled into being no more than an obedient instrument, the staff could do nothing of itself for the general good.[35]

The Cossacks prowled the flanks and rear, butchering the sick, the exhausted and the straggler. Yet by a mercy the weather still remained mild for Russia at this season, even though night frosts warned that winter could spring its ambush at any moment.

Thus far Bonaparte himself 'still did not or would not admit' the true condition of the army[36] or its danger. He looked to Smolensk and its magazines as to a sanctuary. While Kutusov would grow weaker as he advanced, so Bonaparte believed, he himself would find copious stores and reinforcements, enabling him to go into winter quarters.[37] He issued instructions for the gathering and issue of rations that belonged wholly to the realm of dreams.[38]

On 29 October the Grande Armée traversed the field of Borodino, where 30,000 rotting corpses served as a ghastly reminder of the futility of the sacrifices both of the dead and of the still living. Two days later it reached Viazma, its numbers reduced to 65,000 from the 100,000 deployed at Malo-Yaroslavetz barely a week before.[39] The weather now turned dry and bitterly cold; the horses, unprovided with frost nails, slipped in droves on the frozen mud, many too weak to rise again, many breaking their legs. On 7 November the snow came at last.

It was at this time of gathering calamity that Bonaparte received news from Paris which brought home to him just how insubstantial his regime remained even after some twelve years' existence and in spite of all his apparent triumphs. A former general, one named Malet, had escaped from a lunatic asylum and succeeded for several hours in convincing civil and military authorities in the capital that Bonaparte was dead, his Empire at an end, and that he, Malet, had assumed power in the name of the exiled Moreau. Bonaparte was deeply mortified at the willingness of some senior officials to believe Malet and co-operate with him, and by the general failure to rally to the Empress and the King of Rome during the shortlived *coup d'état*. 'The French are like women,' he indignantly remarked to Caulaincourt, 'one must not stay away from them too long. You cannot tell what intrigues they might be persuaded into – and what might happen – if they were too long without news of me.'[40]

The last stages of the retreat from Moscow, 1812. In fact the Grande Armée suffered more from Bonaparte's own mismanagement than the weather. Contemporary painting. *Bildarchiv Preussischer Kulturbesitz, Berlin*

While Ney and the rearguard fought daily to hold off the vengeful enemy, the army dragged itself on through the snow towards the haven of Smolensk. Bonaparte himself, sometimes riding in his carriage, sometimes walking with a stick amid the Guard, had lost his cockiness now; his manner had become 'grave, silent and resigned; suffering physically less than others, but spiritually much more.'[41]

Between 9 and 14 November 1812 the Grande Armée, now no more than 50,000 strong, straggled into Smolensk, the thought of whose stores of food and clothing had kept it going; the city which Bonaparte intended to form the advanced base of his winter quarters.[42] But instead Smolensk proved the climactic example of the incompetence of French military administration during the Napoleonic era. In the first place the magazines were only half-stocked; it had proved easier for Bonaparte to issue instructions to have them filled than to carry out the instructions in a stripped countryside and without ready cash to buy provisions from far afield through Jewish merchants. Secondly, the French army, accustomed to the system of living by pillage, lacked efficient commissariat officers experienced in the complex task of swiftly issuing rations from a depot to an army. The result was, as the Duke of Wellington wrote later, that the commissariat in Smolensk performed the task 'but slowly, and men who were starving with hunger and cold were little disposed to wait to satisfy their appetites until these persons had gone through all the formalities.'[43] The desperate soldiery therefore simply broke into the magazines by main force and pillaged them. In the chaos that followed, all the stocks were dissipated within twenty-four hours. In General de Fezensac's words, 'they pillaged and they starved.'[44]

During his stay in Smolensk Bonaparte learned that a Russian army under

Wittgenstein had captured Vitebsk, on the road to Vilna. Though this finally shattered his hopes of establishing winter quarters round Vitebsk, he deluded himself afresh that he could still do so further west. As Caulaincourt remarks: 'It seemed as if the Emperor were expecting some miracle to alter the climate and end the ruin that was descending upon us from every side . . .'[45]

The Grande Armée, its numbers now down to 36,000, fell back from Smolensk, which was to have restored it, in a state more deliquescent and despairing than ever. Now began that episode of final disintegration in the snow popularly remembered to this day as 'the retreat from Moscow'. Kutusov relentlessly pressed the rearguard; Wittgenstein threatened the line of retreat from the north; Admiral Chichagov and a third Russian army took Minsk, a main French base to which Bonaparte had been looking for his next refuge. Now he was forced to direct his army's retreat to Vilna by a new route via Borisov on the River Beresina. Amid the wreck of his grandest adventure and the ruin of his army, these most immediate of realities, Bonaparte could still cover his mind with tatters of illusion. 'Hope, the merest suggestion of success,' wrote Caulaincourt, 'exalted him more excessively than the worst reverses disheartened him . .'[46] General de Ségur recalled that in Bonaparte's eyes 'and in the midst of these deserts of mud and ice, this handful of men was still the Grande Armée and he the conqueror of Europe!'[47]

On 21 November Chichagov's army blocked the crossing of the Beresina at Borisov. French engineers thereupon built two trestle bridges over the river some five miles to the north; a truly heroic performance. On 25–29 November a chaotic, panic-stricken mass of men, women, beasts and vehicles struggled frantically across these fragile structures while the rearguard fought off the eager Russians. Thirteen thousand corpses, frozen hard as stone, enabled the enemy to make a grisly reckoning of those who failed to reach the bridges.

Nothing was left now of the Grande Armée but a rabble of 16,000–20,000 men bereft of all fighting power and fleeing for the sanctuary of Vilna. Yet even while Bonaparte was acknowledging to his foreign minister in Vilna that the army was so exhausted and disbanded that it could do no more, not even if it were a question of defending Paris, the fantasist in him was assuring the same minister that 'ten days' rest and plenty of victuals will restore discipline.'[48] If it were not for Chichagov taking Minsk, so the fantasist Bonaparte averred to the minister, and for the inaction of certain of his own commanders, 'I would have remained at Smolensk, Vitebsk, Orcha, Moghilev.'[49]

At Smorghoni on 5 December 1812 Bonaparte, deciding that his fortunes demanded his earliest presence in Paris, set off post-haste for home. He bequeathed Murat the unattractive task of rallying the army. Two days beforehand, at Molodechno, he had drafted his now famous 29th Bulletin,[50] a lurid catalogue of sufferings and disasters which for the first time revealed to France and Europe the extent of the Grande Armée's destruction. Bonaparte concluded his narration of this the most colossal catastrophe in the history of war, the cause of grief to hundreds of thousands of families throughout Europe, by reassuring his readers that 'His Majesty's health has never been better.'[51]

Yet although the 29th Bulletin did not unduly gloss over the ruin of the Grande Armée, it nevertheless launched a fresh Bonapartian legend on its way – the legend that it was the retreat alone which destroyed the army, and above all the Russian winter. 'This army', wrote Bonaparte, 'so fine on 6 November, was very different from the 14th onwards; almost without cavalry, without artillery, without transport.' But in fact the Grande Armée lost more than 350,000 men during the advance to Moscow; only some 80,000 during the retreat. It lost 35,000 men in fair weather in one week between the eve of Malo-Yaroslavetz (including 5,000 casualties in the battle) and the arrival at Viazma; 15,000–20,000 during that particular week of snowfall between Viazma and Smolensk cited by Bonaparte as the beginning of the catastrophe. Moreover, very many of the army's horses succumbed to hunger and overwork before the cold struck.[52]

By transforming the sorry tale of its author's military incompetence into the epic of any army's courage, the 29th Bulletin fostered Bonaparte's legend in ways that he could not have foreseen. For 'The Retreat From Moscow' – humanity pitting its spirit against savage nature and malign fate – was to capture the romantic imagination of the nineteenth century, inspiring painters and writers alike to graphic reconstruction of its horrors. Bonaparte amid the snows came to acquire something of the character of Lear on the storm-blasted heath; a tragic hero whose more-than-human stature was paradoxically even enhanced in Bonaparte's case by the very immensity of the catastrophe he had brought about.

But all this lay in the future. In December 1812, when Bonaparte set off for Paris in order to restore his fortunes, the sixteen-year spell of his success had just been spectacularly broken. As a consequence, he had lost more than the greatest of all his campaigns, more than the largest army he was ever to command; he had lost the essential stock-in-trade of a speculator such as he – his credit.

XIV

AFTER SUCH BUTCHERY, NO RESULT

IT HAD TAKEN BONAPARTE sixteen years to rise from command of the Army of Italy to the throne of apparent power and success he enjoyed on the eve of the Russian adventure. After his return from that adventure, sixteen months sufficed for him to lose it all.

This helter-skelter decline and fall was caused by the continued destruction of the military strength which alone maintained his unstable empire. And that destruction, in turn, was caused by Bonaparte himself. But it was not, as some historians have argued, that his military talents and energies had decayed. His performance as a strategist and a commander in 1813–14 was neither better nor worse than in 1796–7; his vigour (measured by correspondence and strenuousness of activity) even greater. Rather it was that he failed to perceive that he was now operating in a fundamentally different political and military environment; failed therefore to adapt himself accordingly. Instead, he went on stubbornly repeating his old formulas of diplomacy and strategy like a gambler sticking to his system even though the game has swung persistently against him, even though each further throw leads to fresh calamitous loss. For these reasons there is a curious quality of *déjà-vu* about the campaigns of 1813 and 1814 – and 1815 too.

IN THE EVENT the wreckage of the Grande Armée could not hold East Prussia and the Grand-Duchy of Warsaw, let alone Vilna. Early in March 1813 Eugène (who had replaced Murat) gave up the line of the Oder, evacuated Berlin and fell back behind the Elbe in the face of the inexorable Russian advance. On 15 March the King of Prussia, the shackles of Bonapartian oppression lifting after seven years, signed an alliance with the Tsar; next day he declared war on France. So Prussia took the field again – but a new Prussia, with an army and state reformed and modernized under the sting of her defeat in 1806; champion-in-arms of awakened German nationalism. Yet only a year earlier Bonaparte had asserted that nothing need be feared from the Germans, 'a people so wise, so reasonable, so tolerant . . .'[1] Now he discovered that Germans too, like Italians, like Spaniards, could be goaded into a people's war; he received afresh an unlearned lesson that force as a tool of statecraft eventually rebounds on the user. The poets and philosophers proclaimed the cause of German freedom; the bands crashed out 'Preussens Gloria'; young patriots flocked to the colours. Germany, Bonaparte's base of operations, became a clogging swamp of armed hostility, like northern Italy in 1796. Here then was the first *déjà-vu* of 1813. The second lay in Bonaparte's own response to this self-induced problem: 'At the least sign of hostility from a Prussian town or village,' he ordered Eugène, 'have it burned down . . .'[2]

Meanwhile, Austria was deftly edging away from her alliance with Bonaparte into neutrality; a first step towards possible belligerence. Bonaparte had really believed that by marrying Marie-Louise he had secured the Emperor Francis' undying support. Quite blind to the effect on Austria of his cumulative tramplings on her power and influence, he could actually interpret her new policy as 'desertion'. It rankled, and continued to do so.[3]

English diplomacy now seized its moment; the Fifth Coalition against France since 1792 began to take shape. In the early months of 1813, therefore, Bonaparte confronted an old and familiar problem. The true interests of France herself now demanded a compromise peace even more urgently than in late 1795, when the Directory (advised by Bonaparte) instead first began the endless search for a 'glorious peace' by opting for the invasion of Italy. In spring 1813 the allies offered such a compromise settlement, generously based in the circumstances on the Treaty of Lunéville of 1801. Bonaparte was to keep domination of Italy and the Low Countries, but evacuate Spain and give up Germany beyond the 'natural frontiers' of the Rhine. Bonaparte turned down these proposals. As always he meant to dictate his own peace at gun-point after a great victory. However, this refusal prodded Austria into taking a slow road to war. Once again then – another *déjà-vu* – Bonaparte had helped England to create her coalition.[4]

And so once again armed force was to serve as a substitute for statecraft instead of its instrument; France was to wage yet another needless campaign. Therefore, in a replay of 1800 before Marengo or 1809 before Eckmühl, Bonaparte had now to improvise a new army in desperate haste. But never had he poured forth instructions in such quantity or detail; a vast paper monument to a will to power that the Russian catastrophe, instead of taming, only served to madden.

Yet for all his unprecedented exertions, the army of 1813 was the most ramshackle he had ever led; its rank and file largely young conscripts, some of whom did not receive muskets until in Germany; many of its officers and non-commissioned officers elderly dug-outs or newly promoted and inexperienced. It proved impossible to re-create the cavalry arm destroyed in Russia owing to shortages of horses and trained troopers. Supplies of all kinds were desperately scarce; so too cash to buy them, forcing Bonaparte again to dip into his own imperial treasure.[5] As Marshal Marmont reported from Germany to Berthier in April, '. . . there is a large collection of men here, but there is not an organized army . . .'[6] In the light of such military realities Bonaparte's decision to resort to force rather than a compromise peace becomes the more irresponsible.

In his place a prudent commander such as the elder Moltke might have minimized the army's shortcomings by standing on the defensive well back behind the barrier of the Rhine and its fortresses.[7] Instead Bonaparte, true to character, opted for his favourite strategic cure-all, a fast-moving offensive with the aim of deciding the campaign at a stroke. He intended to destroy the Russians and Prussians before the Austrians, not yet ready, could join in; rather as in 1805 he had dealt with the Austrians at Ulm before the Russians could take the field. Speed was – as ever – of the essence; time as ever his self-made enemy.

In the last days of April Bonaparte led his army eastwards across the River Saale from its assembly area in central Germany near the old battlefield of Jena-Auerstädt. Of his strength in Germany of 225,000 men and 457 guns, the garrisoning of fortresses and the need to defend depots and communications against partisans left barely 150,000 and 372 guns as a field army under his own command. In infantry he was superior to the allied forces; in cavalry he could oppose only 8,000 to 24,000, a heavy handicap for an attacking army.[8] The French moved forward in the customary higgledy-piggledy jostling of men, vehicles and beasts, coupled with the no less habitual random marauding and destruction.[9] Since his lack of cavalry left Bonaparte with only the sketchiest notion of the enemy's dispositions, his advance marked yet another hopeful lunge in the dark.

On 2 May 1813, when the French army had reached a front Leipzig-Lützen, Bonaparte was surprised by a violent enemy offensive against his right-flank corps at Lützen. There began a scrambling battle in which the French corps reached the decisive point one by one and just in time – Rivoli or Eylau or Marengo again. One corps (Bertrand's) was left stationary for two hours within sound of the guns for want of orders, like Bernadotte's at Jena-Auerstädt. Bonaparte himself for once reverted to the front-line leader of Lodi and Arcola, knowing how imperative it was to open his campaign with a success. His unfledged troops fought bravely but amateurishly. At the end of a day's murderous struggle and after a bombardment by an eighty-gun battery and an onslaught by the Guard, he had his victory; but another Wagram or Borodino, not Austerlitz. The French lost 18,000 killed, wounded and missing; the allies only 11,500. And the allies drew off in good order.[10]

On 8 May Bonaparte entered Dresden, capital of Saxony. It seemed that the Russians had retreated east through Bautzen, but where now were the Prussians? Bonaparte guessed that they had moved north to cover Berlin. He therefore split up his own army, directing Ney with the smaller portion to Luckau, midway between Dresden and Berlin. He reckoned that he and Ney, though physically separated, would still remain strategically united, each able to close in quickly on the other as necessary; a characteristic Bonapartian arrangement.[11]

But in the event, and by no means for the first time in his career, Bonaparte failed to unite his divided army on the decisive battlefield according to plan. On 14 May he received news that the Prussians were actually rallying on the Russians at Bautzen. He thereupon resolved to advance and attack the allies again, hoping this time to gain a decisive victory that would, among other things, deter Austria from entering the war. However, he ordered Ney to march southeast on Bautzen with only part of his force; two of his corps were to advance north on Berlin. Then – an echo of Marengo and Desaix – he countermanded the order; Ney was to march on Bautzen with his entire force in order to take the enemy in the right flank and rear. But the two corps destined for Berlin had already taken the road. Unlike Desaix in 1800 they countermarched too late to reach the Bautzen battlefield in time.

Ney's impact on the battle was further weakened because of an ambiguously worded order about his role from Bonaparte in his own execrable hand – echoes here of his failure to give Bernadotte clear orders at Jena-Auerstädt or any orders at all at Eylau, or to order Ney at Eylau to close in on the main body in time. It did not occur to Bonaparte to ride a distance of less than ten miles and take personal command of Ney's vital outflanking stroke.[12]

As a consequence of these confusions Ney entirely failed to fall upon the enemy rear like an avalanche as Bonaparte intended. The two-day Battle of Bautzen (20– 21 May 1813) turned out to be another series of bloody French frontal attacks, this time costing 20,000 casualties, followed by another orderly enemy withdrawal. In words uncannily like Ney's after Eylau Bonaparte remarked: 'What! After such butchery, no result! No prisoners at all!'[13] Disappointment changed to grief a few minutes later when Duroc, his Grand Marshal of the Palace, and a man for whom he seemed to entertain genuine feeling, was disembowelled by a round-shot and died slowly in agony. Still, Bonaparte's visit to Duroc's deathbed made wonderful copy for an imperial bulletin; just as good as Lannes' death after Aspern. Duroc, we are told:

> . . . seized the Emperor's hand and carried it to his lips. 'All my life,' he told him, 'has been dedicated to your service . . .' 'Duroc,' said the Emperor, 'there is another life! There you will be waiting for me and we will meet again one day . . .'[14]

Although Bonaparte's successes had fallen well short of the great victory he had looked for, he had none the less inflicted two reverses on the allies and driven them back over two hundred miles into Silesia. Now was the time, it might seem, to push his offensive to the hilt in true Napoleonic fashion. Instead, on 4 June, he concluded an armistice, to run until 20 July, later extended to 17 August. For his military position was such that he simply had to have a respite, just as in the case of the peace of Leoben in 1797 and the armistice after Marengo in 1800; another *déjà-vu*. He had outrun his supplies. His communications were infested with Cossacks and German partisans. Long marches and little food had played havoc with his conscripts, putting 30,000 on the sick list. Ammunition stocks were low; his scant cavalry ruined by poor horsemastership.[15]

Bonaparte's gamble on deciding the campaign by a single offensive rush had therefore miscarried. He would have to march further, fight further battles; yet one more of the *déja-vus* of 1813.

AFTER CONSULTATION with the allies Austria now offered Bonaparte her armed mediation: that is, if Bonaparte refused her terms for a peace settlement, she would enter the war on the allied side. Such an event would place him in double jeopardy, both by swinging the military balance heavily against him and because the Austrian army in Bohemia would threaten his rear, especially his main base at Dresden. It was therefore of capital importance to him to keep Austria neutral. On 26 June he met the Austrian Chancellor, Metternich, in Dresden, favouring him, according to Metternich, with 'a series of professions of friendship alternating with the most violent of outbursts.'[16]

> What! Not only Illyria, but half Italy and the return of the Pope to Rome! and Poland and giving up Spain! and Holland, and the Confederation of the Rhine, and Switzerland! This is what you call your spirit of moderation! . . . In a word you want nothing else but the dismemberment of the French Empire . . .[17]

Bonaparte denounced Austria for demanding from him 'a vast capitulation' without even drawing the sword and 'when my victorious army is at the gates of Berlin and Breslau.'[18] Far from accepting the Austrian conditions, which included the provision that Prussia be restored to her 1805 boundaries, Bonaparte asserted that 'I will not cede an inch of land: I will make peace on the basis of the *status quo ante bellum* . . .'[19] He would go no further than offering Austria a bribe of Illyria to stay neutral.

Later, however, he consented to send Caulaincourt to a peace conference at Prague. But his purpose was not peace but the gaining of time for military preparations. Deviously he refrained from issuing Caulaincourt with instructions until 22 July and full powers to treat until 13 August. By then it was too late; the allies, tired of his chicaning, had already broken off the negotiations. They had drawn fresh heart from news that the Marquis of Wellington had routed Bonaparte's Army of Spain at the Battle of Vittoria on 20 June, so liquidating brother Joseph's kingdom. On 12 August Austria declared war.

So now for the first time in his career Bonaparte had to fight the armies of Russia, Austria and Prussia simultaneously; and it was entirely his own doing, the gift of Bonaparte the egoist to Bonaparte the soldier.

Bonaparte's defence of his dominion over Germany in the second German campaign of 1813 bears curious resemblances to his defence of northern Italy against Austrian offensives in 1796–7. In both cases his strategy was tethered by the need to shield a major fortress and base from enemy thrusts – in Italy Mantua, held by the Austrians but besieged by himself; in Germany Dresden, his own forward base and capital of his ally the King of Saxony. In both cases he had to defend a wide front: in Italy from west of Lake Garda to east of Legnago on the Adige; in Germany from Magdeburg along the Elbe, thence east into Silesia and finally west again to cover Dresden from the south. In both cases too the menace of converging enemy attacks left him guessing to the last moment as to the principal danger, so inducing him to deploy his army in widely separated groups rather than concentrated in a central position. Once again he would have to rely on being able to concentrate at the decisive point in a last-minute pell-mell rush.

Yet in other respects the anatomy of this campaign differed radically from Bonaparte's defence of northern Italy. In 1796–7 it had been the Austrians' main purpose to relieve Mantua. Hence they were always willing to fight a decisive battle in order to clear their path. In 1813 the allies lay under no strategic compulsion to present Bonaparte with the gift of such a battle. On the contrary they had decided on a strategy of evasion and protracted conflict. If one of their armies were attacked by Bonaparte, it was to retire while other armies took the opportunity to close on Bonaparte's *derrières*. The allies meant to compel Bonaparte to wear out his army in forced marches to and fro until he was ripe for dispatch.

Then again the scales of numbers and distances were so much greater in Germany in 1813 than in Italy seventeen years earlier: a front of five hundred miles (indeed six hundred if the French corps at Hamburg be included) instead of one hundred; more than 400,000 men to control instead of a tenth that figure in Italy. Bonaparte's rigidly centralized system of command had more than once come to grief even in the Italian campaign; in Germany the problems of personally directing far-flung operations in detail proved altogether too much even for him. Moreover, commanders and staffs brought up not to think but to obey proved singularly unfitted for the independent roles with which sheer circumstance now forced Bonaparte to entrust them.

And finally there were the differences between the fighting quality of the combatants in 1796 and 1813. In Italy Bonaparte had commanded a unique force of war-hardened and patriotic veterans whose skill and dash had time and again got him out of difficulty. In Germany he was leading – apart from some formations like the Guard – a scratch array of relatively green troops. And whereas in 1796 he had been opposed by an army of the *ancien régime* cramped by eighteenth-century rules, in 1813 he faced armies reforged in the crucible of war, and directed by generals and governments inspired by a relentless determination to fight on until they brought him down. In Italy in 1796–7 Bonaparte had begun the process of debasing warfare from a regulated institution to the level of a Corsican blood-feud, no holds barred; in 1813 he became in due turn the victim of the resulting vendetta.

'. . . Bonaparte's curious scorn for especially dangerous enemies . . .': the Prussian Marshal Prince Blücher (1749–1819). Painting by Sir Thomas Lawrence, 1814. *Copyright Reserved*

AFTER FINDING GARRISONS for Hamburg, Dresden and various fortresses, Bonaparte mustered a field army of 375,000 men against an allied total of over 480,000. The allies had divided their strength into three armies (each of mixed nationality) for the purpose of gradually netting him from north, east and south: the Army of the North under the Swedish Crown Prince (the former French Marshal, Bernadotte) covering Berlin, 125,000 men; the Army of Silesia under the Prussian Blücher, 104,000; and the Army of Bohemia under the Austrian Schwarzenberg, 254,000. Schwarzenberg, with the largest force, was charged with advancing from the south on Bonaparte's main base of Dresden.

Hampered as so often by poor operational intelligence, Bonaparte wrongly judged Schwarzenberg's army to number only 100,000, and believed that Blücher offered the main threat. He therefore deployed his own main weight in the east and north, neglecting his right, or southern flank. Oudinot with 72,000 men was to advance on Berlin while Macdonald (lying some 120 miles east of Dresden) with 102,000 men protected his right flank against Blücher. Bonaparte himself, at Bautzen with the remaining 201,000, would act as central reserve, moving to support the others as necessary. Bonaparte had thus dispersed his strength rather than concentrated it. But in fact Oudinot's advance on Berlin marked a return to a strategy that had attracted Bonaparte since the inception of the 1813 campaign – that of an offensive through Berlin on Danzig. This would serve to 'punish' Prussia for her 'desertion' and knock her out of the war. At the same time it would draw the Russian army northwards away from the Austrians by threatening the main Russian line of communication. It was a typical Bonapartian conception: simple, grand, bold, but quite outrunning his real military means and taking too little note of the enemy's own capability. For in fact Bonaparte lost the initiative almost as soon as the campaign began again in August. On the 20th, learning that Blücher was advancing westward from Silesia, Bonaparte marched to join Macdonald and attack him. Blücher, however, retired out of reach according to plan as soon as he knew that he faced Bonaparte in person. At this point Bonaparte received news that Schwarzenberg, advancing north from Bohemia, was threatening Dresden far in his rear. He flung himself westward across country in order to save it, the Guard marching the hundred and twenty miles in four days; a repetition of those lightning marches in Italy to meet the surprise appearances of Wurmser or Alvinzi. *En route* for Dresden Bonaparte decided to sweep south into Bohemia past Schwarzenberg's right flank, cut his communications with Prague and destroy him like Mack at Ulm. He ordered Vandamme's corps to act as advanced guard, promising him the immediate support of the Young Guard.[20] But the danger to Dresden appeared too urgent; he changed his mind and instead marched straight to the city's rescue, leaving Vandamme and the Guard to execute the turning movement alone.

On 26 August Bonaparte held off Schwarzenberg south of Dresden with 70,000 to 150,000. Next day, two more corps having arrived, he furiously attacked the Austrian commander. But although he inflicted some 38,000 casualties (including 13,000 prisoners), it was only a partial success, and Schwarzenberg retired southwards in good order.

On 28 August Bonaparte ordered Vandamme to press on and cut Schwarzenberg's retreat. Later that day, however, he learned that Macdonald had been badly beaten by Blücher on the River Katzbach and Oudinot likewise by Prussians of Bernadotte's army at Gross-Beeren twelve miles south of Berlin. He therefore recalled the Young Guard from its march in support of Vandamme. But, by a not unfamiliar kind of breakdown in staffwork, Vandamme was neither recalled himself nor told that the Guard had been recalled. As a consequence Vandamme, advancing in isolation, was ambushed and destroyed at Kulm in Bohemia. Bonaparte of course blamed Vandamme, even denying he had given him orders to advance.[21]

Bonaparte now decided to attack in the north again, with Berlin once more as his objective. But instead he was compelled to turn east to support Macdonald, hard-pressed by Blücher. In the first week of September Bonaparte attacked the Prussian commander for the second time; and for the second time Blücher ducked the punch by retiring. From that day onwards Bonaparte came to suspect the existence of an allied strategy of denying him a decisive battle. This suspicion caused him, as his Saxon aide-de-camp, Odeleben, put it, to exhibit 'a great deal of ill-humour . . .'[22] On 6 September a renewed threat to Dresden by Schwarzenberg brought Bonaparte pounding westward again. And in Dresden two days later he learned that Ney (whom he had appointed in the north to replace Oudinot) had been shatteringly defeated at Dennewitz with the loss of 20,000 men.

Bonaparte's campaign, more, his entire control over events, was fast disintegrating. He found himself compelled by the enemy's strategy to bolt to and fro like a rabbit tennis player. And every forced march further wore out his unfledged troops, especially since they were expected to march on an empty stomach, for as Bonaparte admitted on 23 September, '. . . this army is in no way fed.'[23] He now had 50,000 men sick on top of 150,000 men lost in action or fallen out on the march.

Doubt, and with doubt something like fear, now began to knife through the thick padding of his belief in his star and his own infallibility.[24] Earlier in the year he had been his usual cocksure self, strutting among his soldiers to flatter them and pinch their cheeks; chucking books that bored him out of his carriage window on to the road;[25] reproving Marie-Louise for receiving the Arch-Chancellor while in bed, conduct 'only permissible to those over thirty.'[26] But now he became moody and introspective; given to ferocious outbursts of rage against those whom he wished to blame for his difficulties. Once he went so far as to smack a general's face in public.[27] On 12 September he even admitted to Marmont that 'The chess-board is highly confused,' but added immediately: 'I alone know what I am about.'[28] But was it true? In a long memorandum of 30 August he balanced one possible strategy against another, as if to resolve his own perplexities.[29] He again pondered a march on Prague, only to perceive in advance for once the basic drawbacks of his own system of warfare: 'I could not take Prague, a fortress; Bohemia would rise against us; I should be placed in an awkward situation . . .'[30] Yet at other times his old self-delusion fumed his mind. On 3 October, for instance, he upbraided Berthier: 'One must not give vent to alarm too easily . . .'[31]

By now, however, the allies were pulling their net closer and closer about him. On 3 October Blücher and Bernadotte crossed the Elbe and together began to advance on Leipzig from the north with 140,000 men, while Schwarzenberg came up from the south with 180,000 men. Bonaparte was threatened by a double envelopment. Nor could he repeat his Italian trick of throwing his strength first against one opponent and then the other, because under attack each allied army would simply have temporarily retired out of reach.

On 12 October Bonaparte decided to concentrate round Leipzig for battle against the converging enemy forces. Only once before had he fought while virtually surrounded, and that was at Rivoli. Then the lie of the ground, enabling him to bottle up part of the Austrian army in the Adige gorge, and the fighting qualities of the Army of Italy had been in his favour. But the Leipzig battlefield was a saucer of low ground cut up by several rivers, offering no advantages, while this time Bonaparte's own army enjoyed little if any superiority in fighting skill over the enemy. Furthermore by the eve of battle Bonaparte's sole line of retreat westwards in the event of defeat lay across a single bridge and along a single road. Why then did he choose to fight in such a potential trap? It seems probable that he meant his very inferiority of numbers and disadvantageous strategic situation to serve as baits to draw the enemy at last into a decisive battle; trusting to his own genius, to his 'star', to win him deliverance in the actual fighting, as at Rivoli. Perhaps too he was moved by sheer eagerness to have done with the business; certainly his correspondence breathes anticipation.

On 16 October 1813 the Battle of Leipzig, later celebrated as 'the Battle of the Nations' opened with a concentric attack by some 300,000 allied troops on a hungry and tired-out French army of fewer than 190,000 men. In a fresh example of Bonaparte's curious scorn for especially dangerous enemies, he underestimated Blücher now as he had done throughout the campaign, and left only covering forces against him along the northern sector of the Leipzig perimeter. Instead,

he concentrated in the south against Schwarzenberg, even ordering Ney
(commanding the northern sector) on the morning of the battle to send him an
extra corps. But Blücher's fierce onslaughts pressed Ney so hard that he recalled this
corps (the 3rd, under Souham) to shore up his own front. Souham, the recipient of
orders and counter-orders as the battle crises waxed and waned, was to march to
and fro all day without firing a shot on either sector.[32]

Meanwhile, Bonaparte's attack on Schwarzenberg with the aim of crushing his
right flank had been delayed and weakened by the failure of Souham to arrive.
Instead of a smashing blow and a decisive success, there took place a day of brutally
hard fighting. It ended in stalemate despite a final onslaught by 10,000 horsemen
supported by Macdonald's corps and the fire of a 150-gun battery. And stalemate in
Bonaparte's position meant defeat. He tried an old ruse by asking the allies for an
armistice in order to discuss peace terms; no takers. He began to make preparations
for a retreat, but, with typical reluctance to acknowledge reality, still hung on
round Leipzig. On 17 October both sides rested in preparation for another struggle;
rain poured steadily down; 'a gloomy silence reigned round the bivouac of the
Emperor.'[33] Bernadotte belatedly came into the allied line with 60,000 men;
Bennigsen was arriving with 40,000 more Russians; another Austrian corps was on
its way. Yet Bonaparte himself had again failed to concentrate all his available forces

on the decisive battlefield. For he had left 30,000 men in Dresden, Augereau's corps at Wurzburg and Davout's round Hamburg.

On 18 October, a day dismal with mist and rain, the allies attacked again from all sides simultaneously. Outfought and overborne, given no chance to launch some 'Napoleonic' stroke, Bonaparte at last gave the order to retreat. Now he paid the full penalty for accepting battle in so perilous a strategic situation. In the panic struggle to get through Dresden and across the one bridge to safety, the army dissolved into chaos. To complete the catastrophe, a nervous sapper blew the bridge prematurely and stranded between 15,000 and 20,000 men on the enemy side of the river. The three-day 'Battle of the Nations' ended in a scene of apocalypse worthy of the painter John Martin, a flame-lit night of terror and vengeance on the vastest scale.

As for Bonaparte, the cause of it all, Marshal Marmont recorded that when he met him next day some ten miles west of Leipzig:

> He was sunk in gloom, and he had reason to be. Hardly two months had elapsed and an immense army, an army of more than 400,000 men, had melted away in his hands. It was the second time in a year that such a spectacle of destruction had been presented to the world, and one otherwise without parallel in modern times. Only about 60,000 men remained to him . . .[34]

When this demoralized remnant straggled into the sanctuary of the Rhine fortresses at the beginning of November, it found neither supplies nor hospitals to succour it; only an outbreak of typhus which cost another 14,000 lives.[35]

On 7 November Bonaparte took coach from Mainz to Paris, in order to start the process all over again.

NOW BONAPARTE's entire power structure was collapsing or shaking on the point of collapse. Germany was lost and his German allies had deserted him. His Iberian enterprise too had wound up in bankruptcy, for Wellington was through the Pyrenees and advancing on Bayonne – the first allied commander to tread French soil for more than twenty years. The loss of Germany and the Iberian Peninsula irreparably smashed the Continental System. English goods cascaded into liberated Europe; the English economy boomed again; English gold in fresh abundance soldered the alliance together. Bonaparte on the other hand found himself back in that very dilemma from which his first Italian campaign had promised to release the Directory – that of the impossibility of waging war out of France's own resources without incurring the nation's politically dangerous resentment. Under the impact of defeat and of harsh new taxes and conscriptions, the French people, so long Bonaparte's docile supporting cast, began to stand away from him; even his imperial aristocracy, even his bureaucrats. The royalists in the provinces too snuffed his downfall, and busied themselves in the hope of a Bourbon restoration. Even within the *Corps Legislatif*, quiescent since Bonaparte's purges in 1803, opposition revived. In December 1813 the *Corps* demanded peace and political liberty by twenty-nine votes out of thirty-one. Bonaparte retorted in traditional style by dismissing the *Corps*, taking the opportunity to restate his political philosophy: 'What are you within the Constitution? You are nothing . . . It

'So at last he had his heir; his Empire a future beyond his own lifetime': Bonaparte's second wife, Marie-Louise, daughter of the Austrian Emperor, and their baby son the King of Rome. Painting by Joseph Franque. *Musée de Versailles. Photo: Musées Nationaux*

is the throne which is the Constitution; everything resides in the throne . . . I am one of those men who triumphs or dies . . .'[36]

So even now Bonaparte proved unable to transcend his egotism. In a national crisis which demanded selfless statesmanship he remained just a soldier of fortune who had learned nothing from two catastrophes in two years, and who meant once again to hazard the interests of France on a needless gamble, and this time at far longer odds than ever before.

In November 1813 the Continental allies offered Bonaparte the 'natural frontiers' again, in the wake of Leipzig a generous enough proposal. He was to give up Italy, Switzerland and Holland (which in any case drove out his garrison that month), but keep the Rhineland and Belgium – the greater France that Louis XIV had sought in vain to achieve. Deviously procrastinating as he had during the June–August armistice, Bonaparte accepted the offer only after the allies had withdrawn it.[37] By January 1814, with their armies on French soil, the allied terms hardened: France must now be reduced to her 1792 frontiers. Yet even these terms left her the initial gains of revolutionary expansion. Bonaparte would have none of it; he now demanded the 'natural frontiers' which he had been so slow to accept earlier. 'France', he wrote to Caulaincourt, now his Foreign Minister, 'without her natural frontiers, without Ostend, without Antwerp, would no longer be on a level with the other powers of Europe.'[38] The truth was that to accept France's pre-Bonapartian frontiers meant acknowledging that all his marches and victories, all the killing, all the waste and destruction, had been for nothing.

'If the country backs me up,' asserted Bonaparte to Caulaincourt, 'the enemy will march to his doom.'[39] The country, as he ought to have known, was unlikely to back him up more than it had to. He could only oppose some 60,000 men ready for the field against allied armies of nearly 200,000. Militarily as well as diplomatically, therefore, Bonaparte's decision to fight in 1814 instead of making peace marks the supreme example of his irresponsibility as a national leader.

Bonaparte himself in that grim winter after Leipzig alternated between hopeful fantasy, as when, in Marmont's words, he 'succumbed to the idea that the enemy would not undertake a winter campaign against us',[40] and a feeling, according to Méneval, 'that luck was no longer with him'.[41] This time all his efforts to raise men, money and supplies only resulted in a field army for the defence of northern France less than a third the size of that assembled in Germany at the start of the previous year's campaign and even worse trained, equipped and fed. Many of Bonaparte's new recruits received only a shako, an overcoat and a musket – which not every man knew how to load and fire.[42] To pit these sorry youths without necessity against the arrayed armies of Europe verged on the criminal. Yet they too were to pass into the Napoleonic legend, romantically nicknamed 'les Marie-Louises' after the Empress, who as regent while Bonaparte was still in Germany had signed the decree for the levy.

When long ago in Italy as a mere general-in-chief he had scented disaster he had vented his fears to his government, appealing almost frantically for help and reinforcement. Now he *was* the government, the plight of his own making; and there was no one to whom to appeal. And yet in a curious way he did turn to Marie-

Russian troops entering Paris in April 1814 wearing stolen garments and loaded with plunder; a sour French version of the event. In fact the Grande Armée had looked much the same during *its* advances. *Weaver Smith Collection, Thames Television*

'To pit these sorry youths against the arrayed armies of Europe . . . verged on criminal. Yet they too were to pass into Napoleonic legend . . .': the boy recruits of 1814 romantically rendered by the artist Auguste Raffet. The original caption reads: 'Sire, you can count on us as on the Old Guard.' *British Museum*

Louise, his strapping young Habsburg wife, as if he saw in her a talisman of strength and success. He again appointed her regent during his absence in the field, a trust he had never confided to Josephine. But Josephine was not forgotten. Just before he left to join the army in January 1814 he visited her at Malmaison to bid farewell; a last farewell as it proved, for they never saw each other again. According to Josephine, 'nothing could assuage his feelings of despair.'[43]

On 25 January he bid farewell to his wife and son, the last time also he was to set eyes on them, and the coach rattled away.

'Come,' remarked Bonaparte to Berthier, 'we must repeat the campaign of Italy.'[44] And this is indeed how generations of military historians have seen the French campaign of 1814 – Bonaparte at his most dynamic and brilliant, superbly exploiting the central position to inflict defeat after defeat on an allied army immensely superior in numbers. But this is to repeat their error of interpretation with regard to the Italian campaign itself and divorce the conduct of war from its political context, treating it again almost as a sport where a player's virtuoso performance is to be admired for its own sake. The folly of Bonaparte's decision as head of state to undertake this foredoomed campaign at all wholly eclipses any mere operational skill he may have displayed as a general.

Yet even his military conduct of the campaign is open to question. He failed again to concentrate all his combat-ready forces in the decisive area, having left some 120,000 men locked up in German fortresses and another 12,000 in Verdun and Metz.[45] Instead of opting for a defensive in a strong position, as a Moltke or a Wellington might have done, partly in order to spare an army of raw recruits, he again chose an offensive strategy; a *déjà-vu* of 1813, itself a *déjà-vu* of 1796–7. His chosen arena of battle was not northern Italy, however but Champagne, and Champagne in mid-winter, almost without shelter, scoured by freezing winds, a forager's nightmare. A report from Marmont to Bonaparte on 8 February says it all:

> The troops have suffered much from this evening's march over bad roads through thick darkness; they stand in extreme need of victuals. The villages of this province are nothing.[46]

However impressive on the map, therefore, Bonaparte's lightning thrusts first at this allied army and then at the other merely served rapidly to wear out his own green troops.

He struck first at the northern arm of the allied invasion, Blücher's army, which had advanced through the Rhineland and Lorraine, but nevertheless failed to prevent Blücher joining Schwarzenberg, who had advanced via Basle and Chaumont. On 1 February Bonaparte offered battle to three times his number at La Rothière. Beaten, he had to retire fifty miles westward to Nogent. Meanwhile, a peace conference had opened at Châtillon, where on 7 February Caulaincourt, the French delegate, was handed the allied terms. These, as before, reduced France to her 1792 boundaries. When Caulaincourt's report reached Bonaparte that night, 'his cries were those of a trapped lion.'[47] Nevertheless, with his campaign thus far going badly and the realist in him uppermost for the moment, he decided to accept the allied terms. But next morning he learned that Blücher had separated from Schwarzenberg and was advancing toward Paris well strung out, his flank exposed, on the Châlons–Meaux road. Hope flashed again; Bonaparte rejected the terms after all, remarking: 'Do not let us rush anything; there will always be time for us to sign a peace such as they now propose.'[48]

Hurrying his soldiers northward, he struck three successive blows at Blücher's divided corps: at Champaubert on 10 February, at Montmirail on the 11th and at Château-Thierry on the 13th. On the 14th he attacked Blücher's main body at Vauchamps, almost severing his retreat. Bloody-headed, Blücher retired to Châlons. On 16 February, after a southward march of more than eighty miles in two days, Bonaparte fell upon Schwarzenberg at Montereau, some fifty miles southeast of Paris, forcing that somewhat nervous Austrian into retreating via Troyes.

This was the nearest Bonaparte came to bringing off his gamble. A momentary flurry of panic seized the allied leaders. There was talk of armistices. But Lord Castlereagh, the English Foreign Minister, would hear of no such thing, and his was the hand that held the guineas. The panic quickly ebbed. Moreover, Bonaparte's salvo of attacks had only inflicted superficial damage on the allied armies, temporary rebuffs. Soon old Blücher was on the Paris road again, this time via Sézanne.

Yet Bonaparte believed he had smashed Blücher and won the campaign. After his first success at Champaubert he was, wrote Marmont, 'drunk with joy,' predicting that after another such victory, 'the enemy will recross the Rhine faster than he crossed it. I will be on the Vistula.'[49] There was no question now of accepting the allied terms. In vain did Caulaincourt urge him that 'We must make sacrifices and we must make them in good time.'[50] Remarked Bonaparte to a

POLITICAL CHESS PLAYERS, or Boney Bewilder'd - John Bull supporting the Table .

'Meanwhile, a peaceful conference had opened at Châtillon . . .': John Bull holds up the globe, the upper part of which is a chess-board, while Bonaparte and allied sovereigns and generals play their grand-strategical game. An English cartoon published in 1814. *British Museum*

subordinate, 'I do not read Caulaincourt's letters; tell him they tire and bore me beyond limit.'[51]

He missed his last chance of a negotiated peace, and, as it was to prove, his last chance of keeping his throne. On 9 March the allies signed a treaty of grand alliance, committing themselves to fight on until their full war aims were achieved. On the 19th they broke off the Châtillon conference. By this time Bonaparte had come to realize that he had not won the campaign after all. On 8 March he had attacked Blücher in a strong position near Laon with 40,000 men against 100,000; a bloody failure. His famished, freezing, exhausted troops could no longer sustain the shock of action or the strain of forced marching. Even the Young Guard was, Bonaparte admitted, 'melting away like snow.'[52] On 11 March he gave orders for redoubts to be constructed on Montmartre.[53] On the 13th he won a partial success against Blücher at Rheims ('I am still the man of Wagram and Austerlitz,' he bragged in a letter to Fouché, Minister of Police).[54] A week later he had hustled his woebegone army forty-five miles to the south in order to strike at Schwarzenberg near Arcis-sur-Aube; another bloody French rebuff like Laon. This was 1813 all over again, with the enemy columns closing relentlessly back towards Paris despite all Bonaparte's frantic marching and hitting, just as the previous year they had closed on Dresden and Leipzig.

Unwilling to accept the fact of defeat, Bonaparte took refuge once more in make-believe. Deluding himself that Blücher was no longer capable of the offensive,[55] he decided to leave Marmont and Mortier with 17,000 men to defend Paris while he took the main body of the army off into eastern France, picked up fortress garrisons to swell his strength, and win the campaign by cutting the enemy communications. The drawback of this manoeuvre lay in that it equally left 200,000 enemy troops on his own *derrières*. Bonaparte sealed the blunder by sending an uncoded letter about his plan to Marie-Louise. Intercepted by a Cossack patrol, it emboldened the allies to ignore Bonaparte's gesturing behind them and plough straight on to Paris, smashing Marmont's and Mortier's troops at La Fère-Champenoise on the way.

On 30 March Marmont formally surrendered the capital and retired to the south. On the 31st the allies marched in. That same day Bonaparte, furiously counter-marching as soon as he learned of the disaster at La Fère-Champenoise, reached Fontainebleau, too late by a few hours to fight for Paris. The gamble of 1814 was over.

War, for twenty years a French export, becomes an import at last. Cossacks bivouacking along the Champs-Elysées after the allied occupation of Paris on 31 March 1814. Engraved by Jazet from a drawing by Sauerweid. *British Museum*

BONAPARTE had always conceived of society as a machine. Machines do not, however, evince loyalty towards their engineers. Nor did French society evince loyalty towards Bonaparte now that his hand was off the levers of power. The organs of state hastened to make their peace with the allied powers; the Paris populace welcomed the allied troops rather than otherwise; even most of Bonaparte's marshals turned against him, urging him to abdicate in favour of his son. On 3 April the Senate proclaimed Bonaparte to be deposed and on the 6th invited Louis XVIII, Louis XVI's brother, to the throne. On 8 April the allied sovereigns had

Marie-Louise and the King of Rome brought under escort from Blois, where they had taken refuge, to safe keeping at Rambouillet. Except for his personal entourage Bonaparte now found himself almost entirely forsaken; the nemesis of an egotist.

Yet for a week after his arrival at Fontainebleau his will had still twitched like a reflex. He issued orders for a new campaign based on Orleans. To avoid pointless bloodshed Marmont wrecked the scheme by taking his corps over to the allies.

On 11 April Bonaparte yielded to an allied demand that he should abdicate unconditionally:

> The allied powers having proclaimed that the Emperor Napoleon was the sole obstacle to re-establishing peace in Europe, the Emperor Napoleon, faithful to his word, declares that he renounces for himself and his heirs, the thrones of France and Italy, and that there is no personal sacrifice, even life itself, which he is not ready to make for the good of France.[56]

Either that night or the night after, Bonaparte, in the classic pattern of the gambler leaving the casino utterly ruined, sought to take his life with poison which he had carried with him ever since the retreat from Moscow. But after convulsive vomiting he recovered. He took this as a sign. 'Fate has decided,' he announced to his entourage, 'I must live and await all that providence has in store for me.'[57] And what could that be, except the exile of the island of Elba to which his vanquishers had condemned him? In a remark made 'with remarkable serenity' to one of his staff perhaps lay a clue: 'I abdicate and I yield nothing.'[58]

'Blücher the Brave extracting the groan of abdication from the Corsican Bloodhound' – cartoon by Thomas Rowlandson, April 1814. *British Museum*

XV

GLORY IS IN MOURNING

ON 20 APRIL 1814 he bid farewell to the Guard in the courtyard at Fontaine-bleau which was later to be renamed *le Cours des Adieus*; a scene that was to form one of the great sentimental set-pieces of Napoleonic iconography – something of a Last Supper.

> Goodbye, my children! I wish I could press you all to my heart; let me at least embrace your flag![1]

On that day he also wrote to Marie-Louise to express the hope that she could rejoin him. 'Farewell my good Louise. You can always count on your husband's courage, calm and goodwill. A kiss for the little King.'[2]

Then he was on his way to Fréjus under escort to take ship for Elba, all the power and pomp stripped away from him, just a fat, balding middle-aged man frightened of being manhandled or killed by the hostile crowds in the towns along the route.[3]

NOW HE FOUND HIMSELF back again in the small world of a Mediterranean island, thrown suddenly like any newly-retired head of a firm on his own internal resources. The English commissioner on Elba, Sir Neil Campbell, noted:

> I have never seen a man in any situation in life with so much personal activity and restless perseverance. He appears to take so much pleasure in perpetual movement . . . [that] I do not think it possible for him to sit down to study, or any pursuits of retirement, as proclaimed by him to be his intention . . .[4]

So, playing the Emperor in miniature, Bonaparte encouraged local industries; reviewed the 1,000 soldiers of the Guard allowed him by the allied powers; held levées for the *bon-ton* of Porto Ferrajo, a burlesque of the Court of the Tuileries. His sister Pauline loyally came to share his exile. His mother Letizia paid him a visit; so too did loyal, simple Marie Walewska, bringing their four-year-old son Alexandre with her. But he longed in vain to be joined by his wife and the King of Rome. In 1810 the interest of the Habsburg monarchy had placed Marie-Louise in Bonaparte's bed; now it had removed her and for good. She and her son had been taken to live in gilded custody in Vienna, where she was soon consoled by her equerry Count Neipperg, a dashing hussar – the more dashing because of a black patch over one eye. The Emperor Francis was no doubt heartless to deprive Bonaparte of his wife and son, yet hardly more so than Bonaparte himself, when, equally for reasons of state, he deprived his brother Jerome of his first (and pregnant) wife and later sought to deprive his brother Lucien of *his* wife as well.

Nevertheless, Bonaparte harboured a grievance. Nor was it his only grievance: though pressed to do so by the allies, the Bourbon monarchy failed to pay him the

'A Grand Manoeuvre! Or, The Rogue's March to the Island of Elba', by George Cruikshank. Bonapart was in truth much in fear of the hostile crowds along his route. *British Museum*

pension due to him under the terms of his abdication. His restlessness was further stirred by the news he received from France. The nation resented the reappearance of the forms and some of the institutions of the *ancien régime*; the army even more so, as when the Old Guard was abolished in favour of a corps composed purely of noblemen, the *Maison du Roi*. Old soldiers grumbled in the cafés, recalling the great days of conquest. Returned *émigré* nobles took the plum jobs at Louis XVIII's Court while the imperial nobility found itself snubbed. Conspiracies abounded. Disgruntled generals plotted armed rebellion. As the months passed Bonaparte brooded and measured his chances. On 16 February 1815 he ordered the brig *Inconstant* to be prepared for sea and painted like an English warship.[5] On 20 February an emissary arrived on the island from his former Foreign Minister, Maret, and one of his most fanatical adherents, with a report on the supposedly promising state of affairs in France. At nine o'clock at night on 26 February, two days after this emissary's departure and while Sir Neil Campbell was temporarily absent from the island, Bonaparte made his escape from Elba in the *Inconstant* and set sail for France.

NOW BEGAN THE EPISODE in his adventurer's life which came nearest to pure adventure story: the reconquest of a country and a throne with no greater resources than himself, his legend and a thousand soldiers. Successfully slipping past or bluffing guardships on patrol, Bonaparte made landfall at Golfe Juan on 1 March 1815. Rather than take the direct route to Paris via the Rhône valley, where he had encountered such hostility on his journey to Elba, he led his handful of guardsmen up amid the wild mountains of Haute Provence; a romantic journey in the best style of Mrs Radcliffe's Gothick novels. Indeed, the author of *Clisson et Eugénie* had not lost his own narrative touch. At Gap, where the road from Castellane and Grasse winds down out of the sky into the wide valley of the Durance, he published a proclamation promising that 'The eagle will fly from steeple to steeple until it reaches the towers of Notre-Dame.'[6] So it proved. Just south of Grenoble, at Laffrey, in scenery exactly to the right romantic specification – a path through a narrow pasture clinging to a mountainside, a landscape of soaring buttresses of rock bewigged with snow – there took place on 7 March an encounter ever to be celebrated in Napoleonic legend. A battalion of the royal army deployed to block Bonaparte's march; Bonaparte stepped towards the levelled muskets and opened wide his coat: 'Soldiers, if there is one among you who wishes to kill his Emperor he can do so. Here I am!' But instead came a shout of '*Vive l'Empéreur!*'[7]

By sheer force of personality Bonaparte had decided the fortune of his march. Grenoble opened its gates; Lyon too. The always volatile Ney joined him instead of bringing him back 'in an iron cage' as he promised Louis XVIII. Louis XVIII and his Court departed in haste for Ghent. On 20 March Bonaparte entered the Tuileries, almost carried up the grand staircase by enthusiastic supporters, 'his eyes half closed,' says an eyewitness, 'his hands extended before him like a blind man, and expressing his joy only by a smile.'[8] If the farewell to the Guard at Fontainebleau had been the Napoleonic Last Supper, this was surely the Resurrection.

HE INAUGURATED HIS NEW REGIME with a resounding lie. According to a proclamation to the French people, it was only because of Marmont's 'treason' in surrendering Paris that the campaign of 1814 had not ended in victory.[9] Having thus tidied up the immediate past, he proceeded to grapple with the present, which was not so readily arranged.

For Bonaparte soon realized that he had been misled by his adherents about the likely warmth of the French people's welcome; 'They let me come,' he told a courtier, 'just as they let the other fellow [Louis XVIII] go.'[10] Although the Bonaparte clan, even Lucien, rallied to him, nine marshals, including the sick and ageing Berthier, refused to serve his cause again.

In terms of grand strategy Bonaparte had locked himself straight back into the dilemma of early 1814. He once more confronted a European coalition of overwhelming strength resolved to bring him down cost what it might. On 13 March 1815 – before he even reached Paris – the allied leaders at the Congress of Vienna declared that 'Napoleon Buonaparte (sic) had placed himself outside the pale of political and social relations.'[11] Five days later they revived the Treaty of Chaumont and pledged themselves each to place 150,000 men in the field until Bonaparte was crushed (England's contribution to be partly naval and financial). Bonaparte could entertain no hope at all of matching these forces. Immediate recourse to mass conscription was out of the question for political reasons, while in any case a shortage of muskets and manufacturing bottlenecks made it hard enough even to equip existing reservists.[12]

If strategically Bonaparte was back in 1814, in terms of domestic politics he found himself replaying 1799, with his personal authority under challenge from both Jacobins (now metamorphosed into liberals) and royalists. Old opponents like Benjamin Constant and Madame de Staël hotly demanded constitutional

'His sister Pauline came loyally to share his exile': Princess Pauline Borghese (1780–1825) by Robert Lefevre. *Wellington Museum, Apsley House, London. Photo: Crown Copyright*

government on the English model. In 1799 Bonaparte had solved the problem of liberal opposition by means of repression and exile. In 1815 he allowed himself to be persuaded by brother Lucien (and partly too by Joseph) that his survival depended on rallying the liberal bourgeoisie behind him by concessions.[13] After a month of backstage haggling Bonaparte proclaimed an *Acte Additionel* to the imperial constitution, largely drafted by Constant, which went far to transforming his old tyranny into a parliamentary monarchy. Yet far from winning him middle-class support, it exposed him afresh to the kind of attack inside the constitutional organs that had so enraged him in 1799–1803. Under one such attack in the Council of State Bonaparte lost his temper and revealed how little his political ideas had really changed:

> You are weakening and chaining me . . . France is asking what has become of the Emperor's arm, this arm which she needs to master Europe. Why speak to me of goodness, abstract justice, and of natural laws? The first law is necessity; the first justice is the public safety.[14]

Still, the *Acte Additionel* at least enabled legend to present Bonaparte as a liberal and a lover of freedom at heart; more, a man whose conquests had all been inspired, as the *Acte* put it, by the aim of 'organizing a great European federal system . . . in accord with the spirit of the century and for the sake of the progress of civilization.'[15]

With powerful opposition at home and gathering dangers abroad, it was little wonder that Bonaparte's exultation at being back on the throne soon yielded to despondency. Marie-Louise and his son remained far off in Vienna despite his appeals to Francis I to reunite husband and wife. Josephine lay in her tomb, dead of angina since May 1814. Méneval noted that Bonaparte's talk was now:

> . . . stamped with a calm sadness and resignation . . . I did not find in him that certainty of success which had made him so confident in the past; it seems as if that faith in his star which had inspired him to venture on the hazardous enterprise of returning from Elba, and which had borne him up during his march across France deserted him from the moment he reached Paris . . .[16]

SINCE THE ALLIES returned no answer to his appeals for peace, having heard it all before, the soldier of fortune would again have to trust to his sword. But by July allied armies totalling 650,000 men would be invading France from the north, east and southeast. Bonaparte's only hope lay therefore as always in quickly beating the nearest enemy force before the rest could get into the field. As a victim he chose the allied army in Belgium, composed of the Anglo-Dutch under Wellington and the Prussians under Blücher. A sensational victory followed by the occupation of Brussels would rekindle French enthusiasm and consolidate his authority again. With Wellington and Blücher defeated, he could swing south and smash Schwarzenberg in turn. The coalition would then fall apart.

Here was the old, old routine which had only narrowly succeeded even during his earlier career, and which had utterly failed in 1812, 1813 and 1814. It was even less likely to succeed in 1815, for the odds against him had never been heavier; his enemies' determination never more resolute. They had decided to follow the same strategy of evasion and protracted war as in 1813 and 1814: if one army were defeated or forced back, the others would exploit the opportunity to thrust deeper towards Paris. It is therefore a fair surmise that even if Bonaparte had won the Battle of Waterloo, it would only have proved another Lützen or Bautzen or Champaubert; a delusory prelude to inexorable defeat.

On 13 June 1815 Bonaparte took personal command of the Armée du Nord, now lying concentrated just southwest of the Belgian frontier opposite Charleroi. In fighting quality and equipment it was greatly superior to the improvised armies of the two previous campaigns, being founded on the Bourbon peacetime regular army, the ranks of which were filled with Bonaparte's own veterans. Its weakness lay in sheer numbers – some 128,000 men (including 22,300 cavalry) and 344 guns,[17] against an allied total in Belgium alone of over 200,000 men (including 25,000 cavalry) and nearly five hundred guns.[18] In the absence of Berthier, who was living in Germany, Bonaparte appointed Marshal Soult, an experienced and methodical soldier, as his chief-of-staff. He chose to leave the particularly able Davout in Paris as Minister of War, possibly because at a time when he could count on the loyalty of few in the capital, he knew he could count on Davout, a marshal notorious for his doglike devotion.

On 14 June Bonaparte issued one of his inspirational orders of the day:

> Soldiers, today is the anniversary of Marengo and Friedland, which twice decided the destinies of Europe. Then, just as after Austerlitz and Wagram, we were too generous; we believed in the oaths and protestations of the princes we left on their thrones! Today, then, in a coalition against us . . . they have begun the most unjust of aggressions. Let us then march to meet them: are not we and they still the same men? . . .
> For every Frenchman with a heart, the moment has come to conquer or perish![19]

Next morning the Armée du Nord began to advance.

FEW CAMPAIGNS have been so closely analysed as that of Waterloo. Since Bonaparte lost in spite of being a 'military genius' and 'the greatest captain of history', much effort has been laid out in explaining how this could come to pass. His subordinates are blamed for blunders in carrying out his orders, although in fact impartial comparison shows that they performed neither better nor worse than subordinates in previous campaigns. They are also blamed either for acting on their own initiative or failing to do so; a neat enough double. Soult in particular is blamed, on the grounds that as chief-of-staff he was nothing like as efficient or as clear in his drafting of orders as Berthier but Berthier himself had been guilty of repeated serious muddles and ambiguities.[20] Then again Bonaparte's own age and state of health are cited in order to prove that, were he still the man he had been, victory must have been inevitable. In fact he was the same age as Wellington and nearly thirty years younger than Blücher, while his leadership during the campaign was much the same in terms of style and of energy expended as, say, during the Austerlitz campaign. But in any case Bonaparte was present in the field out of personal choice, not duty like his two opponents. If indeed he were unfit to command, this would render his return from Elba even more irresponsible a venture.

The truth is that the Waterloo campaign, taken as a whole, amounts to very much an average Bonapartian exercise; indeed a fascinating reprise of patterns and happenings from his previous operations.

H E OPENED THIS, his last campaign, as he had opened his first, the Italian offensive of April 1796, with a stroke at the joint between two allied armies – in the present case, north of Charleroi, between the Anglo-Dutch under Wellington and the Prussians under Blücher. So well did he hide the concentration of his own army that he achieved a complete strategic surprise, catching the allies still spread out in peacetime cantonments. By the end of the first day, and despite the usual hold-ups owing to poor organization of the march, he had begun to shoulder his way between Wellington and Blücher.

He now decided that while Brussels, covered by Wellington's army, should be his main objective, he must first safeguard his own right flank and rear from Prussian attack by beating Blücher; another echo of spring 1796, when though the Directory instructed him to attack the Piedmontese, he was first compelled to deal with the Austrians at Montenotte.[21] As in 1796 he now divided his army, one wing against each enemy. The Guard, 10,000 strong, formed the reserve under his own command. As he explained to Ney, whom he appointed to command the left wing (45,000–50,000 men) against Wellington, 'I shall move to one wing or the other according to circumstance . . . As necessary I will draw troops from either wing in order to strengthen my reserve . . .'[22] On paper this was an admirably flexible arrangement, a classic Bonapartian deployment: groups which though dispersed could close on each other in any direction to give battle. The only drawback in the past had lain in the frequent failure of the system to work in the event, the separate groups proving unable to unite in time at the decisive point.

For 16 June Bonaparte planned an equally classic Bonapartian manoeuvre. While he in person with his right wing (45,000 men under Marshal Grouchy) and the Guard attacked Blücher's front at Ligny, Ney with the left wing would first march north up the Brussels road to the crossroads of Quatre-Bras, then swing east in a hook round Blücher's right flank and rear. The plan, founded on inaccurate intelligence, did not quite work out. Bonaparte expected Ney easily to brush aside such troops as Wellington could by then deploy at Quatre-Bras. Instead, the English commander rushed up formations in just sufficient quantities to bog Ney down in a fierce encounter battle and then force him back. And Blücher at Ligny had concentrated not just a corps, as Bonaparte reckoned, but 84,000 men, four-fifths of his army. Rather than the expected walkover Bonaparte found himself struggling in one of the hardest fights of his career.

He had to struggle the harder because he left one of his own corps (Lobau's) idle at Charleroi for want of orders – shades of Serrurier during the Castiglione campaign, Bernadotte at the battles of Jena-Auerstädt and Eylau, and Bertrand at Lützen. Far from overwhelmingly outnumbering Blücher, Bonaparte himself was outnumbered. In mid-afternoon he sent Ney an urgent signal of a familiar kind:

At this moment the battle is very severe . . . you are to manoeuvre at once in such a manner as to envelop the enemy's right and fall with all your might on his rear . . . the fate of France is in your hands.[23]

But by this time Ney's own battle had become far too 'severe' for him to be able to carry out this order. Meanwhile – shades of Souham at Leipzig – the 1st Corps under d'Erlon, 20,000 strong, spent the day trudging between each battlefield without firing a shot. At first ordered to support Ney, it was diverted eastwards to join Bonaparte, probably owing to the interfering zeal of one of Bonaparte's aide-de-camps. When it got within sight of Ligny, it was recalled to Quatre-Bras by the now desperately pressed Ney, only to arrive too late to be useful.

Bonaparte therefore managed to fight on both fronts with inferior numbers; not a good advertisement for the Bonapartian maxim of concentration of force. None the less, at Ligny he inflicted a major defeat on Blücher, so proving that his own and his army's pugilistic skills were undiminished. Its centre smashed by a final onset by the Guard, the Prussian army struggled off through a thunderstorm, leaving behind 16,000 killed, wounded and prisoner. Had Bonaparte's broad strategy of driving Blücher away from Wellington succeeded after all? Bonaparte, ever prone to require reality to conform to his desires, believed so. Next morning, 17 June, he informed Ney that 'The Prussian army has been put to rout; General Pajol [with half a cavalry corps] is pursuing it on the roads to Namur and Liège [that is, due east, away from Wellington] . . .'[24] Here again was the euphoria of Champaubert; the euphoria which in 1796 had led Bonaparte on the Po to imagine himself over the Alps into Austria in another month.

It was not a mood conducive to prudent decision or energetic action. That morning he dallied, as he had dallied in Milan before Marengo, instead of pouncing swiftly on Wellington. By the time he and Ney attacked the English position at Quatre-Bras, only Wellington's rearguard remained. Since early morning the English commander had been falling back in perfect order to a defensive position at Mont St Jean, barring the Brussels road two miles south of the village of Waterloo. That evening, after a hectic pursuit of the English rearguard, Bonaparte ordered his cavalry to probe Mont St Jean, whereupon the flare of English cannon-fire in the dusk told him that Wellington intended to stand and fight. Eagerly Bonaparte looked forward to the morrow, when he and his veterans would kick the Englishman's polyglot and largely inexperienced army to pieces.

His elation was misplaced, for the true strategic situation was the very reverse of what he imagined it to be. Far from Blücher's army fleeing eastwards in fragments, it now lay fully concentrated in a strength of 100,000 men only eight miles to Wellington's left, ready to join him next day. And while the allied commanders had thus been working to bring their armies together Bonaparte had perpetuated the dividing of his own. Marshal Grouchy, with a third of Bonaparte's total strength, now lay almost twice as far from the scene of the next day's battle as Blücher.

LIKE THE AUSTRIANS AFTER MONTENOTTE the Prussians after Ligny had retired by a route that would reunite them with their ally; in their case, due north to Wavre and parallel to Wellington's own retreat. Bonaparte's attempt to drive his enemies apart had failed in 1815 as in 1796. At noon on 17 June, feeling belated twinges of doubt as to whether all the Prussians had in fact gone off eastwards to Liège, Bonaparte dispatched Grouchy with 33,000 men and ninety-six guns – a needlessly large force for reconnaissance – in order to find out, 'whether he [Blücher] is separating from the English, or whether they mean to reunite in order to cover Brussels and risk . . . a fresh battle . . .'[25] But Bonaparte ordered Grouchy northeastwards to Gembloux, a direction widely divergent from his own advance northwards on Mont St Jean, and *east* of Blücher's true line of retreat, which as a result was reconnoitred neither by Grouchy nor Bonaparte himself.

During the small hours of 18 June, the day of the Battle of Waterloo, uncertain reports from Grouchy and others made Bonaparte realize that at least a Prussian corps must have retired on Wavre. None the less he still failed to grasp the magnitude of the danger to his own right flank. Instead of ordering Grouchy to march west at utmost speed to join him, he merely ordered him (at 10 a.m.) to advance *northwest* on Wavre, pushing the supposed Prussian 'corps' before him.[26] By the time this order reached Grouchy at about 4 p.m., Grouchy had already been marching on Wavre for several hours.

Bonaparte was therefore about to give battle to Wellington's 68,000 men with only two-thirds of his own army, some 72,000 men present, and while his right flank and rear lay exposed to an advance by Blücher's 100,000. Not he but the allies had proved the more truly 'Napoleonic' in their combinations. Unless Bonaparte could rout Wellington in the few hours that remained before Blücher could deploy *en masse* he would be engulfed by another catastrophe like Leipzig – and that meant final political ruin. Never in his life had Bonaparte stood in such extreme need of rescue by means of victory in battle.

Now at last he found himself face to face with the English. And no man better exemplified the best qualities of the English ruling class than the Duke of Wellington, with his high-nosed aristocratic confidence and direct simplicity of speech and manners; a man remarkable for hard-minded good sense, steady nerve and a character as true and tough as the metal of a cannon. In Wellington Bonaparte had come up against an officer with the same simple resolve to do his duty as Colonel Maillard who had held the Citadel of Ajaccio against him in 1792. In Wellington also Bonaparte had come up against by far the most formidable opponent of his career, alike because of the Englishman's professionalism, his force of leadership and his sheer strength of will.

Bonaparte's flashier victories had been won against opponents willing to meet him in freewheeling battles of manoeuvre. Wellington proposed to offer him no such opening. Instead, like old Kutusov at Borodino, he decided to fight a static defensive battle on carefully chosen ground. For he commanded an international army uneven in skill and reliability: of his 68,000 men 24,000 were from the United Kingdom, 26,000 from various German contingents and 18,000 Dutch-Belgians (Belgium and Holland then forming one kingdom).

Carefully intermingling his various national contingents, Wellington posted his army just behind the crestline of the Mont St Jean ridge, a low hog's back running

east–west across the Brussels road. To the south, towards the French positions on the parallel ridge of La Belle Alliance a mile away, the ground shelves away in treeless, hedgeless fields then tall with corn; the slope was long and gentle on Wellington's left and centre, steeper on his right, but everywhere offering a perfect field of fire for his guns. A few hundred yards in front of this main position Wellington had improvised four fortresses out of big stone-built farmsteads, their buildings grouped round walled courtyards – the Château de Hougoumont on his right, La Haye Sainte protecting his centre, just down the slope beside the Brussels road; Papelotte and La Haye over on his left. Wellington's left flank – towards the Prussians – was covered against an out-flanking movement by tumbled countryside of deep lanes and valley bottoms; his right by a detached force of 17,000 men posted at Hal, some eight miles to the west.

It was a formidable position, rendered the more formidable by its narrow extent of only two and a half miles (twice Bonaparte's front at Austerlitz with similar numbers), so enabling Wellington to deploy in depth, especially behind his right and centre. That morning old Spanish hands among Bonaparte's subordinates tried to warn him that the long innocent-looking crest of Mont St Jean might conceal just such a Wellingtonian defence. Bonaparte swept their advice aside with all his old impatient ridicule, telling Soult:

> Because you have been beaten by Wellington, you consider him a great general. And I tell you that Wellington is a bad general, that the English are bad soldiers, and that the whole thing will be a walkover . . . We shall sleep in Brussels tonight.[27]

Perceiving, then, no need for subtle manoeuvre, Bonaparte proposed simply to smash straight through Wellington's centre beyond La Haye Sainte with a human battering ram of 20,000 men (d'Erlon's corps) preceded by a bombardment from a battery of eighty guns, including twenty-four of his favourite 12-pounders –

Wagram, Friedland or Borodino again.[28] But not until about 11.30 a.m. did Bonaparte and his artillery chief judge the ground to have dried out enough after the rain for cannon-balls to pitch and bound instead of embedding themselves. Bonaparte occupied the time by holding a grand review of the army to impress the enemy, his own soldiers and himself. It was past 1 p.m. before he was ready to launch his attack.

Just as he was about to give the order, dark masses of troops were sighted some five miles off to the east. Could this be Grouchy? A dispatch captured with a Prussian courier revealed their true identity: Bülow's Prussian 4th Corps. To an order just drafted to Grouchy confirming his existing movement on Wavre was now added an urgent postscript: '. . . do not lose an instant in drawing near and joining us, and crushing Bülow, whom you will catch in the very act [of attacking our flank] . . .'[29] Or, as he had more tersely signalled Desaix on the morning of Marengo, 'In the name of God, return if you still can.' But *this* time it was far, far too late for Bonaparte to start reuniting a divided army. His order did not reach Grouchy until after 6 p.m., by which time Grouchy had become hopelessly entangled in a hard-fought action with Blücher's rearguard at Wavre in conformity with Bonaparte's earlier wishes.

Grouchy was, of course, to become a favourite scapegoat for Bonaparte's defeat at Waterloo, accused of being slow in his initial pursuit of the Prussians and then ill-judged in not marching straight to the sound of the guns at Waterloo. Examination of the evidence shows that neither charge carries weight. His pursuit was as swift as the muddy state of the lanes permitted. His march on Wavre had been approved by two successive signals from Bonaparte. Bonaparte in any case expected not initiative from his subordinates but strict obedience to detailed orders. He had reminded Ney of this only two days earlier.[30]

The appearance of Bülow on the eastern skyline compelled Bonaparte straightaway to detach 10,000 men to protect his right flank. He would now have to beat Wellington with inferior numbers. More than ever, therefore, all turned on his conduct of the battle. Yet instead of leading front-line operations in person, as Wellington was to do, Bonaparte followed his usual practice – Austerlitz, Eylau, Wagram – of remaining at a command post in the rear. Here, behind the French centre (some accounts say at La Belle Alliance, some say Rossomme a mile further back), he was not only remote from the swift ebb and flow of tactical events, but also could not even clearly see parts of the battlefield because of the lie of the contours – in particular the low ground round Hougoumont and between La Belle Alliance and Wellington's centre at Mont St Jean on the Brussels road. The fog of powder smoke would further have obscured Bonaparte's distant view.

He entrusted command of forward operations to Marshal Ney, as he had entrusted Soult with the attack on the Pratzen at Austerlitz. Yet Ney was quite unfitted for so crucial a role; a man ginger of hair and ginger of temperament, pink, beefy, brave, but with a long record of impulsive blundering. His appointment casts doubt on Bonaparte's ability at picking men.

As the combined result of Bonaparte's remoteness and Ney's incompetence the French attack never became more that a series of disconnected assaults in which

'. . . one of the great sentimental set-pieces of Napoleonic iconography – something of a Last Supper': Bonaparte's farewell to the Guard at Fontainebleau on 20 April 1814. *Bibliothèque Nationale, Paris*

ADIEUX DE NAPOLEON A SON ARMÉE
(Fontainebleau 20 avril 1814)

there was an almost complete failure to co-ordinate infantry, cavalry and guns. From the very start the battle slewed off its intended path, thanks to Bonaparte's brother Jerome, now commanding a division (another ill-judged appointment), who turned a subsidiary attack on Hougoumont into a major effort that was to keep more than two French divisions occupied for the rest of the day. Meanwhile, the bombardment of Wellington's centre by Bonaparte's eighty-gun battery failed in its purpose because Wellington, unlike Continental generals, did not post his troops in the open, but back behind the crest of the ridge, or even lying down.

At about 1.30 p.m. Bonaparte launched the grand assault by 20,000 infantry against Wellington's centre. It too failed – because of the tactical formation adopted by Ney. Instead of deploying in handy battalion columns or a mixture of line and column, Ney organized three out of the four attacking divisions each in a single clumsy rectangular mass; superb targets for allied guns firing case-shot and the musket volleys of the allied line. Wedged tight together, the French could not deploy in order to return the fire. Helpless, hammered, they gradually melted into a dense crowd of frightened men. Allied bayonets and a cavalry charge in the flank returned them to the foot of the slope. The episode had lasted about two hours.

Wrongly jumping to the conclusion that some of Wellington's units were beginning to break to the rear, Ney now ordered the French cavalry to attack – but omitted to support them with infantry and guns. Between about 3.30 p.m. and 5.30 p.m. massed horsemen rode again and again round the infantry squares of Wellington's right centre; an entirely impotent display of courage because sabres cannot overcome musket-fire or a hedge of bayonets. Bonaparte, watching the first of these charges ebb back down the distant slope, snapped to Soult: 'This is a premature movement which may well have fatal consequences.'[31] Nevertheless, rather than see his cavalry beaten Bonaparte ordered another cavalry corps forward in support. By a misunderstanding the Guard cavalry followed suit as well. Nine thousand horsemen jostled forward, to achieve nothing but blown horses and heavy losses.

By now the Prussians were attacking deep behind Bonaparte's right flank, threatening the road back to Charleroi. At about 6 p.m. Bonaparte therefore ordered Ney to take La Haye Sainte and break Wellington's centre at all cost. This time the French infantry carried the farmstead and achieved a lodgement on the crest of the Mont St Jean ridge. For once Ney had the wit to send up horse artillery; a gap opened in Wellington's line; and for the first and last time the French came close to victory. It only needed another attack with fresh formations to split the Anglo-Dutch army in two. Ney therefore sent an officer back to ask Bonaparte for more troops. Bonaparte helpfully remarked: 'Where do you expect me to get them? Do you expect me to manufacture them?'[32] In fact he still had fourteen battalions of the Guard in reserve. But he was far from Mont St Jean and all too near the Prussians. Instead of sending the Guard or much of it up to Ney, he deployed it on his right flank against Blücher, thereby missing his one great opportunity of the day. For while Ney's emissary was riding on his vain errand, Wellington, present in person at the very point in his line where the French were in danger of breaking through, rapidly switched troops from his left to plug the gap.

The climax of the Battle of Waterloo, 18 June 1815 – Wellington orders the allied army to advance after the repulse of the Imperial Guard by the English Foot Guards. Painting by John Augustus Atkinson, who was an eyewitness. *Bibliothèque Nationale, Paris*

At about 7.30 p.m. Bonaparte, his right flank now bent back at a right angle against the Prussians, belatedly launched eight battalions of the Guard in a final attempt to splinter Wellington's line. But it was Ney, not Bonaparte, who marched at their head. Bonaparte himself made much the same contribution as to Desaix's counter-stroke at Marengo; he harangued the troops. It is possible that, again as at Marengo, looming disaster had paralysed him mentally and morally. For when the Guard too was beaten by the superior firepower of the allied line, and the Armée du Nord, under attack by Wellington from the north and Blücher from the east, struggled in frantic confusion to get home to France through the bottleneck of the narrow, steep and winding village street of Genappes, Bonaparte did not stay to rally his soldiers or conduct their retreat. Instead, he rode for his life from Blücher's vengeful uhlans, a speechless, weeping and terrified man.[33]

F ROM LAON, on his way to Paris, he issued the last of his bulletins. It explained how in fact 'the battle had been won' at Waterloo, when 'a sudden panic terror swept the entire field of battle', with the result that 'in a moment the army became nothing but a confused mass.'[34] Generations of ingenious French historians were to draw inspiration from this theme that Bonaparte had really been victorious at Waterloo, but had been robbed of the match by the celestial referee.

Back in Paris on 21 June, Bonaparte spoke of leading a national resistance to the invader. A mutiny by the Senate and the House of Representatives dispelled this final fantasy. Lucien urged him to quell this mutiny by another '18 Brumaire'. On that occasion Bonaparte had nervously plucked the lip;[35] now he did so again, and with better reason. 'Where is your resolution?' asked Lucien. 'Stop hesitating; you know what the consequences must be if you fail to act boldly.' But Bonaparte only glumly replied: 'I have been only too bold.'[36] It was the moment not only of the final bankruptcy of his fortunes, but also of his will. Faced with an ultimatum from a new provisional government, he abdicated once more and took refuge at Malmaison with his family and his memories of Josephine. The Bonaparte clan decided to sail to a new life in America; Napoleon first, his kin later. The provisional government, eager to be rid of him, ordered him to take ship at Rochefort. On 29 June he bade farewell to his mother: 'Adieu, my son', 'My mother, adieu.'[37]

Barring the exit from Rochefort, however, lay an English ship of the line, H.M.S. *Bellerophon* (Captain Maitland R.N.). Bonaparte therefore addressed to the Prince Regent the last of all his appeals to his foes' better natures:

I come, like Themistocles [who in fact was a renegade], to throw myself upon the hospitality of the British people. I place myself under the protection of their laws, which I ask from Your Royal Highness as the most powerful, the most constant, and the most generous of my enemies.[38]

In all the circumstances it was a letter of quite astonishing cheek. It did not elicit a reply. In the meantime Maitland agreed to take Bonaparte to England on condition that his fate would be at the disposal of the English government. But the nearest Bonaparte got to the country he had so deeply wanted to conquer and humiliate was Torbay, and later Plymouth Sound, where H.M.S. *Bellerophon* anchored while the government decided what to do with him. At the end of July they decided: the other allied governments agreed; and Bonaparte, who had been transferred with his suite to H.M.S. *Northumberland*, sailed for St Helena; *'petite île'*, as he had written in one of his notebooks a quarter of a century ago.[39]

O N 17 OCTOBER 1815 St Helena was sighted on the southern horizon, 'the ugliest and most dismal rock conceivable,' as a British army surgeon described it, 'rising like an enormous black wart from the face of the deep.'[40] Jamestown, the port and only town, lay in a deep ravine between mountains of dark rock, its white church surrounded by English-looking houses. But the grassy plateau in the centre of the island where Bonaparte dwelt for the rest of his existence was, avers the same witness, embellished by 'several really beautiful and romantic spots.'[41]

On St Helena Bonaparte and his entourage settled down to a life that resembled nothing so much as a novel by Jane Austen, first at 'The Briars' and then at Longwood (the very names are redolent). Longwood itself was just such a comfortable country home surrounded by lawns and shrubberies as Mr Woodhouse's Hartfield. The weeks, the months, the years revolved round events like the calling of a visitor, the receipt of a letter, little expeditions, dinners at Plantation House, the English Governor's residence (supplying the place of the Great House in the social life of Jane Austen's villages); occasional balls in Jamestown. When the lamps were lit in the evening the company at Longwood diverted itself with chess, cards, billiards and reading aloud. Bonaparte himself played the role either of Sir William Lucas, boring the room into somnolence with his interminable and repetitious memories of his great days at Court, or of

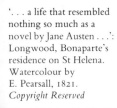

(left) The morning after Waterloo; engraving after a painting by Heavyside. Bonaparte's escape from Elba had cost Europe in all over 60,000 men killed and maimed. *Radio Times Hulton Picture Library*; (insert) A British 6-pounder field gun employed at Waterloo. *Royal Military Academy, Sandhurst. Photo: National Army Museum, London*

'. . . a life that resembled nothing so much as a novel by Jane Austen . . .': Longwood, Bonaparte's residence on St Helena. Watercolour by E. Pearsall, 1821. *Copyright Reserved*

Lady de Bourgh, punctilious observance of rank meaning much to him. He lacked, however, that gentlemanlike air with which Miss Austen invests even her bores and bounders. After meeting Bonaparte in 1817, when he was in his forty-eighth year, a British army surgeon recorded:

> Napoleon's first appearance was far from imposing – the stature was short and thick – head sunk in shoulders – his face with large folds under the chin – the limbs appeared to be stout, but well-proportioned – complexion olive – expression sinister, and rather scowling. The features instantly reminded us of the prints of him we had seen. On the whole, his general look was more that of an obese Spanish or Portuguese friar than the Hero of Modern Times.[42]

This life of rural retirement spelled an anguish of boredom for a man so restless, so barren of internal resources. Moreover, the compulsive urge to manipulate and dominate his fellow men remained as strong as ever. In order to vent this urge he conducted an unscrupulous campaign against the Governor, Sir Hudson Lowe, seeking to wrong-foot him over petty questions of protocol and privilege as he had once wrong-footed the cabinets and courts of Europe in regard to the destinies of nations. Sir Hudson, a Lowland Scots soldier strict of character and rigid in his sense of duty, was only too conscious that he had been charged by the allied governments with custody of one of the most dangerous troublemakers of history. He looked, so wrote a British eyewitness, 'very much like a person who would not let his prisoner escape if he could help it.'[43] After all, Bonaparte's last escape had cost Europe over 60,000 men killed and maimed. Sir Hudson therefore unbendingly applied the rules governing Bonaparte's confinement on the island, lest that wily man should take advantage of him. This enabled Bonaparte's partisans to present Bonaparte as the tortured victim of a harsh jailer. Were it even true, Bonaparte would hardly merit sympathy, for it was he who, having imprisoned the aged Pope, had given the order:

> . . . you will not allow anyone, whoever it may be, to visit him . . . You will take care to remove the Pope's papers, books and any documents . . . You will leave him neither paper, nor pens nor ink, nor any means of writing . . . Furthermore the people of his household can also be confined . . .[44]

Yet one absorbing interest remained to Bonaparte during his years on St Helena – himself. Residence at Longwood afforded him the leisure to rewrite – and retell to eager scribes – the course of his career, explaining away his errors and defeats; pruning the haphazard shape of events into an artistic symmetry. In these accounts luck and self-seeking opportunism became transfigured into the step-by-step execution of a grand work of political architecture. His life, it appeared, had been inspired by love of France; indeed by a wider ideal of a Europe united in liberty and progress. Many were to believe all this. Bonaparte also discoursed at length on the principles of war to which he had been by no means faithful in practice, so deluding generations of soldiers into a naïve belief that the secret of war lies in seeking swift and total victory by an offensive with all forces united, and into the even more naïve belief that Bonaparte's career proved the point. The legend industry of St Helena therefore thrived. Bonaparte was conscious that his very

'... hero-worshipping emotion, indeed religious veneration ...': a French allegorical embroidered and painted picture of Bonaparte arising from his grave at Longwood to immortality, to the chagrin of four watching allied officers. *Collection Malmaison*. Photo: *Studio Laverton*

imprisonment, Prometheus chained to a rock, must appeal to a romantic age:

> Our situation may even have its attractions! . . . The universe is looking at us! . . . We remain the martyrs of an everlasting cause! . . . Millions of men weep for us, the homeland sighs, and glory is in mourning! . . . We struggle here against the oppression of the Gods, and the wishes of the nations are for us![45]

On 5 May 1821 Bonaparte died of cancer of the stomach, like his father, and like two of his sisters.[46] A peculiarly fitting epitaph is supplied by his own words thirty years before in *Le Discours de Lyon*:

> In a disordered imagination lies the source of human unhappiness. It makes us wander across the seas from one fantasy to another, and if its spell leaves us in the end, it is by then too late; the hour strikes and the man dies detesting life . . .[47]

Bonaparte's body, at first buried in the grounds of Longwood, was brought back to France in 1840. Its progress up the Seine to Paris and its ceremonial reburying in the Invalides presented one of the most remarkably successful public-relations exercises in French history; Bonaparte would have much approved. The accompanying uprush of hero-worshipping emotion, indeed religious veneration, marks the moment when the Napoleonic legend, so long in the creating, was fairly launched. Posthumously Bonaparte had consummated his one lasting conquest: the sentimental credulity of men.

214

APPENDICES

BIBLIOGRAPHICAL REFERENCES
AND NOTES

Prologue
1 This anachronistic term is accurate; the situation would have been recognizable to the Germany of the 1920s.
2 This account is based on FREDERIC MASSON *Napoléon Inconnu: Papiers Inédites* Paris, Paul Ollendorff 1895, 2 Vols, II pp. 357–84; ARTHUR CHUQUET *La Jeunesse de Napoléon* Paris, Armand Colin 1897–8, 3 Vols, II *La Révolution* pp. 268–94

Chapter I
1 Chuquet I p. 14
2 C. F. ANTOMMARCHI *Les Derniers Moments de Napoléon 1819–21* Paris 1898, Tome I p. 352
3 Chuquet I p. 13
4 Ibid.
5 *Souvenirs de Madame Mère, dictés par elle à Mlle Rose Mellini* in BARON LARREY *Madame Mère (Napoleonis Mater): Essai Historique* Paris 1892, 2 Vols, I Appendix II p. 528 et seq.
6 JOSEPH BONAPARTE *Mémoires* Paris 1853–4, I p. 40
7 Larrey I p. 528 et seq.
8 Napoleone with stockings at half-mast Makes love to Giacominetta
9 The Buonapartes were among the oldest families in Corsica, having left Italy in the 16th cent. Letizia's family was also noble.
10 Chuquet I p. 82
11 Joseph Bonaparte *Mémoires* I p. 26
12 C. H. *Some Observations on Bonaparte's Early Years* London 1797
13 Ibid.
14 Chuquet I p. 123
15 Masson I pp. 80–1
16 GUY GODLEWSKI *La vie quotidienne de Napoléon à Brienne*; in *Souvenir Napoléonien* No. 265 August 1972
17 Chuquet I p. 263
18 Masson I pp. 94–5
19 Chuquet I p. 293
20 Ibid.
21 Masson I p. 214
22 Op. cit. p. 216
23 Chuquet II p. 2
24 Op. cit. p. 224
25 Masson II p. 328
26 Op. cit. p. 36

27 Masson I pp. 149–50
28 Masson II p. 289
29 Masson I pp. 145–6

Chapter II
1 Chuquet I p. 359
2 Chuquet II p. 102
3 ALFRED COBBAN *A History of Modern France* 2 Vols, Pelican Books, Harmondsworth 1961, I p. 161
4 Masson II pp. 208–9
5 Ibid.
6 Chuquet II p. 231
7 Masson II pp. 341–5
8 Masson II p. 384; Chuquet II p. 294
9 Chuquet III p. 2
10 Op. cit. p. 4
11 Masson II p. 388
12 Op. cit. p. 406
13 Ibid.
14 Chuquet III p. 154
15 Op. cit. p. 172
16 Op. cit. p. 194
17 CORRESPONDANCE No. 1
18 Chuquet III p. 229

Chapter III
1 SIR JAMES MARSHALL-CORNWALL *Napoleon as Military Commander* London, Batsford 1967, p. 43
2 FREDERIC MASSON *Napoléon et les Femmes* Paris, Paul Ollendorf 1894, p. 13
3 Correspondance 42
4 Op. cit. 65
5 Op. cit. 72
6 Masson *Napoléon et les Femmes* p. 17
7 Correspondance 91
8 JEAN COLIN *Education Militaire de Napoléon* Paris, Librarie R. Chapelot 1901, p. 88
9 Correspondance 53. Instructions to the Representatives and the Commander-in-Chief of the Army of Italy. From a rough draft by Buonaparte.
10 Ibid.
11 GUGLIELMO FERRERO *The Gamble: Bonaparte in Italy 1796–7* London, G. Bell 1961, p. 6
12 DUC DE RAGUSE *Mémoires* I Paris 1857, p. 297
13 Correspondance 202
14 Op. cit. 233
15 Op. cit. *passim*
16 Op. cit. 220
17 Op. cit. 234

'. . . the moment when the Napoleonic legend, so long in the making, was fairly launched': medal struck in Paris in 1840 to mark Bonaparte's reburial in the Invalides. *Mansell Collection*

18 Op. cit. 257
19 Op. cit. 347 and 349
20 Raguse I p. 178
21 LEON CERF Lettres de Napoléon à Joséphine Paris. Editions Duchartre et Van Buggenhoudt 1929, pp. 14–15
22 Correspondance 368
23 Op. cit. 443 and 453
24 Op. cit. 503
25 Op. cit. 1078
26 Op. cit. 925
27 Op. cit. 1182
28 Op. cit. 1196
29 Op. cit. 1223
30 Op. cit. 1377
31 Op. cit. 1378
32 Raguse I p. 253
33 Ferrero pp. 156–7
34 Correspondance 1735, 1745 and 1756
35 Op. cit. 1756

Chapter IV
1 Raguse II p. 296
2 Ferrero pp. 227–8
3 Cerf p. 36
4 Op. cit. p. 51
5 Ferrero p. 181
6 Correspondance 2014
7 Op. cit. 2103
8 Op. cit. 2495
9 Op. cit. 2502
10 Ibid.
11 Op. cit. 2570
12 Op. cit. 2723
13 Ibid.
14 Ibid.
15 Op. cit. 2878
16 Ibid.
17 Op. cit. 3259
18 F. CHARLES-ROUX Bonaparte: Governor of Egypt translated by E. W. Dicker. London, Methuen 1937, passim but especially pp. 32–3, 100–6, 180–3, 225–30 and 292–4.
19 Correspondance 2901
20 Op. cit. 3524
21 Op. cit. 3527
22 Op. cit. 3282
23 Op. cit. 3945
24 Op. cit. 4012, 4013 and 4019
25 Op. cit. 4022
26 Op. cit. 3828
27 Op. cit. 4014
28 I am indebted to Major-General B. P. Hughes for this information, and to him and to Brigadier R. G. S. Bidwell for their general advice concerning artillery and its employment in this era.
29 Raguse II p. 11
30 Op. cit. pp. 21–2
31 Correspondance 4124 and 4156
32 Op. cit. 4138
33 Op. cit. 4155
34 Op. cit. 4225, 28 June 1799
35 Charles-Roux p. 328

Chapter V
1 LOUIS DE VILLEFOSSE and JANINE BOUISSOUNOUSE L'Opposition à Napoléon Paris, Flammarion 1969, p. 46
2 LUCIEN BONAPARTE Mémoires Secrets London 1818, 2 Vols, I pp. 62–80
3 Correspondance 4585
4 Ibid.
5 Op. cit. 4422
6 Op. cit. 4499
7 Ibid.
8 Op. cit. 4506
9 Op. cit. 4445–6
10 Op. cit. 4649
11 Ibid.
12 Op. cit. 4695 and 4711
13 Op. cit. 4738
14 According to the new Constitution, the First Consul could not command armies.
15 Ibid.
16 Correspondance 4747
17 Op. cit. 4751
18 Op. cit. 4795
19 Op. cit. 4792
20 Op. cit. 4811
21 DE CUGNAC Campagne de l'Armée de Reserve en 1800 Paris 1900, 2 Vols, I pp. 303 and 435
22 Op. cit. 4816
23 Correspondance 4826
24 de Cugnac I p. 441
25 Ibid.
26 Correspondance 4846
27 Op. cit. 4826
28 de Cugnac I p. 468; Raguse II p. 121
29 Correspondance 4896–7
30 de Cugnac II pp. 372–3
31 Ibid.
32 de Cugnac II p. 395
33 Correspondance 4906: letter of 10 June to his chief commissary: 'Have shoes made ready for us, because we are all going barefoot.'
34 de Cugnac II p. 397; Raguse II p. 132
35 Correspondance 4910
36 Raguse II p. 142
37 Correspondance of Charles, First Marquis of Cornwallis edited by C. Ross. London 1859, 3 Vols, III p. 457

Chapter VI
1 Correspondance 4786
2 Op. cit. 4909
3 Op. cit. 4806
4 Raguse I pp. 297–8
5 Correspondance 797
6 Larrey Madame Mère I p. 327
7 M. A. LE NORMAND The Historical and Secret Memoirs of the Empress Josephine London 1895, 2 Vols, I p. 247
8 de Villefosse and Bouissounouse pp. 82–3
9 Le Normand I p. 229
10 Le Discours de Lyon Masson II p. 322
11 Ibid.
12 Correspondance 5378
13 GEORGE LEFEBVRE Napoléon 1799–1807

Routledge and Kegan Paul 1969, p. 141
14 Correspondance 5647
15 Op. cit. 6246
16 de Villefosse and Bouissounouse p. 168
17 Correspondance 6887
18 Lefebvre p. 125
19 Op. cit. pp. 125–6; de Villefosse and Bouissounouse pp. 150–61
20 Correspondance 7568
21 Masson I p. 149
22 de Villefosse and Bouissounouse p. 175
23 Masson I p. 149
24 Op. cit. pp. 149–50
25 Correspondance 5090
26 Op. cit. 6230
27 This is based on Lefebvre pp. 141–9
28 The poems of Ossian were a literary fake by an ingenious Scot named Macpherson.
29 Lucien Bonaparte p. 166
30 Correspondance 7754
31 Op. cit. 7752
32 To Josephine, Le Normand II p. 28
33 Ibid.
34 Correspondance 7897
35 Ibid.
36 de Villefosse and Bouissounouse p. 258
37 Masson Napoléon Inconnu II p. 327

Chapter VII
1 Correspondance 8203
2 Lefebvre Napoléon 1799–1807 p. 169
3 Correspondance 6414
4 Op. cit. 6276
5 Lefebvre p. 176
6 ARTHUR BRYANT Years of Victory 1802–1812 The Reprint Society 1944, p. 39
7 Whitworth's dispatches of 14 March 1803, quoted in Bryant p. 49
8 Ibid.
9 Masson I pp. 320 and 323
10 Correspondance 9073
11 Le Normand I p. 250
12 Correspondance 6628 and 6814
13 Op. cit. 7026
14 Op. cit. 7030
15 Op. cit. 7186
16 Ibid.
17 Op. cit. 7333
18 Lefebvre pp. 186–7
19 Ibid.
20 Correspondance 7279
21 Op. cit. 7309
22 Le Normand I p. 250
23 Correspondance 8379–81
24 Op. cit. 8379
25 Ibid.
26 JOHN TERRAINE Trafalgar Sidgwick and Jackson 1976, p. 58. This account excels by its succinctness and clarity.
27 Ibid.
28 Ibid.
29 Correspondance 8578
30 Op. cit. 8791
31 Op. cit. 8808

32 Op. cit. 8817
33 Op. cit. 8892
34 Op. cit. 8787
35 Op. cit. 8871
36 Terraine p. 71
37 Correspondance 8985
38 Terraine pp. 90–1
39 Correspondance 8999
40 Op. cit. 8996
41 E. DEBRIERE Projets et Tentatives de Debarquement aux Iles Britanniques Etat-Major, Section Historique, 1793–1805, quoted in Terraine pp. 116–17
42 Correspondance 9073
43 Op. cit. 8076
44 Bryant p. 159
45 Correspondance 9114
46 Op. cit. 9117
47 Op. cit. 9130

Chapter VIII
1 For Franco-Russian relations, 1803–4, see Lefebvre pp. 198–9 and 201–3
2 Correspondance 8796
3 Lefebvre pp. 208–11
4 Correspondance 8905
5 Op. cit. 9070
6 Ibid.
7 Op. cit. 9117
8 It is often stated that Bonaparte greatly benefited from the artillery reforms of the Comte de Gribeauval under Louis XVI, but this has been exaggerated. See Raguse II p. 150
9 Correspondance 9158
10 Op. cit. 9162
11 Ibid.
12 Op. cit. 9217
13 Op. cit. 9245, 9249 and 9254
14 Raguse II p. 307
15 Correspondance 9299
16 Ibid.
17 Op. cit. 9387
18 Op. cit. 9425; and 9426 on the need for shoes.
19 DE FEZENSAC Souvenirs Militaires de 1804 à 1814 Paris 1863, p. 64
20 Op. cit. pp. 64–5
21 Correspondance 9392
22 Op. cit. 9394
23 Op. cit. 9506
24 Op. cit. 9434
25 Op. cit. 9549
26 Op. cit. 9503
27 Op. cit. 9518
28 Op. cit. 9531
29 Ibid.
30 Op. cit. 9541 and 10032
31 Op. cit. 9519
32 Op. cit. 9527
33 ROBERT C. RICHARDSON Larrey: Surgeon to Napoleon's Imperial Guard John Murray 1974, p. 96
34 Correspondance 9532
35 Op. cit. 9535

36 Op. cit. 9533
37 Op. cit. 10032
38 Op. cit. 9533
39 Op. cit. 9547 and 9553
40 Op. cit. 9541

Chapter IX
1 Correspondance 9805
2 Bryant p. 227
3 see de Fezensac passim
4 Correspondance 10597
5 Op. cit. 10660
6 Op. cit. 10696
7 To brother Joseph, 12 September, op. cit. 10771
8 Op. cit. 10764
9 Op. cit. 10757
10 To brother Joseph, March 1806, op. cit. 9997
11 Marshall-Cornwall p. 164. See P. FOUCART Campagne de Prusse: Jéna Paris 1887, pp. 604–6
12 See Colin p. 249 for Bonaparte's views on this topic in 1794
13 Raguse II p. 211
14 Correspondance 11105
15 Lefebvre p. 260
16 Correspondance 11281
17 Op. cit. 11256
18 Op. cit. 11450
19 Op. cit. 11451
20 Op. cit. 11292
21 Op. cit. 11458
22 Op. cit. 11767
23 Op. cit. 11948
24 Op. cit. 11942
25 Lefebvre p. 266
26 Correspondance 9821 and 11292; de Fezensac p. 150
27 de Fezensac Chapter V
28 Op. cit. p. 147
29 Op. cit. p. 149
30 Correspondance 11800
31 Op. cit. 11779 and 12002
32 Op. cit. 11365
33 Op. cit. 11505
34 Masson Napoléon et les Femmes p. 199
35 Op. cit. pp. 203–4
36 Op. cit. pp. 207–8
37 Op. cit. p. 213
38 Lefebvre p. 262
39 Correspondance 12562

Chapter X
1 Correspondance 11948
2 Op. cit. 12015
3 Op. cit. 12380
4 Op. cit. 12758
5 Op. cit. 12815
6 BARON MENEVAL Napoléon et Marie-Louise: Souvenirs Historiques de Baron Méneval Paris 1844, 3 Vols, I p. 186
7 GEORGE LEFEBVRE Napoléon 1807–1815 London, Routledge and Kegan Paul 1969, p. 7
8 Correspondance 13033

9 Op. cit. 499
10 Op. cit. 13283
11 Op. cit. 9053
12 Op. cit. 13402
13 Op. cit. 13550
14 Lefebvre Napoléon 1807–1815 p. 169
15 Op. cit. p. 167
16 Correspondance 12415
17 Op. cit. 13634, 13643, 13691. Cobban p. 37
18 Correspondance 13358
19 Le Normand II p. 281; Lefebvre Napoléon 1807–1815 pp. 194–5
20 Méneval II p. 55
21 Lefebvre Napoléon 1807–1815 p. 193
22 Correspondance 12666
23 J. HOLLAND ROSE The Personality of Napoleon London 1912, p. 143
24 Rose Ibid.; Cobban p. 33
25 Rose Napoleon II p. 133 qu Erinnerungen der Grafin von Voss
26 Méneval III p. 3
27 Bryant FN I p. 12
28 Méneval II p. 3
29 Ibid.
30 Op. cit. p. 125
31 Op. cit. I p. 401
32 Op. cit. p. 194
33 Rose Napoléon II p. 193
34 Méneval I p. 213
35 Op. cit. III pp. 118–19
36 To Decrès, who passed it straight on to Marmont. Raguse II pp. 242–3
37 Masson Napoléon Inconnu II p. 328
38 Correspondance 12947

Chapter XI
1 Correspondance 13327
2 Op. cit. 13351
3 Op. cit. 13327
4 Op. cit. 13416
5 Lefebvre Napoléon 1807–1815 p. 147; Correspondance 16 passim
6 Correspondance 16 p. 498
7 Op. cit. 13738
8 Op. cit. 13750
9 Op. cit. 16 p. 500
10 Op. cit. 13813
11 Rose Napoléon II p. 167
12 Op. cit. FN p. 167
13 Correspondance 13815
14 Ibid.
15 Iberian place-names are spelled according to English usage at that time.
16 Correspondance 14239
17 Op. cit. 14244
18 Op. cit. 14243
19 Ibid.
20 Op. cit. 14234
21 Op. cit. 14244
22 Ibid.
23 ELIZABETH LONGFORD Wellington: The Years of the Sword London, Weidenfeld and Nicolson 1969, p. 139
24 Le Normand II p. 103

25 Correspondance 14269
26 Op. cit. 14275
27 Op. cit. 14473
28 Op. cit. 14603
29 Op. cit. 14378
30 Op. cit. 14620
31 Op. cit. 14715–16
32 Op. cit. 14703
33 Lefebvre *Napoléon 1807–1815* p. 173
34 Correspondance 14975
35 Op. cit. 15087
36 Op. cit. 15203
37 Op. cit. 15196
38 Op. cit. 15246
39 Op. cit. 15508
40 Raguse III p. 343

Chapter XII
1 Masson *Napoléon et les Femmes* p. 127
2 For a discussion of Napoleon's sexual make-up, *see* FRANK RICHARDSON M.D. *Napoleon Bisexual Emperor* William Kimber 1972
3 Méneval I pp. 341–2
4 Ibid.
5 Masson *Napoléon et les Femmes* p. 261
6 Op. cit. p. 262
7 Op. cit. p. 264
8 Op. cit. p. 265
9 Masson *Napoléon Inconnu* II p. 329
10 Chuquet I p. 293
11 Méneval I p. 387
12 Lefebvre *Napoléon 1807–1815* p. 257
13 For the Continental System *see* Lefebvre, op. cit. pp. 107–46 and 232–60; PAUL M. KENNEDY *The Rise and Fall of British Naval Mastery* Allen Lane 1976, Chapter V
14 Correspondance 16031
15 MICHAEL GLOVER *Wellington's Peninsular Victories* Batsford 1965, p. 25
16 Glover pp. 25–6
17 Raguse IV p. 36
18 Op. cit. pp. 9–10
19 Op. cit. p. 101
20 Correspondance 17071
21 PIERRE-LOUIS ROEDERER *Mémoires sur la Révolution, le Consulat et l'Empire* Paris, Plon 1942, p. 263
22 Le Normand II p. 40 FN
23 Op. cit. II p. 293
24 Duroc, who witnessed this scene, recounted it the same day to Marmont. Raguse III pp. 339–40
25 Lefebvre *Napoléon 1807–1815* p. 312
26 Correspondance 18725
27 Op. cit. 18429
28 Op. cit. 18450
29 Op. cit. 18554 and 18556
30 Op. cit. 18789, 18799 and 18800
31 Richardson *Larrey* pp. 150–2
32 Méneval III pp. 3–4
33 Rose *Personality of Napoleon* p. 252, quoting Heine *Englische Fragmente*
34 Correspondance 18769
35 Op. cit. 18781–2

36 Op. cit. 18855
37 Op. cit. 18860

Chapter XIII
1 Correspondance 18893 and 18909–10
2 de Fezensac p. 207; Correspondance 23–4 *passim* but *see especially* 18942
3 Correspondance 18935
4 Op. cit. 18884, 18888, 18915 and 18919
5 Op. cit. 18913
6 To Davout, 9 July, Correspondance 18938
7 Op. cit. 19024
8 Op. cit. 19019
9 RICHARD ALDINGTON *The Duke* Garden City Publishing Co., New York 1943, Appendix 5
10 Ibid.
11 de Fezensac pp. 222–3
12 Ibid.
13 DE SÉGUR *Histoire de Napoléon et la Grande Armée Pendant l'Année 1812* 3rd edition, Paris 1825, Tome I p. 220
14 Correspondance 19052
15 de Ségur I pp. 226–7
16 Op. cit. pp. 229–36; de Fezensac pp. 221–3 JEAN HANOTEAU (Editor) *Memoirs of General de Caulaincourt, Duke of Vicenza, 1812–13* translated by Hamish Miles, London, Cassell 1935, pp. 153–7
17 Correspondance 19085
18 Caulaincourt p. 166
19 de Ségur p. 293
20 Correspondance 19109, 19139 and 19155
21 Op. cit. 19181
22 Op. cit. 19175; Raguse IV pp. 450–62
23 Correspondance 19182
24 de Ségur II pp. 35–6
25 de Fezensac p. 245
26 Correspondance 19213
27 Caulaincourt pp. 236–8 and 252–9
28 Op. cit. p. 260
29 Correspondance 19234
30 Caulaincourt p. 249
31 de Fezensac p. 249; Correspondance 19264
32 Correspondance 19273 and 19275
33 It had occurred at Acre in the Syrian campaign, but that was a sideshow.
34 de Fezensac p. 254
35 Caulaincourt p. 601
36 Op. cit. p. 317
37 Op. cit. pp. 317–20
38 Correspondance 19310, 19311 and 19313
39 Marshall-Cornwall p. 224
40 Caulaincourt p. 331; the actual date Bonaparte received the news of the Malet plot is not certain: *see* op. cit. p. 327 FN 2
41 de Ségur II p. 192
42 Caulaincourt p. 339
43 Aldington Appendix 5
44 de Fezensac p. 276
45 Caulaincourt pp. 341–2
46 Op. cit. p. 379
47 de Ségur II p. 276
48 Letters of 29 and 30 Nov. and 4 Dec. Correspondance 19362, 19363 and 19373

49 Op. cit. 19364
50 Op. cit. 19365
51 It may be that this reference was inserted for political reasons to scotch rumours that he was dead, but the phrasing of the reference and the place chosen for it in the bulletin conveys the Bonapartian concern with self.
52 de Fezensac pp. 258 and 128; Caulaincourt pp. 316–18 and 321

Chapter XIV
1 Letter to Davout, 2 December 1811, Correspondance 18300
2 Op. cit. 19664
3 Instructions to Caulaincourt, 17 May 1813, Op. cit. 20017
4 Lefebvre *Napoléon 1807–1815* pp. 323–7
5 Op. cit. pp. 327–8
6 Raguse V pp. 59–60. For Bonaparte's preparations for the 1813 campaign, *see* Correspondance Tomes 24 and 25 *passim*, but especially 19395, 19401, 19404, 19405, 19419, 19431, 19437, 19452, 19459, 19460, 19461, 19496, 19586, 19602, 19612, 19659, 19689, 19706, 19711, 19717, 19721, 19865 and 19972. *See also* Caulaincourt pp. 619–20; Lefebvre *Napoléon 1807–1815* pp. 327–8
7 Moltke's draft plans for defensive wars against France or Austria, THOMAS E. GRIESS and JAY LUVAAS (Editors) *Strategy: Its Theory and Application: The Wars for German Unification 1866–1871*, reprints and translations of Moltke's papers and Prussian General Staff history of the Austro-Prussian War, Greenwood Press, Westport, Connecticut 1971
8 J. F. C. FULLER *The Decisive Battles of the Western World* Eyre and Spottiswoode 1957, 3 Vols, II pp. 453 and 458; Lefebvre *Napoléon 1807–1815* p. 329
9 BARON VON ODELEBEN *A Circumstantial Narrative of the Campaign in Saxony in the Year 1813* John Murray 1820, 2 Vols, I pp. 13–14 and 24–5
10 Fuller p. 461
11 Correspondance 2006
12 Fuller pp. 462–3
13 Op. cit. p. 464
14 Correspondance 10042
15 Lefebvre *Napoléon 1807–1815* pp. 330–1; Correspondance 20066, 20070, 20071, 20139, 20142 and 20148
16 METTERNICH *Mémoires* Paris 1880, 2 Vols, II p. 461
17 Correspondance 20175, verbatim account by Bonaparte's secretary, Fain.
18 Ibid
19 Metternich p. 462
20 Correspondance 20469
21 Op. cit. 02496; Raguse V pp. 170–1; von Odeleben I pp. 288–90
22 von Odeleben I p. 295
23 Correspondance 20619
24 von Odeleben I p. 301
25 Op. cit. I p. 157

26 Correspondance 20094
27 von Odeleben I pp. 181–3
28 Raguse v p. 256
29 Correspondance 20492
30 Ibid.
31 Op. cit. 10676
32 Raguse v p. 288; Fuller II p. 477
33 von Odeleben II p. 26
34 Raguse v p. 301
35 Op. cit. VI p. 4
36 de Villefosse and Bouissounouse p. 321
37 HAROLD NICOLSON *The Congress of Vienna*
New York, Harcourt Brace 1946 pp. 61–3;
Lefebvre *Napoléon 1807–1815* pp. 339–42
38 Correspondance 21062
39 Ibid.
40 Op. cit. pp. 6–7
41 Méneval I pp. 314–15
42 Raguse VI pp. 7–8 and 51
43 Le Normand II p. 213
44 FELIX MARKHAM *Napoleon* London, New
English Library 1963, p. 198
45 Lefebvre *Napoléon 1807–1815* p. 338;
Correspondance 21538
46 Raguse VI p. 179
47 Nicolson p. 77
48 Op. cit. pp. 77–8
49 Raguse VI p. 52; *see also* Nicolson p. 80
50 Nicolson p. 80
51 Ibid.
52 Correspondance 21461
53 Ibid.
54 *Cambridge Modern History* IX p. 552
55 Correspondance 21522; Raguse VI p. 325
56 Op. cit. 21558
57 Rose *Napoleon* p. 432
58 Op. cit. p. 433

Chapter XV
1 Correspondance 21561
2 Op. cit. 21562
3 *See* journal of the Prussian commissioner,
Count Waldburg-Truchsess, quoted in Raguse
VII pp. 138–41; *see also* Journal of the English
Commissioner, Sir Neil Campbell, p. 192
4 Campbell pp. 243–4
5 Correspondance 21674
6 Op. cit. 21682
7 Rose *Napoleon* II p. 433
8 Op. cit. p. 445
9 Correspondance 21881
10 Mollien, quoted in Raguse VII p. 106 FN
11 Nicolson p. 227
12 Correspondance 21701, 21732, 21798 and
21181
13 de Villefosse and Bouissounouse pp. 330–4
14 Rose *Napoleon* II p. 451
15 Correspondance 218839
16 Méneval II p. 444
17 LT. COL. CHARRAS *Histoire de la Campagne de
1815* London 1857, p. 60
18 Marshall-Cornwall pp. 265–6; Lefebvre
pp. 363–5
19 Correspondance 22052

20 *See especially* CHARLES C. CHESNEY *Waterloo
Lectures: A Study of the Campaign of 1815*
London 1868, pp. 85–8
21 Correspondance 22058
22 Ibid.
23 Charras p. 151
24 Op. cit. p. 213
25 Op. cit. p. 219
26 Op. cit. p. 259
27 Aldington p. 236
28 Correspondance 22060
29 Charras p. 262
30 Correspondance 22058; *see also* Chesney
pp. 148–53 and 159–67; Charras pp. 258–60
31 GENERAL GOURGAUD *The Campaign of 1815*
London 1818, p. 102
32 DUC D'ELCHINGEN *Documents Inédits sur la
Campagne de 1815* Paris 1840, p. 18
33 Eyewitness accounts including Bernard's,
Bonaparte's A.D.C. Raguse VII pp. 121–2
34 Correspondance 22062
35 Le Normand I pp. 201–2
36 Lucien Bonaparte II p. 89
37 Larrey II p. 119
38 Correspondance 22066
39 Masson *Napoléon Inconnu* II p. 49
40 PAT HAYWARD (Editor) *Surgeon Henry's
Trifles: Events of a Military Life* Chatto and
Windus 1975, p. 143
41 Ibid.
42 Op. cit. p. 149
43 Op. cit. p. 147
44 LECESTRE *Lettres Inédites de Napoléon Iᵉʳ*
Paris 1897, II p. 103
45 LAS CASES le comte de, *Memorial de Sainte-
Helène: Journal de la Vie Privée et des
Conversations de l'Empereur Napoléon à Sainte-
Helène* London 1823, Tome I Part I p. 407
46 For discussion of medical evidence *see 20th
Foot and Physician to Napoleon* British Medical
Journal 1975, III pp. 293–5; Hayward Ch. 10
47 Masson *Napoléon Inconnu* II p. 310

SELECT BIBLIOGRAPHY

Aldington, Richard *The Duke* New York, Viking 1943, Garden City Publishing Co. 1946; *Wellington* London, Heinemann 1946

Anon 'C. H.' *Some Observations on Bonaparte's Early Years* London 1797

Antommarchi, C. F. *Mémoires ou les Derniers Moments de Napoléon 1819–21* Paris 1898

Arnott, A. *An Account of the Last Illness, Disease, and Post-Mortem Appearance of Napoleon Bonaparte* London 1822

Bonaparte, Joseph *Mémoires* 10 Vols, Paris 1853–4

Bonaparte, Lucien *Mémoires Secrets* 2 Vols, London 1818

Bourcet, P. *Mémoires historiques sur la guerre 1757–62* Paris 1792

Bryant, Arthur *Years of Victory 1802–1812* London, Collins 1944; New York, Harper 1945

Cerf, Léon *Lettres de Napoléon à Joséphine* Paris, Editions Duchartre et Van Buggenhoudt 1929

Chandler, David *The Campaigns of Napoleon* London, Weidenfeld and Nicolson 1967; New York, Macmillan 1973

Charles-Roux, F. *Bonaparte: Governor of Egypt* translated by E. W. Dicker. London, Methuen 1937

Charras, Lt. Col. *Histoire de la Campagne de 1815* London 1857

Chesney, Charles C. *Waterloo Lectures: A Study of the Campaign of 1815* London 1868

Chuquet, Arthur *La Jeunesse de Napoléon* 3 Vols, Paris, Armand Colin 1897–8

Cobban, Alfred *A History of Modern France* 3 Vols, Pelican Books, Harmondsworth 1961

Colin, Jean L. A. *Education Militaire de Napoléon* Paris, Librarie R. Chapelot 1901

Craig, Gordon A. *Problems of Coalition Warfare: The Military Alliance Against Napoleon, 1813–1814* Colorado, United States Air Force 1965

Crawley, C. W. (Editor) New Cambridge Modern History Vol. IX *War and Peace in an Age of Upheaval 1793–1830* Cambridge University Press 1965

Crouzet, F. *Blockade, and Economic Change in Europe, 1792–1815* in *Journal of Economic History* Vol. 24, No. 4, 1964

Debrière, E. *Projets et Tentatives de Debarquement aux Iles Britanniques* l'Etat Major de l'Armée, Section Historique 1793–1805

de Cugnac, J. *Campagne de l'Armée de Reserve en 1800* 2 Vols, Paris 1900

de Fezensac, R. E. P. J. *Souvenirs Militaires de 1804 à 1814* Paris 1863

de Ségur, P. P. *Histoire de Napoléon et la Grande Armée Pendant l'Année 1812* Paris 1825

de Villefosse, Louis and Bouissounouse, Janine *L'Opposition à Napoléon* Paris, Flammarion 1969

Dufriche-Desgenettes, R. N. *Histoire médicale de l'armée d' orient* 2 Vols, Paris 1802

Elchingen, Duc d' *Documents Inédits sur la Campagne de 1815* Paris 1840

Ferrero, Guglielmo *The Gamble: Bonaparte in Italy 1796–1797* London, G. Bell 1961; New York, Walker & Co.

Foucart, P. *Campagne de Prusse: Jéna* 2 Vols, Paris 1887

Fuller, J. F. C. *The Decisive Battles of the Western World* 3 Vols, London, Eyre & Spottiswoode 1957; New York, Scribner

Geyl, Pieter *Napoleon: For and Against* translated by Olive Renier from Dutch. London, Jonathan Cape 1964; New Jersey, Humanities Press 1974

Glover, Michael *Wellington's Peninsular Victories* New York, Macmillan 1963; London, Batsford 1965

Gourgaud, Gaspard *Journal Inédit de Sainte-Hélène* 2 Vols, Paris 1880

Gourgaud, General *The Campaign of 1815* London 1818

Griess, Thomas E. and Luvaas, Jay (Editors) *Strategy: Its Theory and Application: The Wars for German Unification 1866–1871* Connecticut, Greenwood Press, Westport 1971

Guibert, J. A. H. de *Essai général de tactique* Liège 1775

Hanoteau, Jean (Editor) *Memoirs of General de Caulaincourt, Duke of Vicenza, 1812–13* translated by Hamish Miles. London, Cassell 1935

Hayward, Pat (Editor) *Surgeon Henry's Trifles: Events of a Military Life* London, Chatto & Windus 1975

Hecksher, E. F. *The Continental System: An Economic Interpretation* Oxford 1922

Keegan, John *The Face of Battle* London, Jonathan Cape 1976; New York, Viking

Kennedy, Paul M. *The Rise and Fall of British Naval Mastery* London, Allen Lane 1976

Lachouque, Henry *The Anatomy of Glory* adapted from the French by Anne S. K. Brown. London, Lund Humphries 1961; New York, Brown University Press 1961

Larrey, Baron *Madame Mère (Napoleonis Mater): Essai Historique* 2 Vols, Paris 1892

Las Cases, le comte de *Memorial de Sainte-Hélène: Journal de la Vie Privée et des Conversations de l'Empereur Napoléon à Sainte-Hélène* 4 Vols, London 1823

Lecestre, Léon *Lettres Inédites de Napoléon 1ᵉʳ* 2 Vols, Paris 1897

Lefebvre, George *Napoleon: From Eighteen Brumaire to Tilsit, 1799–1807* translated by Henry F. Stockhold, *Napoleon: From Tilsit to Waterloo, 1807–1815* translated by J. E. Anderson. London, Routledge and Kegan Paul 1969; New York, Columbia University Press 1969

Le Normand, M. A. *The Historical and Secret Memoirs of the Empress Josephine* 2 Vols, London 1895

Longford, Elizabeth *Wellington: The Years of the Sword* London, Weidenfeld & Nicolson 1969; New York, Harper & Row 1970

Madelin, L. *Lettrés Inédites de Napoléon 1ᵉʳ à Marie-Louise* Paris, Editions des Bibliothèques Nationales de France 1935

Markham, Felix *Napoleon* London, New English Library 1963; New York, New American Library 1963

Marshall-Cornwall, Sir James *Napoleon as Military Commander* London, Batsford 1967; New York, Van Nostrand 1967

Martineau, Gilbert *Napoleon's Last Journey* translated by Frances Partridge. London, John Murray 1976

Masson, Frédéric *Napoléon Chez Lui: La Journée de l'Empereur aux Tuileries* Paris 1884; *Napoléon et les Femmes* Paris, Paul Ollendorf 1894; *Napoléon Inconnu: Papiers Inédits* 2 Vols, Paris, Paul Ollendorf 1895

Méneval, Baron *Napoléon et Marie-Louise: Souvenirs Historiques de Baron Méneval* 3 Vols, Paris 1844

Metternich, Prince *Mémoires* 2 Vols, Paris 1880

Nicolson, Harold *The Congress of Vienna* London, Constable 1946; New York, Harcourt Brace 1946

Odeleben, Baron von *A Circumstantial Narrative of the Campaign in Saxony in the Year 1813* 2 Vols, London, John Murray 1820

Pierce Clark, L. *A Psycho-Historical Study of the Epileptic Personality in the Genius* in *The Psychoanalytic Review* Vol. IX October 1922

Raguse, Duc de *Mémoires* 9 Vols, Paris 1857

Richardson, Frank *Napoleon Bisexual Emperor* London, William Kimber 1972, New York, Horizon 1973

Richardson, Robert G. *Larrey: Surgeon to Napoleon's Imperial Guard* London, John Murray 1974; New York, Transatlantic 1975

Roederer, Pierre-Louis *Mémoires sur la Révolution, le Consulat et l'Empire* Paris, 1942

Rose, J. Holland *The Personality of Napoleon* London 1912; *The Life of Napoleon* 2 Vols, London 1902

Ross, C. (Editor) *Correspondance of Charles, First Marquis of Cornwallis* 3 Vols, London 1859

Terraine, John *Trafalgar* London, Sidgwick and Jackson 1976; New York, Military Book Club

INDEX

Bonaparte sketched from life by Samuel Decimus Davies either on HMS *Northumberland* or on St Helena. *Barclays Bank Limited*